# Mysterion Seeking Understanding

# Mysterion Seeking Understanding

*How Sacramentality Can Save the Body of Christ*

Edited by
Ian S. Markham *and*
Jeremy Means-Koss

Foreword by
*Katherine Sonderegger*

☙PICKWICK Publications • Eugene, Oregon

MYSTERION SEEKING UNDERSTANDING
How Sacramentality Can Save the Body of Christ

Copyright © 2022 Wipf and Stock Publishers. All rights reserved. Except for brief quotations in critical publications or reviews, no part of this book may be reproduced in any manner without prior written permission from the publisher. Write: Permissions, Wipf and Stock Publishers, 199 W. 8th Ave., Suite 3, Eugene, OR 97401.

Pickwick Publications
An Imprint of Wipf and Stock Publishers
199 W. 8th Ave., Suite 3
Eugene, OR 97401

www.wipfandstock.com

PAPERBACK ISBN: 978-1-6667-0643-7
HARDCOVER ISBN: 978-1-6667-0644-4
EBOOK ISBN: 978-1-6667-0645-1

*Cataloguing-in-Publication data:*

Names: Markham, Ian S. [editor]. | Means-Koss, Jeremy [editor] | Sonderegger, Katherine [foreword writer]

Title: Mysterion seeking understanding : how sacramentality can save the body of Christ / edited by Ian S. Markham ad Jeremy Means-Koss.

Description: Eugene, OR: Pickwick Publications, 2022 | Includes bibliographical references.

Identifiers: ISBN 978-1-6667-0643-7 (paperback) | ISBN 978-1-6667-0644-4 (hardcover) | ISBN 978-1-6667-0645-1 (ebook)

Subjects: LCSH: Sacraments | Lord's Supper | Theology, Practical | Church | Liturgies | Pastoral care

Classification: BV800 M34 2022 (print) | BV800 (ebook)

12/05/22

Scripture quotations marked (NRSV) are from the New Revised Standard Version Bible, copyright © 1989 the Division of Christian Education of the National Council of the Churches of Christ in the United States of America. Used by permission. All rights reserved.

Scripture quotations marked (RSV) are taken from Revised Standard Version of the Bible, copyright © 1946, 1952, and 1971 National Council of the Churches of Christ in the United States of America. Used by permission. All rights reserved worldwide.

Scripture quotations marked (NIV) are taken from the Holy Bible, New International Version®, NIV®. Copyright © 1973, 1978, 1984, 2011 by Biblica, Inc.™ Used by permission of Zondervan. All rights reserved worldwide. www.zondervan.com The "NIV" and "New International Version" are trademarks registered in the United States Patent and Trademark Office by Biblica, Inc.™

Scripture quotations marked (AMPC) are taken from the Amplified® Bible (AMPC), Copyright © 1954, 1958, 1962, 1964, 1965, 1987 by The Lockman Foundation Used by permission. www.lockman.org

*We dedicate this book to Brendan and Lesley.
Two lives who make us the people we are.*

# Contents

*Foreword* | ix
—Katherine Sonderegger

*Acknowledgements* | xiii

*Contributors* | xv

*Introduction* | xix
—Jeremy Means-Koss and Ian Markham

## Part 1: Saving the Formation of Faith

1. Word and Flesh: Hermeneutical and Phenomenological Approaches to Sacramentality | 3
—Garrett Ayers

2. The Religiously Unaffiliated and the Sacramental Church | 23
—Beverly Eileen Mitchell | 23

3. The Mysterion of God's Devotedness to Human Beings: Northern Realizations | 42
—G. Ronald Murphy

## Part 2: Saving the Church as a Community

4. What Perfect Love Can Be: The Sacraments as Sites of Disunion and Hope in Christ | 63
—Brit Frazier

5   Sacramental and Liturgical Inclusivity through Understanding "Performativity" and "Tribalism" | 80
    —Jeremy Means-Koss

6   Wrapped in Paradox: The Impact of the Church and Its Sacrament of Reconciliation on Political and Social Life | 99
    —Catherine Meeks

7   Addressing Polarization and Apathy through Sacramental Preaching | 111
    —Crystal J. Hardin

8   Intergenerational Worship: The Sacrament of Radical Belonging as the Body of Christ | 131
    —Sarah Bentley Allred |

**Part 3: Saving Ourselves**

9   Ethical Formation through the Liturgy and Sacraments | 151
    —Ian S. Markham

10  Moral Imperatives Brought on by Our Sacramental Participation | 162
    —Cayce Ramey

11  Sacraments and the Transformation of Desire | 183
    —David Tremaine

12  Sacramental Therapy | 198
    —Benjamin B. Hawley

*Postscript on Pastoral Liturgy* | 217
    —Barney Hawkins

*Conclusion* | 225
    —Jeremy Means-Koss and Ian S. Markham

# Foreword

SOME ESSAYS POSSESS THE elixir that makes everything old new. This is one of those collections: the old of Sacramental Theology is made new. In the church we usually imagine we know what Sacramental Theology is all about, its contours, major themes, and controverted questions. We expect, especially in the Latin tradition, to hear about the Augustinian architectonic of thing and sign; we relate that primal distinction to creation as a whole and then its place within Christian worship; we expect historical analysis of source and development of Christian sacraments; numbering, ranking, ordering; then particular gravamen about Scriptural warrant, Christological presence and mode, and sacrificial character; then rounded out by a review of neuralgic controversies that haunt sacramental ecumenism. All this I consider the bedrock of the old. It is the terrain of Sacramental Theology, and like most things old and familiar, it is valuable, well-plowed, and generative. But it does not surprise, nor does it turn over fresh ground. This collection of essays does both.

We might take the measure of its novelty in an odd fashion: there is little of contemporary Sacramental Theology in these pages. Here and there we find a mention of the pioneering work of Alexander Schmemann, or a footnote or two to Louis-Marie Chauvet or Gordon Lathrop or Edward Schillebeeckx. But this collection does not belong to the broad ecumenical movement of Liturgical Renewal, forged at Maria Laach, and refined by de Lubac and the Constitutions of the Second Vatican Council. It rests content to speak of the Augustinian definition of sacraments as the "outward and visible sign of an inner and spiritual grace," a time-honored axiom that has lost luster in recent Sacramental Theologies. It is also notably relaxed about the Scriptural grounding of the sacraments, and it makes little use of the distinction of primary and secondary theology, or of juxtaposition, central to much present-day Liturgical Theology. These pleasing archaisms in the volume tell us that the center of gravity has shifted for these authors. Sacramental Theology for them is concerned with other things, and ordered in a fresh and novel manner.

For the authors of this volume, Sacramental Theology explodes beyond the Church, beyond dogmatic or systematic theology, to encounter and encompass the wider matters of worldly life, of cultural criticism, of race, gender, and class, of contemporary deconstructive and poststructural thought, and of materiality. Even traditional topics, such as the ecumenical convergence on sacraments and orders, are up-rooted from their customary home in comparative dogmatics and planted in the wider field of a cosmos, created and beloved of God. The eloquent essay by Brit Frazier enacts a spiritual grounding and re-framing of the entire enterprise of ecumenical sacramental life, a unity commanded and bestowed by the Lord Christ. So, too, the essays devoted to a particular sacrament—to Baptism or Reconciliation or to Eucharist—move in cross-grained fashion to the traditional format of such discussions. The angle of vision, then, makes the old new, and raises fresh, provocative questions about the sacraments as means of grace.

Consider the essay by G. Ronald Murphy on the place of sacraments within the larger cause of inculturation or "dynamic equivalence." Readers familiar with contextual theology know how such essays go: an appeal to our post-war, global culture; an examination of recent Church encyclicals on the Church within a diverse world; the problematic of the whole; proposed solutions or ameliorations. Not so in this volume! Here Murphy brings us to particular Churches and artefacts of northern Germanic lands, fearlessly taking up the motifs of Nordic and Icelandic cultures, and demonstrating their presence in Church architecture, baptismal fonts, crucifixes, and pulpits. A full-throated traditional appeal to the ancient teaching that paganism too can serve as praeparatio evangelica to Christian revelation is simply assumed from the outset. From there the serpents and world trees and warriors of the older and more recent Eddas are shown to be entwined, figurally and architecturally, in the great Stave Churches of the north country. This is the old, at times the very old, made new through its simple boldness.

Or turn to the essay by Catherine Meeks on the Sacrament of Reconciliation. Here we might expect some of the same Scriptural and historical reflections that trace the development of such a rite, its prominence in Luther, say, or in Tridentine Catholicism, and its transformation under the impress of modernism, or Tillich's chronology of changing existential forms of faith. Instead, we find a firm anchoring in the racialized injustice of American culture, and the refusal by white supremacists to acknowledge the depth, and continuing wound of racism in our society. Carl Jung, rather than canon or dogmatic theologians, serves as chief interlocutor of this sacrament.

Or consider Cayce Ramey's passionate defense of excommunication as a means of Eucharistic devotion. Here is an essay that takes the entire orbit of Christ's presence in the Supper, a topic of splendid delicacy in the tradition, and radically re-orients it to the white Christian disobedience to the living presence of Christ in the slave trade and the riches it produced for slavers and their heirs. To honor Christ's presence in the Eucharist, he argues, white Christians should freely inhibit themselves from Communion, until humility, submission, and reparation break out and radically re-make the racist Church.

Garrett Ayres and Jeremy Means-Koss take up phenomenological, hermeneutical, and post-colonial thought to explore Sacramentality itself. The fleshiness of the very idea of sacrament, its inescapable tactile nature, lies embedded in the sign that is always more than what appears. Not presence but absence, or an absence that gestures toward presence: these are the proper rhythms of a sacramental universe. Even a certain form of Tribalism can be sanctified and put in service of Sacramental unity.

In short, a striking *ethical* tone is invested in Sacramental Theology. We are well beyond the restrictions of canon law, bemoaned by many Liturgical Renewal theologians; we are enclosed within a vibrant moral universe that examines human desire (David Tremaine), human indifference and secularism (Beverly Mitchell), apathy and partisanship in the face of the preached Word (Crystal Hardin), a generational isolation and fragmentation in Christian worship (Sarah Bentley Allred). An ethicist by training, Ian Markham directly addresses the ethical imperatives of sacramental worship, daring to speak directly of sin and human rebellion, unwelcome guests in much contemporary theology. Benjamin Hawley brings his training as a psycho-therapist to bear on these ethical dilemmas that haunt contemporary life. The sacramental anointing for healing is viewed now within the proper search for wholeness, including, in fresh ways, the priesthood of the whole body of Christ. In a fitting conclusion to the whole collection, Barney Hawkins reflects on liturgy as a pastoral act: Sacraments and Sacramentality anchor the Christian life, and the ministers of the Mysteries are no more managers or functionaries than the Sacraments themselves are arcane deposits of an outmoded faith.

To read the old become new is exciting fare. I welcome you into this newly-forged world; you will not see the Sacraments of the Christian faith in the same way again.

Katherine Sonderegger

# Acknowledgements

THE EDITORS ARE GRATEFUL to Robin Parry who advocated for this project. We are grateful to the contributors who added this labor to their lives. We are grateful for all those who embody the truth of the sacramental life in their lives—Martin Smith, Martyn Percy, Ryan Danker, Bob Malm, and Kate Sonderegger.

Finally, we have dedicated this book to our spouses. Without their day-to-day support, we would not be the people we are. Thank you Brendan and Lesley: we are forever grateful.

# Contributors

**Ian S. Markham** is the dean of Virginia Theological Seminary and professor of theology and ethics with degrees from King's London, University of Cambridge, and University of Exeter. He is the author of "The New Apologetics" (Fortress, 2020) and editor of *Reasonable Radical* (with Joshua Daniel) (Pickwick, 2018) and *Demant's Penumbra of Ethics* (with Christine Faulstich) (Cascade, 2019). In addition, he has written many other books and articles. He is a priest associate at St. Paul's Episcopal Church in Alexandria, VA.

**Jeremy Means-Koss** is the Priest-in-Charge of St. Peter's and St. James' Episcopal Churches in southwestern Vermont. He holds degrees from Wesley Theological Seminary, King's College London and American University and earned his Certificate of Anglican Studies from Virginia Theological Seminary. He has also held numerous roles in students affairs/higher education.

**Garrett Ayers** holds a Master of Letters from the Institute for Theology, Imagination, and the Arts at the University of St. Andrews and a Master of Divinity from Virginia Theological Seminary. He is the co-editor of *A Student's Companion to the Daily Office in Greek and Hebrew* (VTS Press) and is currently serving as Assistant Rector as St. John's Episcopal Church in Columbia, South Carolina.

**Sarah Bentley Allred** received her MDiv from Virginia Theological Seminary in May 2019. She now serves as the Associate for Christian Formation and Discipleship as well as the Editor of Building Faith for Lifelong Learning at Virginia Seminary. Sarah is passionate about intergenerational worship, small churches, and children's spirituality.

**Brit Frazier** is the Associate Rector at Saint Mark's Church, Philadelphia. She has served as an advisor on adult formation and education in the Episcopal dioceses of Washington and Pennsylvania and continues to be a guest preacher up and down the eastern seaboard. Her Master in Divinity comes from Virginia Theological Seminary and her Bachelor of Arts from Wellesley College.

**Crystal J. Hardin** is an Episcopal priest and serves as Associate Rector at Saint George's, in Arlington, Virginia. She received her Master of Divinity from Virginia Theological Seminary and graduated magna cum laude from the University of Alabama School of Law, where she was named a Hugo L. Black Scholar, served as an editor of the *Alabama Law Review*, and worked for the Capital Defense Clinic. She is co-editor of the book *Prophetic Preaching: The Hope or the Curse of the Church* (2020). She is passionate about preaching, Flannery O'Connor, lunch, and Jesus.

**Barney Hawkins** is the Arthur Carl Lichtenberger Professor in Pastoral Theology and Continuing Education Emeritus at Virginia Theological Seminary from 2000–2018. He is now Chair of the Bicentennial Celebration and Capital Campaign. His publications include the book *Episcopal Ethics and Etiquette* (Church Publishing, 2010), and, as editor, *The Wiley Companion to the Anglican Communion* (2008), and *Words that Listen* (SPCK and Church Publishing).

**Benjamin Hawley SJ** is an Associate Pastor at Holy Trinity Parish in Washington, DC. He holds degrees from Heythrop College, the University of Chicago, Loyola University, and Cornell. He has previously served as Pastor of St. Mary Student Parish in Ann Arbor, MI, ministering to those at the University of Michigan. Before becoming a Jesuit he served as a Peace Corps Volunteer and Foreign Service Officer.

*Contributors*  xvii

**Catherine Meeks** is the Executive Director of the Absalom Jones Center for Racial Healing. She holds a Master's Degree in Social Work from Clark Atlanta University and PhD from Emory University. Prior to the center's opening she chaired its precursor, Beloved Community: Commission for Dismantling Racism for the Episcopal Diocese of Atlanta. A sought-after teacher and workshop leader, Catherine brings four decades of experience to the work of transforming the dismantling racism work in Atlanta. The core of her work has been with people who have been marginalized because of economic status, race, gender or physical ability as they pursue liberation, justice and access to resources that can help lead them to health, wellness and a more abundant life. Catherine is the retired Clara Carter Acree Distinguished Professor of Socio-Cultural Studies from Wesleyan College and Founding Executive Director of the Lane Center for Community Engagement and Service. She is the author of six books and one inspirational CD and is the editor of the bestselling book, *Living Into God's Dream: Dismantling Racism in America* and co-author of *Passionate for Justice: Ida B Wells as Prophet for Our Times*.

**Beverly Eileen Mitchell** is Professor of Historical Theology at Wesley Theological Seminary in Washington, DC. She holds degrees from Boston College-ANTS, Wesley Theological Seminary, and Temple University. She has researched and taught extensively on Systematic Theology, Church History, human dignity, genocide, global poverty, the African American struggle for justice, Holocaust studies, and the challenge of white supremacy in church and society. She is the author of "Black Abolitionism: The Quest of Human Dignity," "Plantations and Death Camps: Religion, Ideology, and Human Dignity" as well as many other chapters and articles.

**G. Ronald Murphy SJ** is Professor Emeritus of German at Georgetown University. He is the author of numerous books, including *Tree of Salvation: Yggdrasil and the Cross in the North* (Oxford University Press, 2013), *Gemstone of Paradise: The Holy Grail in Wolfram's Parzival* (Oxford University Press, 2006), *The Owl, the Raven, and the Dove: The Religious Meaning of Grimms' Magic Fairy Tales* (Oxford University Press, 2001), and translator, with commentary, of *The Heliand* (Oxford University Press, 1992).

**B. Cayce Ramey** is an Episcopal priest, anti-White Supremacy educator, and author. He holds a Doctor of Ministry from Virginia Union University in sacramental theology and transatlantic slavery. He also holds degrees from Virginia Theological Seminary and the Massachusetts Institute of Technology. He has written for *The Arts in Religion and Theological Studies* and exhibited photo essays on art as prophetic witness.

**David Tremaine** is a husband, father, author, and congregational consultant. He holds a Master of Divinity degree from Virginia Theological Seminary and is currently working on his PhD in practical theology at the University of Aberdeen. He started Troubling The Waters consulting in 2021 and works as a consultant in the Diocese of San Diego. He is the author of *The Beautiful Letdown: An Addict's Theology of Addiction* (Cascade, 2018).

# Introduction

IT IS STRANGE. WE are all so anxious about "church growth," but the majority of "church growth books" are strangely secular. The focus, so often, is sociological. Let us play "praise music" rather than use the organ. Let us be more involved in the community. In short, let us be another social organization that doesn't believe it is divine.

There is, of course, truth in these sociological perspectives, but the idea of this book is that need to focus on what is distinctive about the church—what is divine. The contributors to this book gathered around the conviction that the sacraments are what make the difference. We really do believe that the spiritual infuses the material in the sacraments and are a resource that enable humans to participate in the divine life.

In the wake of a global pandemic, what was a slow decline of church attendance became immediate and severe; and what had been merely a looming question of *why we need the church or her sacraments* altered from a mere dark shadow—slowly brought about through generational changes, secular self-help fads, and popular culture—to a fully corporeal reality of the here and now. If people aren't physically attending church or aren't even going to church at all, if they have decided to find transformation out in the world, secular or otherwise, then what are we missing? What do the sacraments do to/in/for us that we cannot find on our own? Does participation in the ordinances of Jesus Christ actually make our lives better? Does it make the church's life better?

We each have our own personal answers, answers that God put on our hearts about why the sacraments and the church are not just instrumental but necessary for the betterment of our lives. And yet, we wondered if there were universal, shared experiences, that testified to how something so mysterious could be so important.

It is not just that we need to be educated as to why the church and her sacraments are important, we need to prove to the wider world of believers and seekers alike why they should participate and join with the Christian church at all. We recognized we have come to a pivotal point where evangelism and pastoral care to the wider world have come at intersection. For the better part of the last two millennia, the world that was subjected to the colonial ownership of Europe and its traditions were given the title of Christendom—a territory of theocratic culture where laws, customs, and habits were guided in some fashion by the Christian church, catholic, protestant, orthodox or otherwise. If you needed to provide pastoral care or answers to the public, you could do so inside the church walls and reach most people. However, growing scholarship recognizes we are no longer in such a nominal state. Christendom is no more. In 2012, former Archbishop of Canterbury, Rowan Williams, was quoted as admitting that the same country that birthed and spread Anglican Christianity world-wide was itself in a "post-Christian" state of affairs.[1] For Williams and others who are willing to admit that the theological hold and habitual practice of Christianity on North American and European cultures can no longer be presumed, the questions of the church and her sacraments cannot be confined to a conversation with the few still kneeling within her walls. Historically, such quests of thought are called *apologia*—Latin to mean a defense of one's opinions. Famous Christian apologists include Jerome, Origen, Augustine of Hippo and even more recently, C. S. Lewis.

The questions above are an opportunity for the church to produce new apologia, to not merely evangelize but to also justify her place in the ever bustling and vied-for parts of our lives. One cannot deny that the church faces an uphill battle of image and identity. A casual introspective glance and it recognizes a host of issues that plague its attractiveness and ability to retain its historic membership numbers. Empire may have been a way the church has grown but it is certainly not the only way.

---

1. Rowan Williams, "Former Archbishop Declares Britain 'Post-Christian,'" *Church and State* 67 (2014) 22.

Few would disagree that the image of the church is at an all-time low. Even throughout such tumultuous times as the crusades and the reformations, people did not question the need to be in church even if they had questions of which churches to be part. It is this post-Christian landscape that forces us to ponder and wonder what the church and her sacraments have to offer us that personal salvation through faith alone may not. Are the "spiritual but not religious" correct and corporate Christian practice is superfluous to personal evolution? We must address the question of why we need the Christian church and her sacraments not merely for evangelism but for our very corporate survival. Yet the body of Christ must also acknowledge her mission from God as a salve to all of God's children. It is not enough to defend the church's right of being but to delve into the very query to ascertain if the church and her sacraments have something unique for God's children, something that speaks to our very nature and core.

Across the myriad of social disciplines from medical journals to Pew Research studies to Mission Insight demographic data, the research indicates that citizens of the global north-west, the communities that place emphatic value individualism and are products of the Enlightenment, are peoples in need of social interaction, are a people plagued by mental and emotional issues that desire healing, and are a people with a deep desire to better themselves. It is also important to note that does not exclude other peoples around the globe who also exhibit those same behaviors and needs. The data however is less available to make such broad generalizations about other such communities.

In the global north-west, self-help books and courses regarding mental health and happiness fly off the digital and physical bookshelves; online interpersonal technologies such as dating and social media to foster relationships are on an exponential increased use; creative arts such as science-fiction, fantasy, and horror continue to captivate the popular attention in attempts to temporarily escape current world circumstances; uses of violence and oppression have not faltered amid outcries of marginalized peoples; and across all sectors of socially-created population groups such as political and social identity, there is an even higher disgust for people who are different.

We are a broken people with real problems and in need of comfort. While sacramentalism may seem like a circle tool for a square problem, the presence of God in and amidst the practice of our lives is the salve necessary to address all of these challenges.

Pope Emeritus Benedict XVI in *Theology of Liturgy* reminds us that we are all on a quest to understand the sacred. If God is quoted in scripture as saying that should we call out for help, *hosanna in the highest*, that God will indeed come and be with us in the midst of it, can we look to our sacraments, the visible signs of invisible grace, to aid us in our failures and challenges? In *On Christian Theology*, Rowan Williams reminded us that personal holiness is not something esoteric or fictitious but truly realizable. Finally, reformed theologian Jürgen Moltmann, in *Church in the Power of the Spirit*, passionately convicts the church to see itself as an instrument of tomorrow's world here and now, today. If we are to see the sacraments as instruments of the church's work to live into these such directives first we must name what challenges face our modern church.

This book attempts to synthesize these such issues. With any such work of this magnitude much is left out. There simply isn't the room to combine so many fields which could yield books of their own into one collection. The result of this collection however covers a swatch of topics that includes personal meaning-making, community building, pastoral care, and the *mysterion* of Christ as the primary actor in all of it. Our authors come from varied generations, denominations, races, sexualities, and genders yet we recognize there are still some voices missing.

The text is separated into three sections. In the first section, *Saving the Formation of Faith*, this book explores how we as people make meaning. Garrett Ayers explores how we all find and create meaning from the hermeneutical and phenomenological perspectives. Beverly Eileen Mitchell explores how individuals find meaning when they themselves may not hold to denomination-specific dogmatics or allegiances. And G. Ron Murphy concludes the section by showing how a non-Christian culture saw their own values and meanings expressed and brought to fruition by Christ—proving Christ can indeed be at the center of all things.

In the second section, *Saving the Church as a Community*, this book explores how sacramentality can be at the center of a church that invites people in rather than scares them away. Brit Frazier explores how adhering to sacramental importance also means desiring a unified church. Jeremy Means-Koss explores how the desire to increase church membership is not about visitor hospitality but is in the sacramental opportunity of Pentecost. Catherine Meeks explores how sacramental community are reconciling communities. Crystal Hardin explore how sacramentality permeates good preaching to unify; and Sarah Bentley Allred explores how sacramental worship is inherently intergenerational.

*Introduction*

Finally, in the third section, *Saving Ourselves*, this book explores the pastoral, moral, and ethical necessities brought about by sacramental understanding. Ian Markham explores ethical formation brought about by sacramental understanding. Cayce Ramey explores moral imperatives that bubble up when we authentically use sacramental lenses on our lives. David Tremaine explores how sacramentality helps us in confronting our humanity. And Benjamin Hawley explores a sacramentally attuned look at pastoral care. This volume of essays concludes with a moving postscript reflection on the significance of "pastoral liturgy" by Barney Hawkins. The work of any minister—the work of "ministering" to others—is a work that has a certain story. We each make our own journey. Using his own lived biographical assessment, Hawkins explains why the pastoral is central to his identity and his ministry. And while his reflection may be rooted in his tradition, this postscript captures the journey that shapes all of us—at some point God touches our lives to make us realize the centrality of being present to others and drawing on the resources of the Church to help us do that.

The common misconception is that first came the church and then came the sacraments. The reality is that first came God's grace and then came the church and then the church found visible ways to see the invisible grace God bestows. The resulting perspective shift puts Christ where Paul would have us put him, as the head of the church and author or our salvation.

The authors were each invited to see and write about the sacraments not as mere band aids to the problems we face but instead use them as lenses for examining the church. Some of the authors delve deep into intellectual conceptions while others make plain what has always seemed so extravagant. The thread they all hold onto however is the desire to help the reader see sacramentality as something wonderous rather than archaic. Our end hope is that you find deep value for sacramentality and the visible signs of God's invisible grace.

Jeremy Means-Koss and Ian Markham
Epiphany 2022

Part 1

# Saving the Formation of Faith

*Lord I Believe. Help my unbelief.*
(MARK 9:24 NRSV)

# 1

# Word and Flesh

Hermeneutical and Phenomenological
Approaches to Sacramentality

GARRETT AYERS

### Introduction

How can we approach a broad understanding of sacramentality—that *quality* of a sacrament—in light of our minds and our bodies? I think there are two primary images for our thinking here: meaning and touch.

Our Anglican definition inherits an understanding of sacraments as "outward and visible signs of inward and spiritual grace," but I'd like to see if we can expand this definition slightly.[1] There are two primary reasons: first, sacraments—as signs and symbols—present themselves to us as something to be interpreted, or at the very least as meanings to be inhabited;[2] signs, by nature, *point*. But what if *meaning* of the sign is not

---

1. At times, we will have to use "sacrament" and "sacramentality" somewhat seamlessly, because of course we cannot talk about one without talking about the other. However, when I mention "sacrament," I mean in this essay the *locale* of sacramentality, and by sacramentality, I understand the respective sense or quality which makes a sacrament a sacrament. Throughout this paper, I am so much interested in "what is a sacrament?" as I am interested in what kinds of sacrament*ality* are suggested by the disciplines of hermeneutics and phenomenology.

2. The phenomenon of a symbol certainly exceeds the demands of interpretation,

3

altogether discernible, or, not discernible in its entirety? In the normal course of life, we would want to say then that this sign is simply imprecise. It does not clearly lead us toward its own meaning. However, in a sacramental understanding, the matter of *imprecision*, so to speak, opens onto to a number of daily realities in a sacramental life from doubt to the very nature of God's appearing in the world. This, we can say, is sacramentality as a kind of signification of God.

Secondly: in whatever way we receive or participate in a sacrament—with our hands, our lips, or with water over our foreheads—the body is necessarily involved.[3] So, what might sacramentality mean if we take our bodies as a starting point as well? Here too there are consequences for theology to move outside of strictly *noetic* (emphasizing consciousness) approaches to the sacramental life, and into a fuller reflection on what it means to be human. So, the second question moves from *meaning* (noesis) to a theological reflection on *contact*.[4]

Elucidating sacramentality in these ways way will require the help of two different but related disciplines: hermeneutics and phenomenology. If hermeneutics is understood as the study of the meanings of texts, and phenomenology is understood as the study of the appearing of things, then sacramentality sits squarely in the crosshairs here, whether we consider sacramentality a relationship to meaning (hermeneutics) or the relationship to the presence of otherness (phenomenology). Each methodological disposition in turn opens up a specific type of mystery, whether the textual mystery (hermeneutics) or the intersubjective mystery (phenomenology): word and flesh. Understanding that some of this terminology can be somewhat niche, a good bit of each section will

---

admittedly, so it is less accurate here to say that they provide a strict signification. Symbols, as we will see, create a *world* or are bearers of a whole order with each symbolic instantiation. So, the task is less to interpret a symbol than it is to let it interpret *us*, as it were. We will have more to say about this below.

3. I am opting for the conservative number of sacraments in the Anglican tradition, if only to make our task simpler. To add an underdeveloped point, we might say that whether two or seven sacraments, I would suggest that each of them still has some relation to the flesh: lived experience, or affectivity. The phenomenological category of the flesh will be elucidated below in the second section.

4. This essay was written under the circumstances of COVID-19, and an emphasis on contact here is not lost on me. It seems to me that responses to sacramentality throughout the pandemic can be considered in this way: is the sacrament something we receive merely *noetically*, as simply a sign (virtual communion, for instance), or is there necessarily more involved in the "sacramentality of a sacrament," wherein touch is not merely a feature but a necessity?

be devoted to explaining terminology: what is hermeneutics, and why should I care? what is a "phenomenology of flesh," and how does this differ from normal Christian usage of the term "flesh"?

Ultimately, as unique points of God's disclosure, sacraments are those very moments wherein "things are more than they are,"[5] and this "more-ness" is precisely what we are calling *sacramentality*. The task is now to consider this "more-ness" across two primary axes: interpretation and incorporation, or, hermeneutics and phenomenology.

## I: *Logos* and the Text: Hermeneutical Sacramentality

To begin, the following section will evaluate sacramentality through existential hermeneutics. Initially, by hermeneutics, I am following Paul Ricœur to mean the practices governing interpretation, and by interpretation, I mean, "the work of thought which consists in deciphering the hidden meaning in the apparent meaning, in unfolding the levels of meaning implied in the literal meaning."[6] I am interested, above all, in the ways that sacramentality is related to acts of interpretation, but *also* in the ways that sacramentality exceeds interpretation, or even oversaturates it. Thus, by attempting to discover in what way *hermeneutical* life elucidates *sacramental* life, we may discover something even more rich—*mystery*, or, what the text cannot give us.

### Paul Ricœur and the World of the Text

To begin, it will be helpful to understand in what way a text relates to our life in the world. In framing the discussion of sacramentality through existential hermeneutics, we will be interested not only in the meaning of this or that sign or symbol, but what that condition of meaning tells us about our lives.[7] Sacraments are not merely nodes of meaning, but have a unique bearing on the way our lives are oriented. Likewise, a text

---

5. Williams, *Grace and Necessity*, 53.

6. Ricœur, "Existence and Hermeneutics," 13.

7. In another context, we might have had occasion to consider the work of Marie-Louis Chauvet, specifically, his text *Symbol and Sacrament: Sacramental Reinterpretation of Christian Existence*. Chauvet takes up some of these very same existential terms and understands their relationship to the sacraments as bearers of existence. However, Chauvet's approach is less hermeneutical (strictly speaking) and generally Heideggerian. As such, his work falls just out of the purview of our inquiry here.

governs this orientation. Or, consulting Paul Ricœur, we can say here that in existential hermeneutics, a text is not merely a document, but "The text speaks of a possible world and a possible way of orienting oneself within it. The dimensions of this world are properly opened up by and disclosed by the text . . . [such that here] showing is at the same time *creating a new mode of being*."[8] But we are getting ahead of ourselves. It stands to be shown how this is the case, and what it has to do with sacramentality.

In an essay titled, "Biblical Hermeneutics and Philosophical Hermeneutics," Paul Ricœur sets up his theory of interpretation against the background of one particular model of biblical interpretation—the historical critical model—which, for Ricœur, tries only to discover original author, original context, and original audience. The task of Biblical hermeneutics had become not one of *responding* to the text, a search for "*the means* or other *circumstances* of the act of writing, which suffice to explain how and why it was written and not otherwise."[9] Similarly, historian and theologian Justo González writes of his own formation, saying, "[For a time, to] teach the Bible became synonymous with explaining the historical setting of texts, and the process by which they had been redacted and transmitted."[10] This meant that the text of the Bible was often looked *behind* but not *looked at*; it was not *itself* a source for its own meaning. Biblical hermeneutics, for Ricœur, was simply a means of discovering the world "*behind* the text."[11]

By way of example, consider what this kind of theory would mean for an approach to the liturgy. Applying this method would involve merely attending to the layers of its historical composition—what prayers came from where, what was the context in which one hymn was written, which practices arose at what time, and from whom. This is, of course, not how we engage with liturgy when we are worshipping.[12] More than anything, liturgy *places* us and gives us a new sense of belonging and understanding

---

8. Ricœur, *Interpretation Theory*, 88.
9. Falque, *Crossing the Rubicon*, 32.
10. Gonzalez, *Santa Biblia*, 23.
11. Ricœur, *Interpretation Theory*, 87.
12. Like the historical critical model, this approach is not always and everywhere wrong or misguided. I am only saying that they cannot exhaust what we do with a text, and that liturgically, this hypothetical historical approach is qualitatively different than simply arriving for worship, and would feel a bit strange there too.

through its whole order.[13] Worshipping, we are most interested in how the liturgy draws us into *itself*.

In a similar way, Ricœur asserts that the Biblical text is *its own world*, and that the task of hermeneutics is not to peer back the curtain *behind* this world, but "to allow the world of being that is the 'thing' of the biblical text unfold."[14] He does this by bracketing out those very historical considerations.[15] In so doing, Ricœur allows readers once again to find how Scripture enfolds us within its "strange new *world*" (Barth).

There are two implications of this move for our purposes here. First, by breaking from a certain historical critical model, Ricœur emancipates the Biblical text from being merely a tool by which one discovers another world, thus allowing the Bible to become *its own* world. Because the Bible has been set up as its *own* world, and not in the first place referential to *another* world, Biblical hermeneutics thus takes on an *existential* relation for the biblical reader. It is no longer simply a source of meaning, but a source of *being* for us. Reading the Bible, we come to understand ourselves wholly "in front of the text."

The second implication has to do with the relationship between Biblical hermeneutics and general (or philosophical) hermeneutics. Ricœur not only says that "Biblical hermeneutics is a *regional* hermeneutics in relation to philosophical hermeneutics,"[16] but even more strongly that, "Theological hermeneutics presents features that are *so original* that the relation [between biblical and philosophical hermeneutics] is gradually inverted, and theological hermeneutics subordinates philosophical hermeneutics to its own organon."[17] This is a dramatic reversal. Even if Biblical hermeneutics shares features common to general hermeneutics, Ricœur tells us that is because they are all derived from this "subordinating" approach. In other words, the same sort of "bracketing" that Ricœur

---

13. Writing on the Medieval Roman Rite, Catherine Pickstock writes that in liturgy, "the question 'where am I' precedes 'who am I,' underlining the embodied nature of the worshipper, and the importance of place and physicality." See Pickstock, *After Writing*, 183.

14. Ricœur, "Biblical Hermeneutics," 96.

15. The move itself is a phenomenological one, derived from Edmund Husserl's processes of attending to the "things themselves," or "the world itself." It stands to reason whether this is entirely possible, especially in Husserl's analyses, but this consideration should not necessarily take away the value of Ricœur's breakthrough as a methodological emancipation from *only* historical or redactional concerns.

16. Ricœur, "Biblical Hermeneutics," 89.

17. Ricœur, "Biblical Hermeneutics," 90.

undertakes with Biblical Hermeneutics, readers should undertake with *every* text. This means that if the Biblical text is a world, likewise *every* text is a kind of world. Building from our first implication, reading a text is not *ultimately* a quest to discover facts about the author, nor the original intended audience, but is ultimately a task of finding *oneself* situated in *its* world.

Admittedly, these are both phenomenological claims, insofar as the philosophical category of "world" is both the place in which we "live and move and have our being" (Acts 17:28),[18] but also the place from which we derive all sorts of expectations *about* our life. Philosophically, a world is not merely a locale (Earth or Mars), but something of a cradle of our very existence. Indeed, the world is "there prior to every analysis that I could give of it,"[19] and even, "the natural *milieu* and field of all my thoughts and of all my explicit perceptions."[20] So, Ricœur develops these phenomenological themes toward the Biblical text, and then text itself. The text is what forms the cradle of our existence, is the "natural milieu" of all my life. Consider, for example, the way that St. Augustine in *Confessions* tells the entire story of his birth, life, and conversion through a host of scriptural allusions, quoting so often that Augustine never understands his life *apart* from the text. Here is that natural milieu. In the same way, what keeps Ricœur's approach fundamentally *hermeneutical*, then, is that for him, text and world overlap. Existentially, the *text* forms that very world that recedes into the background of our perception, even to make my perception possible. To say that we understand ourselves in front of the (biblical) text is to say that it alone circumscribes our very perception, engagement, and anticipation of this life. The text is an existential locale.

Thus, hermeneutics is not *merely* a method of reading and interpreting a document like the Bible, but the process whereby I expose myself "*to the text and receiving from it an enlarged self.*"[21]

Let us return to our liturgical example. In the Fall of 2019, I attended a non-denominational worship service in the DC area with a few fellow students from seminary. The sanctuary was a former Roman Catholic Church; its interior was recarpeted, its altar was replaced with a stage,

---

18. Unless otherwise noted, all biblical citations in this chapter are from the NIV.
19. Merleau-Ponty, *Phenomenology of Perception*, lxxiii.
20. Merleau-Ponty, *Phenomenology of Perception*, lxxiv.
21. Ricoeur, "Distanciation," in Ricoeur, *Hermeneutics and the Human Sciences*, 88.

and its stained-glass windows were boarded up. The new community had created a worship hall that, above all, did not feel overly religious.

Given the conscious departure from some dominant, institutional liturgical practices, we were struck by how this church community had nevertheless, in effect, rediscovered several of the liturgical features of a distinctly "high" liturgy by entirely different means, or, had at least discovered the aesthetic and theological *purposes* for them. Instead of stained glass, there were roving lights, dappling the seats and hands, and sometimes stopping at a wide angle to cut across the room like a morning light through high windows. The church used its light to give one a sense of otherworldliness, heavenly light, bursts of color. In a space that (most likely) had previously undertaken a procession of incense, there was a gentle smoke emanating from in front of the stage, even catching the light. The two were cooperating together in a distinct liturgical experience which simultaneously reengaged the whole person and created a sense that we were in quite different world from the one in which we parked our car.

In the first analysis, what liturgy offers by way of "worldifying"[22] us, all texts can offer insofar as we approach them not with reference to the world *behind* the text, but with respect to the world opened up *in front of the text*. The text draws us into *its* semantic order and presents us with a host of symbols, signs, movements and sings not only to understand those signs, but even to offer us a new understanding of ourselves by being newly "placed," so to speak.

In the second analysis, this example also shows us how "life itself is a hermeneutical venture," in which, daily, "encounter the world and entities within the world 'as' something."[23] To step into the liturgy at all is to begin the work of interpretation, to begin "the work of thought which consists in deciphering the hidden meaning in the apparent meaning"[24] Indeed, *all* self-understanding for Ricœur is "*mediated* by signs, symbols, and texts; in the last resort understanding coincides with the interpretation given to these mediating terms."[25] Thus, the task of hermeneutics spreads out to a mode of existence, and reading is bound up intimately

---

22. The phrase is Emmanuel Falque's as he comments on Ricœur in *Crossing the Rubicon*, 32.

23. Smith, *The Fall of Interpretation*, 96.

24. Ricœur, "Existence and Hermeneutics," 13.

25. Ricœur, "On Interpretation," in Ricœur, *Hermeneutics and the Human Sciences*, 15.

with perception itself. Each of us is wrapped up in "exegesis of his [or her] own life."[26]

## Hermeneutical Sacramentality

We are beginning to see the consequences of Ricœur's thought for our hermeneutical sacramentality.[27] At the outset, we would need to say two things about this kind of method: first, as features of a distinct liturgical world, sacraments give us a new place of belonging by the world they bring, and second, as features of the text, these sacraments also mediate to us the presence of God through those hidden meanings they give. Thus, the act of interpretation steps up as a means now of "deciphering the hidden meaning [of God] in the apparent meaning, [thereby] unfolding the levels of meaning implied in the literal meaning."[28] Hermeneutically, the hidden meaning of God is what makes a sacrament sacrament*al*.

Why not simply stop here, and pronounce sacramentality a quality—the signification of God in sacraments? We would have strong footing, whether we articulated a sacrament as a sign, one thing "used in order to signify something else,"[29] or whether we articulated a sacrament as a symbol: "double- or multiple-meaning expressions whose semantic texture is correlative to the work of interpretation that explicates their second or multiple meanings."[30] Sacramentality (a quality) is thus either the possibility of signifying in relation to God, or the process whereby double-meaning comes about in materiality. In the last analysis, what Ricœur says of philosophy can just as well apply to our inquiry here: "[sacramentality] remains a hermeneutics, that is, a reading of the hidden

---

26. Ricœur, "Existence and Hermeneutics," 11.

27. This would need to be differentiated from a sacramental hermeneutics, along the lines of John Macquarrie's helpful "sacramental universe." See Macquarrie, *A Guide to the Sacraments*, 7: "When we talk of a sacramental universe, we are implying that God is not only a transcendent reality beyond the world he has made, but an immanent reality who dwells within his world and is active in it." In other words, a sacramental hermeneutics is an existential position which sees in all things the potential to disclose the presence of God, and interprets them as such, whereas a hermeneutical sacramentality is simply an approach to sacramentality through hermeneutics. The difference is in the starting points of each.

28. Ricœur, "Existence and Hermeneutics," 13.

29. Augustine, *Teaching*, 107.

30. Ricœur, *Freud and Philosophy*, 13.

meaning inside the text of the apparent meaning."[31] In sum, sacramentality appears to be a relationship to a *given meaning*.

One of the dangers of articulating sacramentality as the relationship to a *given* meaning is that we run the risk of collapsing the boundary here between meaning and sense, such that they have to occur together, and governed by the horizon of the text. But this does not have to be the case. In fact, when it comes to sacraments, sense is often given *without* meaning; I can intuit a presence that I cannot explain. This is precisely what Jean-Luc Marion has called the "saturated phenomenon." Marion writes that "in the case of the saturated phenomenon, intuition [or, sense] by definition passes *beyond* what meaning a hermeneutic of the concept can provide, a fortiori a hermeneutic practiced by a finite I, which will always have less givable *meaning* (concept, intentionality, signification, noesis, etc.) than the intuitive *calls for*."[32] In the same way, restricting sacramentality to the meaning that appears through the sacrament is, I think, to restrict to the condition of *intuition* to the text, or, *to the world*; the text *as* horizon would then close a certain degree of phenomenality that, it seems to me, is necessary for a sacrament to eschew. This is not to say that we should dispense "with a horizon [or text] altogether, since this would no doubt forbid any and all manifestation; it means using the horizon in another way so as to be free of its delimiting anteriority, which can only enter into a phenomenon's claim to absolute appearing."[33] While it seems that at this point with Marion, we are jumping the gun on a pass to phenomenology, Marion's insight here is critical for hermeneutics: the text *reveals* a sacrament as the thing for which it cannot account, and therefore allows it to be "intuited" but not "intended," allows it to be *sensed* but not *understood*. Sacramentality, understood within hermeneutics, is that very freed, extra-textual quality. To return to the conversation about "world," is does not, in short arrive first and foremost from within my world, but characteristically from outside of it.[34]

In short, it appears to me that sacramentality *can* be understood as a relationship to meaning (thus keeping its hermeneutical ties), but a meaning that is first of all *open*. To say that in sacraments I *sense* the presence of God is not necessarily the same thing as saying I can always *explain* that

---

31. Ricœur, "Existence and Hermeneutics," 22.

32. Marion, *Being Given*, 217; emphasis added.

33. Marion, *Being Given*, 209.

34. Marion, *Being Given*, 212: "It is freed because it does not depend on any horizon."

meaning. Likewise, to say that the sense of God appears *within* the text is not to say that it comes only according to the meaning the text would give it (mere signification).[35] Sacramentality is that very openness.

This, then, shows us how we might approach a hermeneutical sacramentality as a relationship to meaning. Rather than collapsing sense and meaning (what I can be aware of, versus what I can explain), a hermeneutical sacramentality is attentive to the sense that escapes interpretation—the meaning that is *not* given, but the sense that *is* given. I have in mind a kind hermeneutical sacramentality along the lines of John Caputo's "radical hermeneutics," in which he writes, "There are certain breaking points, let us say, in the habits and practices, the works and days of our mundane existence where the flux is exposed, where the whole trembles and the play irrupts."[36] Where habits and practices reflect liturgy or ritual, the breaking points are what we have called sacraments. In such a case, the role of a sacramental hermeneutics "is not so much to 'come to grips' with [the breaking points]," so much as "to cope with it, or best of all, to stay in play with it."[37] In short, for our purposes "the task of [sacramental] thinking, which is conducted in the ground of the soul is to keep *open to the mystery*, to keep play in play . . . not to decipher the speaker behind the mask but to alert us to the distance between them—and then to preserve and keep it open."[38] I am not going to go so far as to call this hermeneutical sacramentality a "radical" sacramentality, insofar as *mystery* (conceived first as an opening in the text), is built into the sacraments as such, but a hermeneutical sacramentality shows us the opening of meaning, where the gap is not closed.

In conclusion, another one of the functions beginning our consideration of sacramentality with hermeneutics is likewise to expose the places where hermeneutics cannot speak—the places where we are sorely at a loss of what the *meaning* is. This is, paradoxically, precisely why it is essential *not* to leave hermeneutics behind when it comes to constructing a theology of sacramentality. We can say with confidence that the dynamics of interpretation, meaning, and sense the text gives to us *are* essential to the task

---

35. In this way, we are able to preserve the necessity of the text for understanding the signs that appear within the text, and, more importantly, we are able to say that the text forms for *me* a set of meanings. If meaning appears first of all mediated by the text, that which exists *outside* of the text can be given as *sense*, but not meaning.

36. Caputo, *Radical Hermeneutics*, 269.

37. Caputo, *Radical Hermeneutics*, 271.

38. Caputo, *Radical Hermeneutics*, 289–90; emphasis added.

of understanding liturgy and of understanding ourselves *within* the liturgy. We should only also say, constructively, that we also do not *want* to be able to *explain* exhaustively what any given sacrament means. There is a surplus of meaning as well that gives us far more than mere signification.

## II: Intersubjectivity: Phenomenological Sacramentality

After all has been said and done about hermeneutics and sacramentality, we would still be at a loss if we thought hermeneutics could tell us everything, even in pointing us to its own limit. To get a fuller understanding of sacramentality, we need a pivot—not rejecting hermeneutics or what it taught us, but undertaking an altogether different approach: phenomenology of touch.[39] The sacraments often escape what we can say about them not only because they are given as something beyond the horizon of the text, but also because they are not *only* given to us in the order of language. Even if we need to be accountable to the many ways that our bodies always already interpret existence,[40] bump into a table which is taken *as* a table (or even as an antagonist), we are adapting Levinas' stance to say that "it isn't [only] in terms of writing that problems [of sacramentality] come to me."[41] Or, with Emmanuel Falque, we can claim that "a hermeneutic is *fundamental* only insofar as it is grounded in a mode of existence adequate to its object."[42]

While in the first instance, hermeneutics *is* an adequate engagement for sacraments (they *are* signs, even if surpassing signification) the bodily mode of reception calls for a different kind of treatment in addition to hermeneutics.[43] Sacraments, aside from their relationship

---

39. Emmanuel Levinas terms this same approach "phenomenology of voluptuousness," but for the sake of clarity, I've decided to just use the word "touch." Something is lost in a matter of the intentionality and tenderness of Levinas' term voluptuousness (as well as something erotic), but touch seems more direct for our purposes. See Levinas, *Time and the Other*, 89–90. See also Levinas, *Totality and Infinity*, 265–66.

40. Richard Kearney has called this dynamic "carnal hermeneutics." See Kearney and Treanor, *Carnal Hermeneutics*, 15–75.

41. Levinas, *Alterity and Transcendence*, 173. This quote plays a pivotal role in Emmanuel Falque's critique of "fundamental hermeneutics," which sits in the background of our considerations here. See Falque, *Crossing the Rubicon*, 44.

42. Falque, *Crossing the Rubicon*, 29.

43. Again, I am not suggesting even that the hermeneutical or semiotic or linguistic model is wholesale *wrong* with respect to an approach to sacramentality. I am merely suggesting that (the) *meaning* (of God) is not all that is going on, not simply for

to symbols, signs, rites and rituals, likewise are given to us through touch. Water is poured over our heads, hosts are placed in our hands, and a chalice to our lips. We would need to say at least preliminarily, then, that a sacrament is not merely a visible sign, but a *tangible* sign. There is a presence here, and it is this *presence* which we are considering phenomenologically as sacramentality.

## Identifying Terms

Definitions of phenomenology are notoriously elusive. It is regarded as an academic field, a spirit, a method of inquiry, un-methodical, considered an art, a science, the telos of metaphysics and ontology, and the end of metaphysics and ontology. Again, elusive. While I will not give a summative definition (it is best understood in context), we ought to understand phenomenology as, basically, the study of phenomena (manifested things), and how they have come to be manifest at all. The term lends itself to studies of consciousness, but it is perhaps most concerned with the appearing of things in their locales, and they ways in which we are aware of these manifestations.

One avenue for a phenomenological account of sacramentality could very well again turn to Jean-Luc Marion and investigate a chapter (serendipitously) titled, "The Phenomenality of the Sacrament." In the essay, he is ultimately concerned, like us, with "the sacramentality of the sacrament."[44] Thus he sets out an investigation of how its *phenomenality* is sacramental, that is, how God has *appeared* in the sacrament qua sacrament. His essay is extremely helpful, but I want to take us in a different direction, largely because we would be treading some similar ground to our first section. If Marion is interested in the "noematic kernel"[45] of a sacrament, we are interested in some "intersubjective kernel" (to say it awkwardly). In other words, besides the level of noematic appearing, or appearing the consciousness per se, I am interested in the sacramentality of the sacrament in the fullness of the way that I experience it, which is above all *bodily*. This calls for a different kind of approach—not rationality, but an experience of the *flesh*. In this section, we will consider the flesh as one such locale for manifestation of sacramental "more-ness."

---

the reasons we have shown, but also because of the unique way in which we undertake sacramental rites in the church.

44. Marion, "Phenomenality of the Sacrament," 102.
45. Marion, "Phenomenality of the Sacrament," 104.

Additionally, we ought to consider how I am using the word "flesh," because for a Christian audience, flesh is a loaded term. I am not, strictly, opposing flesh to spirit in the classic Platonic Christian sense, and especially not assigning it moral value as a symbol for sinful life.[46] The *phenomenological* category of the flesh designates, above all, the experience of one's body, "the identity of what touches with the medium where this touching takes place (Aristotle), therefore of the felt with what feels (Husserl), but also of the seen and the seeing or the heard and the hearing—in short, of the *affected with the affecting*."[47] More simply, as the "immediate inner experience of *my* body," the flesh is precisely "the 'me' that is co-indicated in bodily acts."[48]

To explain, we can get a sense of this mode of affection when we retrieve the classic phenomenological distinction between on the one hand, the objective body (*Körper*), and on the other, the phenomenological body (*Leib*). Placing one hand on top of the other, we are aware of a *double-sensation*: both of the hand doing the touch, and the hand that is touched. Both, of course, vacillate between each position—each touches even as it is touched—but the important distinction is to recognize in the body both an *objective* quality, that is, the capacity to be seen, touched, investigated like an object in space, *and* a subjective quality, an immanent *mineness* (*Jemeinigkeit*). This subjective quality of the body is what is often called *the flesh*: the capacity my body has *to be mine at all*, to be experienced as mine, to be affected, to be touched and take up sensation into myself. What has now become an axiom of a phenomenology of the flesh since Michel Henry, we do not say "my ears hear," but "*I* hear." This hearing capacity, altogether different from tracing it in the hand, is what we are calling the flesh: *the lived experience* of the body.[49]

## Sacramentality and Phenomenology of Touch

From here, we can begin to sketch out an *intersubjective* sacramentality through a phenomenology of the flesh. By intersubjective, I mean a

---

46. Biblically, it's important to note that while flesh (σάρξ) is sometimes opposed to spirit (πνεῦμα), body (σῶμα) is almost never opposed to spirit.

47. Marion, *Being Given*, 231.

48. Matthew Farley, "Introduction," in Falque *Crossing the Rubicon*, 6.

49. This is the formulation Emmanuel Falque uses throughout his work, and it is just as appropriate here.

relation between two or more subjects, and more particularly here, the relation that is mediated by the flesh: subjects in contact. Where in the first section we were interested in processes of interpretation, and the meaning(s) that sacraments yield, here we are interested in the way that sacraments meet up with the lived experience of my body, that is, with my flesh. Sacramentality, from this starting point, takes stock of the lived experience of the body, and can be understood the kind of *fleshly* encounter with God that arises in the sacraments.

Emmanuel Levinas, in two great works—*Time and the Other* and *Totality and Infinity: An Essay on Exteriority*—takes up the modality of the flesh in order to investigate the act of "the caress," not simply as a sign of affection, but even more as a unique moment of *intersubjectivity*, where, mysteriously, two people are joined together through touch. The caress, he writes, "is a mode of the subject's being, where the subject who is in contact with another goes *beyond* this contact."[50] For Levinas, who is always meditating on what is *not* given, because "it is not the softness or the warmth of the hand given in contact that the caress seeks,"[51] but, we can say simply, that the caress seeks the being of another. To Levinas' point, when we hug someone we loved, grab their hand, scoot closer, can we say that we are *merely* interested in what this proximity, this contact feels like for our hands, our embrace? More likely, these gestures, like the caress, are undertaken as means of searching out the being of the other: "what is caressed is *not* touched, properly speaking."[52] That is to say initially, we are less interested in the qualities of the hand than in *whose* hand it is and *whom* we are searching out with our touch. We will have an opportunity to return to Levinas, but we might say here that something of a "mineness" reaches out to their "mineness."

Emmanuel Falque develops this thought towards an explanation of incorporation. Incorporation for Falque is understood in a remarkably similar way to Levinas' idea of "the caress." Indeed, Falque even stops by Levinas' thought on the way to his comments about the bleeding woman in Mark 5. Where Levinas was interested in the way that I search out another by my contact with them, Falque is interested in the way that my body is affected by the body of another, such that incorporation involves the "intersecting of fleshes."[53] As the woman reaches out to touch Jesus,

---

50. Levinas, *Time and the Other*, 89; emphasis added.
51. Levinas, *Time and the Other*, 40.
52. Levinas, *Time and the Other*, 40.
53. Falque, *Guide to Gethsemane*, 90.

this double-awareness provides for Falque a prime example of the way that bodies in contact become aware of one another at the phenomenological level of the flesh. This is not to say, however, that every touch is incorporative. Jean-Luc Marion has shown how the flesh of the other can be quite simply, denied; never moving past the status of an object in space, the body of another can be no different for me than a chair I accidentally nick, a table I *almost* walk around.[54] One only needs to think of the kind of interactions on subways, busses, or airplanes to understand this sense of an isolating bump.

For the woman in Mark 5, however, the intention of her touch allows a kind of *intersubjective* awareness, by which not only is she aware of the person and power of Christ, but by which Christ himself is aware of her. In the midst of the crowd pressing in all around him, Jesus feels *her* touch. Falque writes, "When the woman touches Jesus through his clothes ('who touched my clothes?') she does not jostle him with impunity, as in some kind of rough bodily bump, when passengers on a train collide with one another, in a hurry and squeezed together," but instead, "her touching is *animated* by her intention . . . to *incorporate* herself with the flesh of the Son by touching his garment."[55] Extending past Levinas, Falque asserts that through this kind of animated touch, "The bodies of the woman with hemorrhages and that of Jesus are thus in a way specifically 'con-tingent' with one another," so as to found, in "con-tact or an 'intersecting of fleshes [*cum-tangere* (to touch with)]."[56] Finally, related through touch, we can say that the two are "incorporated" by "a touch *in the form of a caress* (rather than the collision of or contact of bodies that remain in total exteriority)."[57] Each is aware of the other not merely cognitively, but corporally, and the other's body becomes part of their immanent experience.

By way of review, both the caress and the "animated" touch reveal modes of an intersubjective relationship in which our lived experience meets up with the lived experience of another, such that we can no longer say that the other is *just* another object for us (remaining in total exteriority), but that we are brought into an awareness of the other. For Levinas, this relation came about through the caress, in which my touch goes

---

54. Marion, *Prolegomena to Charity*, 165.
55. Falque, *Guide to Gethsemane*, 89–90; emphasis added.
56. Falque, *Guide to Gethsemane*, 90.
57. Falque, *Guide to Gethsemane*, 90; emphasis added.

*beyond* contact. Building on the caress, Falque suggests that this touch goes beyond contact and brings the other person into view, or, brings about a kind of touch in which the objectifying touch gives way to the intersubjective touch: incorporation. Incorporation involves not merely my intentional touch, as the woman who touched Jesus, but involves the other's recognition and participation in that touch as well: "Who touched my clothes?"

These two approaches can help foreground how we are understanding a sacramentality of touch. Sacramentality is a kind of *intersubjective contact*, an *incorporation*, a relation to Christ through touch. Much in the same way that the woman reaches out to Christ and hopes only to touch him through his garment, the sacraments offer us a similar kind of being-in-contact. Not that the very historical Christ is present, but that through the unique media of water, bread, and wine, Christ is present to our very flesh—our affectivity—and we are given to a kind of *incorporation* into Christ by this intentional touch we undertake.[58] Just as the woman and Christ found themselves at an intersection of the flesh, so even "we take part in the life of the Resurrected One in its otherness; we make our communion with his Life rather than focusing on ourselves or confining ourselves solely within our egoisms."[59] Sacramentality derived from an attention to the flesh discovers the very presence of God as something which presents itself to be "searched out" within our very *selves* (incorporation).

Why not just stop here and pronounce sacramentality the experience of incorporation which sacraments offer? Falque writes as much, in that incorporation is "a going out and into an other who is not me and will never be reducible to me."[60] But phrases like "total identification," and "total integration,"[61] suggest perhaps less intersubjective distance than I am recommending here. We would like to nuance the claim a bit. Again, Levinas reminds us that "what is caressed is *not* touched, properly speaking." The caress is a searching, but not a *grasping*.

Better yet, Levinas tells us that in the caress, we are precisely aware of the *depth* of the other, not as something uncovered, but something

---

58. Marion, *Prolegomena to Charity*, 160: "Only love opens up the knowledge of the other as such."

59. Falque, *Wedding Feast*, 206.

60. Falque, *Wedding Feast*, 207.

61. Falque, *Wedding Feast*, 206–8.

which remains "clandestine in discovery."[62] That is, we are aware of a *hiddenness*: "The hidden—never hidden enough—is beyond the personal and as its reverse, refractory to the light, a category exterior to the play of being and nothingness, beyond the possible, for absolutely ungraspable."[63] Playing with mythic categories of darkness and light, Levinas reminds us that no incorporation is total, and where presence is given first of all to light, there is an intersubjective *reserve* typologized in darkness—that which is categorically hidden. I am certainly aware of the being and even flesh of another ("Who touched my cloak"), but I am likewise exposed to what has *not*, and *will not*, come to light in our intersubjectivity. This is perhaps the only way to be aware of another's flesh (*Leib*), insofar as it remains *their* flesh, that is, their "mineness." It is made known to us *as* something hidden, quite literally, the "mystery" of the other's alterity.[64]

In the same way, as if led to a cave we have no means to explore, I am both intimately aware of the presence of Christ and yet identically aware of the hiddenness of Christ in a sacrament—that which has not yet come into the light of contact, the intersubjective reserve. In this sense, sacramentally, we cannot merely speak of the saturated phenomenon (Marion), nor the limited phenomenon (Falque), but the *hidden phenomenon*: that which gives itself not in brightness, but in darkness and reservation.[65] As opposed to oversignification (saturated phenomenon),

62. Levinas, *Totality and Infinity*, 265.

63. Levinas, *Totality and Infinity*, 264.

64. Levinas, *Time and the Other*, 87.

65. We are, really, a razor's edge away from Falque's understanding of the "limited phenomenon," which he describes as, "that [which] *lies beneath signification*" (Falque, *Wedding Feast*, 12). Where the two concepts diverge is more likely in terminology; Falque opts for language of "Chaos," and "limit," and I am opting for "reserve" and "hiddenness." Consider Falque's summation here, "Chaos is invasion. It is the impossibility of coming to terms with the 'mass of sensations'—not simply in that it breaks open the framework of what we can come to terms with, to signify in another way (saturated phenomenon), but, inversely, because it shows us that it is not able to formulate itself (the limited phenomenon). . . . It comes from accepting a limit that Chaos overflows, without ever being received or transformed into consciousness" (Falque, *Wedding Feast*, 22). Falque has in mind a kind of internal Chaos that is never appears to us, and what the Eucharist ultimately plumbs and transforms. In that sense, Chaos is abated, even if not signified. For our purposes, while it may be true that the Eucharist plumbs this internal Chaos of my being, we need a different category (one not loaded with moral significance, like Chaos) in order to suggest a *reciprocal* limit, or better, *hiddenness* of God which will never surface to signification, but which is nonetheless not necessarily "chaotic." For Falque's description of the limited phenomenon, see Falque, *Wedding Feast*, 5–30.

the hidden phenomenon gives itself as too *deep* to grasp. Sacramentally speaking, at the level of touch, the presence of Christ is this hidden phenomenon; Christ is present here for incorporation *and* is nevertheless the as-yet-ungraspable, *hidden* presence which I still intuit. This is a sacramentality of touch.

I become uniquely aware of the presence of Christ in a sacrament, even to suggest a kind of "animated touch" that draws Christ into my lived experience, or, my flesh. This possibility is the first order of sacramentality. But the second order involves the way that sacramentality is not merely the presence of Christ I encounter, but also a *depth* of Christ that I will nonetheless never fully grasp. What makes a sacrament a sacrament is, in part, that Christ is *hidden* there. Just as in the first section, mystery was understood as an intuition without a meaning, here mystery is an *intuition without a complete contact*. We can conceive of sacramentality in precisely this fashion: the intuition which a sacrament brings *to my flesh* of the in-contactable being of God.

## Conclusion

A fuller understanding of sacramentality, it seems, takes text and flesh together. Some of the most significant theological consequences of our approach have to do with the diverse reality of lives within the pews. The de-emphasis of strict signification I think leaves room for the reality of doubt, while it also paves way for a sacramentality that is accountable to developmental differences. If cognition is not the essence of our encounter with God, then we are in a better place to think about whether or not cognition ought to be the essence of our sacramentality at all.

Additionally, it appears that we have grounds, then, to broaden the standard Anglican (Thomistic) definition of a sacrament as "outward and visible signs of an inward and spiritual grace." We would want to include *tangible* to the list of adjectives. A sacrament is not merely a visible thing, but always also a *tangible* thing, which nevertheless gives rise to the mystery of the other through touch. Touch plays a central role here as we begin to think through not merely the life of the mind in worship, but the life of the body as well.

To sum up, in the introduction, we called attention to a "more-ness," and here we can see better how more-ness means both overabundance *and* hiddenness. In an Easter sermon on the Johannine Resurrection scene, the seventeenth century Anglican bishop Lancelot Andrewes meditates on Mary Magdalene weeping at the tomb of Jesus. Beautifully, he says, "She weeps, because she found the grave emptie, which God forbid she should have found full, for then Christ must have been dead still, and so, no Resurrection."[66] Another way to sum up this paper would be through Lancelot's Andrewes incredible turn here to reinvest emptiness with a terrific assurance of faith, rather than its abandonment. Throughout the essay, I have tried to expose a kind of emptiness that is really at the heart of sacramentality.

In either respect, the more-ness means either something more than signification (hermeneutics), or something beyond touch (phenomenology). It is my overall claim here that sacramentality is not ultimately about signification, in the same way that this resurrection scene is not about a full tomb, but is about intuition, an empty tomb. Lancelot Andrewes reminds us that Christ's *absence* from the tomb is far more important than his presence here. In the same way, sacramentality is an *opening* in the possibilities of interpretation, an intuition of presence without an attributable meaning *to* that presence.

If sacramentality is not ultimately about signification, then what is it about? Where first Christ appeared disguised, it is only when Christ *addresses* Mary that she cries out "Rabbouni!" (John 20:16). Ultimately, sacramentality is about the way in which we, too, find ourselves addressed by a God hidden (disguised) in these material things like wine, bread, or water. Sacramentality is not simply the meaning it bears in a service, but the way that we find ourselves addressed in a sacrament, called by name into the newness of life, that we might in turn respond, "Rabbouni!"

## Bibliography

Andrewes, Lancelot. *Selected Sermons*. Edited with introduction and commentary by Peter McCullough. Oxford: Oxford University Press, 2005.

Augustine, St. *Teaching Christianity (De Doctrina Christiana)*. Translated with notes by Edmund J. Hill. Hyde Park, NY: New City, 1996.

Caputo, John. *Radical Hermeneutics: Repetition, Deconstruction, and Hermeneutics*. Bloomington: Indiana University Press, 1987.

Falque, Emmanuel. *Crossing the Rubicon: The Borderlands of Philosophy and Theology*. Translated by George Hughes. New York: Fordham University Press, 2016.

———. *The Guide to Gethsemane: Anxiety, Suffering, and Death*. Translated by George Hughes. New York: Fordham University Press, 2019.

---

66. Andrewes, *Selected Sermons*, 232.

———. *The Wedding Feast of the Lamb: Eros, the Body, and the Eucharist*. Translated by George Hughes. New York: Fordham University Press, 2016.

Gonzalez, Justo L. *Santa Biblia: The Bible through Hispanic Eyes*. Nashville: Abingdon, 1996.

Kearney, Richard, and Brian Treanor, eds. *Carnal Hermeneutics*. New York: Fordham University Press, 2015.

Levinas, Emmanuel. *Alterity and Transcendence*. Translated by Michael B. Smith. New York: Columbia University Press, 1999.

———. *Time and the Other*. Translated by Richard A. Cohen. Pittsburgh: Duquesne University Press, 1987.

———. *Totality and Infinity: An Essay on Exteriority*. Translated by Alphonso Lingis. Pittsburgh: Duquesne University Press, 1969.

Macquarrie, John. *A Guide to the Sacraments*. New York: Continuum, 1997.

Marion, Jean-Luc. *Being Given: Toward a Phenomenology of Givenness*. Translated by Jeffery L. Kosky. Stanford: Stanford University Press, 2002.

———. "The Phenomenality of the Sacrament." In *Believing in Order to See: On the Rationality of Revelation and the Irrationality of Some Believers*, translated by Christina Gschwandtner, 102–15. New York: Fordham University Press, 2017.

———. *Prolegomena to Charity*. Translated by Stephen E. Lewis. New York: Fordham University Press, 2002.

Merleau-Ponty, Maurice. *Phenomenology of Perception*. Translated by Donald A. Landes. London: Routledge, 2012.

Pickstock, Catherine. *After Writing: On the Liturgical Consummation of Philosophy*. Malden, MA: Blackwell, 1997.

Ricœur, Paul. "Existence and Hermeneutics." In *The Conflict of Interpretations: Essays in Hermeneutics*, translated by Kathleen McLaughlin, 3–24. Evanston, IL: Northwestern University Press, 2007.

———. *Freud and Philosophy: An Essay on Interpretation*. Translated by Denis Savage. New Haven: Yale University Press, 1970.

———. *Hermeneutics and the Human Sciences: Essays on Language, Action, and Interpretation*. New York: Cambridge University Press, 2016.

———. *Interpretation Theory: Discourse and the Surplus of Meaning*. Fort Worth: Texas Christian University Press, 1976.

———. "Philosophical Hermeneutics and Biblical Hermeneutics." In *From Text to Action: Essays in Hermeneutics II*, translated by Katheen Blamey and John B. Thompson, 89–101. Evanston, IL: Northwestern University Press, 2007.

Smith, James K. A. *The Fall of Interpretation: Philosophical Foundations for a Creational Hermeneutic*. Grand Rapids: Baker Academic, 2012.

Williams, Rowan. *Grace and Necessity*. Harrisburg: Morehouse, 2005.

2

# The Religiously Unaffiliated and the Sacramental Church

*Beverly Eileen Mitchell*

Our churches are concerned with the challenge of secularism in our society, and its impact on the stability of the Christian church as a force for individual and social transformation. This concern has been heightened by growing data which indicates that more than half of the American population report that they are unaffiliated with a community of faith. Those religionists who fear that the U.S. is being overtaken by secular humanism, may take some comfort in the fact that research results indicate that the decline in regular church attendance does not support the conclusion that the unaffiliated are without faith or lacking in spiritual desire. This essay will unpack the distinctions between those who identify as "spiritual but not religious" and those who assert that they "love Jesus but not the church," and reimagine the challenge of secularism as an opportunity to reclaim our understanding of the church as a sacrament of Christ and a viable path toward church renewal.

## "Religious" or "Spiritual"

The landscape of the religiously unaffiliated is complicated. Those who seek to understand why so many Americans indicate no allegiance to the institutional church must first reckon with the distinction between spirituality and religion. Patrick Love's examination of these terms is very helpful for enabling us to understand what people are affirming and denying when they speak about being "spiritual but not religious." While some people who readily acknowledge the distinction between the two terms, there are others who use the term "spiritual" and "religious" interchangeably.[1] Love makes a strong case for differentiating spirituality from religion. Drawing from the *Random House Dictionary of the English Language* (1979) definition of both terms, Love identifies important characteristics of a useful definition of the word "religion."[2] These characteristics are:

1. Religion speaks to the concern over *what exists beyond the visible world*. It does this by way of faith and intuition, as opposed to reason.

2. Religion includes the idea of the *existence of a single being*, a group of beings, an eternal principle or a transcendent spiritual entity that has created the world, governs it, and either controls the destiny of that world or may intervene occasionally in the natural course of its history.

3. Religion is a specific set of fundamental *beliefs and practices* that are generally accepted by a number of persons.

4. Religion is the idea that *ritual, prayer, spiritual exercises, or certain principles and conduct* arise naturally as a human response to the belief in such a being or eternal principle.

These components of the definition of religion can be applied to many of the major religious traditions in American society.[3] While there may be other components one might add, I believe these characteristics constitute several of the major components of religion in the United States. These four components include a recognition that there is a dimension

---

1. Love, "Differentiating Spirituality from Religion."

2. A quick review of the copyrighted 2021 version of the *Random House Dictionary of the English Language* online includes aspects of the 1979 entry. I affirm Love's preference for the 1979 version.

3. Love, "Differentiating Spirituality from Religion."

of reality which is not fully captured by what we can perceive with our physical senses; that there is a transcendent being or entity that creates and preserves the material world; that our lives are governed by beliefs and practices that keep us mindful of the continual need to align ourselves with this transcendent being; and that our commitment to honor and worship this divine being is nurtured by diverse practices and rituals that keep this connection between ourselves and the transcendent alive. Religion may be expressed individually and communally, is related to but not identical with that vitality and energy that enriches and enlivens our us beyond our material needs. That which taps into this vitality and feeds our hunger for transcendence can be called "spirituality."

As Love indicates, and I agree, that spirituality is a concept whose definition is more diffuse and because of this diffusion and ambiguity there is less consensus regarding its meaning. In an article Love coauthors with Donna Talbot, they synthesize a number of definitions of spirituality taken from theology, social science, and the helping professions, (e.g., nursing, counseling, and social work).[4] Love and Talbot identify five components of spirituality:

1. Spirituality is an *internal path* of seeking personal authenticity, genuineness, and wholeness as an aspect of identity development.

2. Spirituality involves a process of continually *transcending one's current locus* of centricity, rather than egocentricity.

3. Spirituality involves a greater *connectedness to self and others* through relationships and union with community.

4. Spirituality is a *path in which meaning, purpose, and direction* in one's life may be sought.

5. Spirituality can involve an *increasing openness to explore a relationship with an intangible and pervasive power or essence or center of value* that exists beyond human existence and rational human knowing.

These components strongly indicate an inward, personal focus. They suggest a struggle to attain mastery over that which fragments the individual from everything and everyone else. They recognize the interconnectedness each individual has to everyone else. There is a desire to establish a deep connection with that transcendent entity or being. There is a trajectory toward fulfillment of a telos toward which one focuses one's life.

4. Love and Talbot, "Defining Spiritual Development."

In reviewing the features of religion and spirituality, it is obvious that there are areas of overlap, such as both have a concern for that which exists beyond the corporeal, rational, and visible universe. Both seek to provide a means for understanding that which lies beyond our physical, time-bound world. One aspect of this transcendence is the notion of a supreme being. In religion, the transcendent being is identified. However, in spirituality there may be an *openness* to a supreme being, or even a belief of something transcendent from what we can see, but there is a "tentativeness" about just who or what that transcendent entity might be. Although the idea of a transcendent aspect exists in both religion and spirituality, the two define that transcendence differently. Love maintains that a spiritually developed *religious* person may identify that entity as God. However, a spiritually developed *nonreligious* person may have no means (or no need) to define that which lies beyond rational knowing. Love and Talbot note that when looking at spirituality, *the supernatural is used explicitly* in the sense of that which exists beyond the natural world. However, matters regarding *deity* and *divine power* are addressed in the realm of religion.[5]

In reflecting on the differences between that which deals with religion and that which deals with spirituality, Love draws from the work of Sharon Parks.[6] She maintains that religion begins as an *external* phenomenon, and that its primary concern is external to the visible world. It is centered on the existence of a supreme being or eternal principle, and includes an agreed upon set of beliefs and practices that are external to the individual. Religion, she maintains, can exist separate and apart from the individual; however, this is not so for spirituality. Spirituality, in contrast, begins and remains a perpetually *internal* process, though there can be movement outward from oneself through self-transcendence. Spirituality is more personal rather than a public search for meaning, transcendence, wholeness, purpose, and apprehension of spirit (or Spirit), as the essence of life. Her view refines the distinction between religion and spirituality rather well for the purposes of this chapter.[7]

This discussion of the distinction between religion and spirituality will be useful for unpacking the research data regarding the "spiritual but not religious" and those who "love Jesus but not the church."

---

5. Love and Talbot, "Defining Spiritual Development."
6. Parks, *Big Questions, Worthy Dreams*.
7. Love and Talbot, "Defining Spiritual Development."

## "Spiritual but Not Religious"

The Barna Group is one organization that has been interested in examining the steady decrease in the number of Americans who have opted not to identify as "religious" and yet they consider themselves as "spiritual."[8] In a published 2017 survey, Barna looked at who the "spiritual but not religious" (SBNR) are, what they believe, and how they live out their spirituality daily. They determined that the SBNRs should be divided into two groups, which are individually described as follows:

> *Group #1 of the SBNRs: They view themselves as "spiritual" but say their religious faith is not a very important factor in their lives.* Some may self-identify as members of a religious tradition (Christian or non-Christian), but in many ways they could be classified as non-observant. For instance, an overwhelming majority have not attended a religious service in the past six months. Within this group, a sizable majority do not identify with a religious tradition at all.[9]

> *Group #2 of the SBNRs: They claim no faith at all, but around one-third of these say they are "spiritual."* More than half self-identify as "unaffiliated;" and nearly one-third identify as agnostic, and a very small number indicate that they are atheists. Of all who claim "no faith," around one-third say they are "spiritual."[10]

Both SBNR groups share key qualities and reflect similar trends despite representing two different kinds of American adults. One group is more "religiously literate" than the other.[11] The Report concludes, with justification, that whether individuals are classified in Groups #1 or #2, religious affiliation or the lack thereof has not affected the practices and beliefs which they have adopted. Neither group views religion as a central tenet of their lives nor does it hold any sway over their

---

8. The Barna Group is a research and resource company that tracks the role of faith and its intersection with American culture. It has developed into one of this country's most comprehensive databases of spiritual indicators through it thirty-year history. It has become a leading research organization for churches, nonprofits, and businesses in the U.S. and overseas.

9. To view the actual percentages represented in each category, please see the report, Barna Group, "Meet the Spiritual but not Religious."

10. Barna Group, "Meet the Spiritual but not Religious."

11. The researchers offer no explanation of what they mean by "religiously literate"; however, my sense is that the researchers are referring to those who have some prior background in or exposure to a religious tradition.

spiritual practices. The SBNRs hold less informed ideas about God, spiritual practices, and religion.[12]

The views of God and religion in both groups of SBNRs are fluid and lack precision. They are likely to believe that God represents a state of higher consciousness that a person may reach, rather than an all-powerful, all-knowing, perfect creator of the universe who rules the world. They are just as likely to be polytheistic as monotheistic. What constitutes "God" for the SBNRs is contested among them. Both SBNRs appear to be ambivalent about the value of religion in general. In line with a broader cultural resistance to institutions, SBNRs are generally suspicious of religion and so they seek autonomy from religious authority. As outsiders in terms of religious institutions, SBNRs tend to lack inside knowledge of religious institutions; therefore, they can be prone to hold unexamined assumptions regarding particular religious traditions. A majority of both SBNR groups are convinced that "all religions basically teach the same thing." SBNRs eschew definitions of terms and do not seem to have boundary markers regarding various religious traditions and practices. They also deny that any single religion has a monopoly on ultimate reality.[13]

Research results indicate that the orientation of their spirituality is focused inward. To be an SBNR is to possess a deeply personal and private spirituality, which is consistent with their general orientation toward autonomy from religious authority. If religions point outside oneself to a higher power for wisdom and guidance, a spirituality which is divorced from a religious tradition looks within. Only a small fraction of the two SBNR groups talk often with their friends about spiritual matters. In fact, they are more likely to *never* talk with their friends and family about spiritual matters, unlike practicing Christians.[14]

Regarding how SBNRs are spiritually fed, they are likely to engage in informal practices with an individualistic orientation. Such informal practices may involve yoga, meditation, silence and/or solitude. The most common spiritual practice for both SBNR groups is spending time in nature for reflection. Their manner of practice suggests an emphasis on personal autonomy or lack of accountability to religious authority or even a

---

12. Barna Group, "Meet the Spiritual but not Religious."
13. Barna Group, "Meet the Spiritual but not Religious."
14. Barna Group, "Meet the Spiritual but not Religious."

community.¹⁵ These two SBNR groups are different from a third group of the religiously unaffiliated: those who "Love Jesus But Not the Church."

## Those Who "Love Jesus but Not the Church"

The Barna Group also released a report in 2017 on a survey of those who "Love Jesus but Not the Church" (LJNC). The majority in this category are women and a large percentage are between the ages thirty-three and seventy. Only a small number of millennials fit into this category, even though they are the most unaffiliated generation. Their numbers are low in this group because millennials are the least likely to either identify as Christian or to indicate that faith is very important to their lives.¹⁶

Though LJNCs have attended church in the past, they had not done so in the last six months or more. They report having a "sincere" faith, but they choose not to attend church.¹⁷ Despite their lack of church attendance, they strongly affirm that their religious faith is very important in their lives. Their beliefs about God are not only "robustly orthodox," but rival their churchgoing counterparts, and are more traditional than the general population. Their view of God's attributes fits a classical definition of divinity: God as omnipotent, omniscient, omnipresent—a "perfect creator of the universe who rules the world today."¹⁸ The LJNCs retain a positive view of religion, aligning with their churchgoing counterparts, despite the former's discomfort with the institutional church. They also appear to be more open to the claims of other religious traditions and to seek common ground.¹⁹

LJNCs also tend to nurture a private spirituality. They prefer to keep spiritual matters to themselves and, in general, do not feel an obligation to evangelize; sharing their faith is a low priority. Though they actively practice their faith, they do so in less traditional ways.²⁰ They

---

15. Barna Group, "Meet the Spiritual but not Religious."

16. Barna Group, "They 'Love Jesus but Not the Church.'"

17. The Barna Group recognizes that church attendance is not necessarily a good measure of commitment to the faith and the strength of a person's spiritual practices.

18. It is interesting to note that the attribute of God as all-loving or omnibenevolent is missing from this list of traits of the divine.

19. Barna Group, "They 'Love Jesus but not the Church.'"

20. Because of their enduring religious affiliation and overt religious faith, they fall *outside* of the characterization of adults who are "spiritual but not religious." Note, however, that both some SBNRs and most, if not all, LJNCs affirm that they are attentive to the spiritual dimension of their lives.

may maintain an active prayer life, but only read scripture half as much as the average practicing Christian. They are also much less likely too read a book on spiritual topics and they never attend group meetings or retreats. Although LJNCs are less connected to an established religious identity, e.g., denomination or religious tradition, they still seek experiences of God; but are more likely to do so in nature and through informal practices such as meditation, yoga, silence and solitude.[21]

## Interpreting the Barna Research Results

There are aspects of these studies that are worth noting in terms of capturing the distinctions between the SBNRs and the LJNCs. As Barna editor Roxanne Stone explains, the intent of the study of the "Spiritual but Not Religious," was to explore what spirituality *outside of religious faith* looks like. By contrast, the study of the "I Love Jesus but Not the Church," explored what religious faith *outside of institutional religion* looks like. There were key differences between these groups. Those who describe themselves as loving Jesus but not the church are disenchanted with the *church*. Those who self-identify as spiritual but not religious are disenchanted with *religion*.[22]

The lovers of Jesus but not the church hold tightly to their Christian belief, but find little value in the church as a component of that belief. The spiritual but not religious reject religion and are determined to define the boundaries of their own spirituality. To do so, they will mix beliefs and practices from a variety of religions and traditions.[23]

The "spiritual but not religious" and the "I love Jesus but not the church" groups represent an equal percentage of the American population. All indicators suggest to Barna researchers that both groups are growing. The lovers of Jesus but not the church are more open to religion and may be more receptive to re-joining the church at some point. However, Barna researchers suggest that the spiritual but not religious are not to be discounted. Because they are distinct among their non-religious peers in their spiritual curiosity and openness, there may be ways in which this group can be reached. This is something for those who

---

21. Barna Group, "They Love Jesus but Not the Church."
22. Stone, Barna Group, "Meet the Spiritual but Not Religious."
23. Stone, Barna Group, "Meet the Spiritual but Not Religious."

have a heart for evangelism to consider.[24] It is also critical to note that the majority of those who have rejected religious faith do *not* describe themselves as "spiritual." Similarly, two-thirds of those with no faith at all do not identify themselves as "spiritual" (SBNR group #2). One bright spot regarding those of the "spiritual but not religious" group, who do view themselves as spiritual (SBNR group #1), is that they do display an "uncommon" inclination to think beyond the material and to experience the transcendent. Barna believes, and rightly so, this *could* open the door to deep, spiritual conversations and, even a willingness to hear about Christian spirituality.[25]

Conversations between those who love Jesus but not the church will be very different from those who self-describe as non-religious. As the Barna Group rightly points out in their analysis, the wounds and suspicions toward church will come from different places, as well as their understanding of what spirituality entails. Both groups represent people who are outside the church, though they have an internal attraction to the spiritual side of life. This clearly suggests that the spiritual hunger is there, and reaching them is possible.[26]

I am not unsympathetic to those who assert that they are "spiritual but not religious." The claim to be "spiritual" among the SBNRs in group #1 suggests that there is a spark of desire in the individual who recognizes the need to strive for a life of integrity, (e.g., their interior life and its exterior expression are consistent); there is a hunger to transcend the limitations of the human condition; a recognition of there being more to life than what can be grasped in the material world; and a longing to connect with something or Someone greater than oneself. This "spiritual" dimension may be expressed in some form of theism or non-theism, but there is an inchoate sense that there is more to a meaningful life then eating, drinking, and making merry.

I can easily identify at times with those who "love Jesus but not the church." I do so because I understand the "allergic reaction" to religious institutions and aspects of congregational life. To some extent, I have suffered from that same allergy. I have seen the underside of church life and church-related institutions, including an experience or two of "church

---

24. Having said this, I would also caution that traditional forms of evangelism are not likely to be effective. Exploration of the reasons for the reasons for the SBNR's disaffection would have to be done.
25. Barna Group, "Meet the Spiritual but Not Religious."
26. Barna Group, "Meet the Spiritual but Not Religious."

hurt." As one who cherishes solitude and silence, I tend to chafe at the give-and-take of social interaction and the superficial engagement that frequently accompanies congregational life. My temptation is to journey alone. However, I am always reminded of the stern warning that Dietrich Bonhoeffer gives in *Life Together*. Though he definitely recognizes the need for solitude and silence, he also asserts that communal gathering is not only essential, but a "gift" of grace to us.[27] Solitude *and* community are the warp and woof of faithful discipleship: *"Let him who cannot be alone beware of community. . . . Let him who is not in community beware of being alone."*[28]

Beyond coming together and then being apart, what do we do *after* our weekly worship hour and our regular time apart in our personal spiritual practices? To what extent do our participation and solitude facilitate not only our own spiritual transformation but also that of others, who may not be part of our faith community? After the hymns are sung, the Scripture is read, the gospel is preached, and the Lord's Supper is celebrated, *How then shall we live?* Does being a church member make us love our neighbors more? Do these activities make a difference in our interactions with strangers, acquaintances, or even family? Are we more generous to those who have less? Are we more courageous in the long fight for injustice? *What is the purpose of the church, and what is its role in the world?*

## An Epiphany at the Church of the Epiphany

In the earlier years of the second Gulf War, when I was in the middle of a season of absence from corporate worship life, I felt that the pretext for war was a moral outrage and this matter troubled me deeply. I began to look for a church that I could regularly attend because I strongly sensed that I needed to be part of a faith community while I engaged in my small acts of resistance to the war. I stumbled upon a relatively small Episcopal church in downtown Washington, DC, which I frequently passed by on my walks to the Metro Center Station. I noticed that they held mid-day services most weekdays. One day I finally came to one of those services. A very small group was gathered for that service and the vibrant, white-haired, lanky, middle-aged pastor gave a short reflection, in which he

---

27. Bonhoeffer, *Life Together*, 20.
28. Bonhoeffer, *Life Together*, 77.

briefly mentioned the war. I cannot remember what scriptural passage he had read or what the key point of his homily was. However, what I *heard* resonated with me. Moreover, what he said indicated that perhaps this church did not focus exclusively on the business of preserving this particular church, but that he knew that whatever holy rituals were observed within this congregation, the church has a responsibility to care about some of the troubling things that were happening in the nation's capital and in the world as a *person of faith*. This church did not reside in a bubble of its own, but was aware of the suffering of the world.

With my appetite whet, I decided to attend a worship service the very next Sunday. I opted to attend the 8 am service. I thought I could slip in quietly, hopefully unnoticed, and leave without fanfare. I walked into the church that morning and was astonished at the number in attendance. The church was full of people! However, the greater shock came as I settled into a pew and noticed *who* was there. Many of the people sitting in the red-cushioned pews were homeless. Some of them came with large bags containing all of their possessions. Some sat quietly, but others walked around at will, whether the scripture was being read or someone was praying or even while the minister was preaching. Some showed signs of mental illness or inebriation, a few were either talking to themselves or staring bleary-eyed or with eyes unfocused. In the midst of those who would be perceived as alien in "polite" society, there was a smattering of people who sat among them who looked "normal."

I had never seen anything like it. As a habitual walker in the downtown DC area, I was sadly quite familiar with unhoused people who congregated at the entrances to Metro rail stations, abandoned stores, nearby parks, and even on the steps of local churches. However, here, at this church, the homeless were not shooed away so as not to offend the sensibilities or to disturb worshippers coming in from the suburbs. The unhoused were *welcomed* in, invited to sit in the pews, and encouraged but never forced to participate. In fact this 8:00 am service was dedicated to them.

The hymns sung were from an African American hymnal. The liturgy was uncomplicated but intensely meaningful. Scripture passages were read by members of the homeless community. A homily was given with illustrations with which the unhoused and unemployed might be able to connect. The culmination of worship was the celebration of the Lord's Supper. *All* were invited to the Welcome Table. After the service was over, those who had signed up for breakfast following communion quietly waited for their name to be called so that they could have a hearty meal. I was wowed by what I had witnessed. I came back for more, week after week for some time. I realized that the Word of God was being read and preached and communion was served and no one was left out. This was all done without patronizing fanfare. With elation, I found myself thinking, "Now *this* is church! This is what the church is *really* about." What I experienced there was meant to be expressed beyond what had transpired within the walls of that church. After the benediction was pronounced, we were all invited to "go and do likewise" (Luke 10:37). What I have come to realize is that what I experienced at Church of the Epiphany was a community of faith living as a *sacramental* church that pointed not to itself but pointed outward to the One we were invited to follow.

## Church: The Sacrament of Christ's Presence in the World

In local Baptist churches, such as the black American Baptist church in which I was raised and nurtured, you are unlikely to hear the term "sacrament" used. In Baptist theology, baptism and communion are considered "ordinances" not "sacraments." Both rituals of initiation into Christian discipleship are observances that Jesus himself commanded that his disciples should do. Our participation in both rites are seen as acts of obedience. They are treated as important rites which the Baptist church observes and should be undertaken with reverence and solemnity. During my youth and young adulthood, this was a satisfactory explanation of the significance of baptism and the Lord's Supper for the church. However, I will limit my discussion regarding this to the Lord's Supper.

The exposition of the Baptist perspective on the Lord's Supper has been theologically satisfying to me for several reasons. As a young member of the Baptist congregation to which I belonged as a child, the emphasis regarding communion was on what I did as a believer, e.g., I was to approach this ritual with solemnity and great reverence. I was to remember that Jesus died for my sins. I was to live according to the Baptismal Covenant; otherwise, God would not be pleased with me. Looking back, there is nothing inherently wrong with being mindful of these matters; however, as one can clearly see, the emphasis is placed upon *me*, e.g., how *I* approached the communion table, what *I* was to remember, and how *I* was to live. As Stanley J. Grenz explains, baptism and the Lord's Supper point to God's saving activity, understood as the eschatological transformation of all believers within the context of the establishment of the new creation. They point toward the work that is already being accomplished by the renewing work of the indwelling Holy Spirit, whose presence is a pledge of the eschatological fullness of salvation.[29] With Grenz's explanation one can clearly see that baptism and the Lord's Supper point to what *God* has done, is doing, and will yet do. God's saving activity is not something limited to the past; but rather, continues now and into the future. Such an expansive understanding of God's saving activity reveals good news that has meaning and value to not only me but to the community of faith *and* the world at large.

In contrast to a Baptist perspective on baptism and the Lord's Supper, Article 25 of the *Thirty-Nine Articles* of the Church of England, presents a view of these two rites in sacramental terms, e.g., "outward and visible signs of inward and spiritual grace,"[30] stating in part:

> The sacraments instituted by Christ are not only badges or tokens of the profession of Christians but also sure witnesses and effectual signs of God's grace and good will towards us. Through them he works invisibly within us, both bringing to life and also strengthening and confirming our faith in him. There are two sacraments instituted by Christ our Lord in the Gospel—baptism and the Lord's Supper.[31]

Although the articulation of this Anglican view of the sacraments expressed in the *Articles* has been helpful, it was not compelling enough to change my view of the two rites of initiation beyond my Baptist upbringing. However, a definition of sacraments by British Baptist Paul Fiddes nudged me forward. Fiddes writes,

> The sacraments are pieces of matter that God takes and uses as special places of encounter with [Godself]; grace transforms nature, and grace is nothing less than God's gracious coming to us and to God's world. . . . In the sacraments, God's action in creation and redemption . . . fuses into a particular focus.[32]

---

29. Grenz, "Baptism and the Lord's Supper as Community Acts," 77, 80, 81. Current Baptist scholars have been reconsidering the traditional stance against sacraments and have been engaged in much discussion regarding the extent to which the notion of "sacraments" could be embraced in Baptist theology.

30. Episcopal Church, *Book of Common Prayer*, 857.

31. Church of England, "The Articles of Religion," art. 25.

32. Fiddes, "Baptism and Creation," quoted in Cross and Thompson, *Baptist Sacramentalism*, 1:2.

Connecting the idea of God's taking and using "pieces of matter" as special places of encounter with God with the incarnation, whereby the "Word became flesh," I have been able to move closer toward a theology of the sacraments. Regarding the Lord's Supper, interpreted as Fiddes does above, although theologically I affirm that there is a qualitative distinction between God and creation or nature, I am reminded that God does not abhor creation because of sin. Rather, God's creation is good enough to be used as a vessel in which God's saving activity is revealed. This is so, not because of any innate quality of creation itself, but because God's grace accompanies God's presence and activity.

Roman Catholic theologian Nicholas Lash makes the case for speaking of the Christian *church* as a sacrament of Christ's presence in the world. His discussion has been most instrumental in shifting my view of the term "sacrament" and has given me language to interpret theologically what I experienced at Church of the Epiphany. Lash rightly observes that in the New Testament, what constituted the primitive church was

> the consciousness of this community that it only existed, as a community, in the presence of the Spirit of the risen Christ. The church's role is to proclaim the gospel—that is, the good news of Christ. What this good news concerns is the here-and-now availability of the resources with which to "revolutionize" human society in the love of God.[33] What do I think of this latter assertion?

In this passage, Lash makes a salient point worth emphasizing: that the New Testament church's awareness was that the community only exists, "in the presence of the Spirit of the risen Christ." Thus, the community does not exist because groups of believers have gathered together to form a "club of like-minded" people; but rather, the church is formed and depends upon who and what the triune God is and does. In other words, the church is not "self-made." Further, if the church's role is to "proclaim the gospel," then the church bears witness to a reality which has been revealed to it. As Barth noted long ago, as a witness, the church bears witness to God, not to itself. Again, the subject is *God*—not what we do or do not do. To me, a focus placed upon God, indicates that the foundation for the existence of the church and its rites and ministries rest upon a solid foundation "not made with hands."

---

33. Lash, "The Eucharist," 172. Here, Lash draws from Article 7 of the *Constitution on the Liturgy*.

It is Lash's discussion of the *church* as a sacrament that has made sacramental language more compelling to me. It is more compelling to me because there is substance to and integration of how he expresses here the dynamic richness that is present when we elaborate more fully upon what it is that the sacramental elements signify. This is the beauty of theological reflection! We are encouraged to move beyond our embedded theology to a deliberative theology that dares to go deeper in its apprehension of what it is that God is saying to us.

Lash sees Christ as present in three forms: (1) the gathered community, (2) his presence in the word, and (3) his presence in the food. As a faithful Catholic, he affirms that the risen Christ is really, truly and substantially present under the forms of bread and wine. But he also points out that the most casual reading of the New Testament makes clear that the gospel writers understood that Christ is present *in the Spirit in the hearts and minds of the Christian community*. He reminds us that the message of the New Testament is about *people*, about humanity renewed, reborn to freedom and the love of God through water and the Holy Spirit. So, asks Lash, in what way is Christ really present in the Church?

This assertion does not deny that there may be other modes of Christ's presence in the world, but that his presence in those other modes is there *for the sake of his presence in his people*.[34] Moreover, the "even better way" of Christ's presence in the New Testament refers primarily to his presence in the people who live, now not they, but Christ lives in them.[35] Accordingly, the fundamental presence in the world of the risen Christ is his presence in people. But his presence is not first achieved in individuals, who then happen to come together to acknowledge the fact nor is the church simply a free association of individuals who decide to meet to further some common interest.[36] Again the importance of this lies in the recognition of *who* lays the foundation, *who* undergirds and supports the community of the gathered, and *who* draws people to God.

Acknowledging the fracturing of relationships between God and humans and between each other, Lash goes on to say that the redemptive love of God unites people with each other and with God. It is this redemptive love that creates human community. The work of our redemption is the work of building human community. The work of redemption

---

34. Lash, "The Eucharist," 173–74.

35. Lash, "The Eucharist," 174. Here, Lash paraphrases the Apostle Paul in Gal 2:20.

36. Lash, "The Eucharist," 174.

is the work of God; therefore in Christ, renewed human community pre-exists the recognition and acceptance of it by the individual. We are *called* to renewed community by God, through Christ, in the Spirit. Our coming together as the community of believers is the expression of our acceptance of this call in which, by faith, we find ourselves.[37]

It is clear from Lash, that *we* do not make community; rather, the act of Christian community is an act of God. If we think *we* are the ones who "make community," we import our own notions of what community is; we establish an "ideal" that we worship because we think it is our idea, our work. We think we are in charge. It is a recipe for disenchantment, disappointment, frustration, and pain. The issue is that this matter of community is not about what *we* do to create it. It is about what has been done on our behalf in Christ. Lash concludes by saying that the sacramental presence, sign-presence of Christ, in the form of bread and wine, can only be understood in the context of his presence in the believing community.[38] Moreover, it seems to me that the sacraments do not point to themselves, they point to God in Christ.

What I saw at Epiphany was a particular community of faith in which its members exemplified what one might call a community that believed that an integral part of their understanding of mission meant being open to the wounded, marginalized, ignored people in an economically comfortable society. This openness was neither half-hearted nor condescending. It was inclusive in the sense that those without a home and with frayed relationships with family and former friends and acquaintances now had a place of sanctuary whereby both their material and spiritual needs could be addressed. These social "outsiders" were treated as the fully human beings they were. They were neither treated as recipients of our largesse nor were perceived as having little or nothing to offer a congregation that by global standards was well-off. We were bearers of each other. Although no community, religious or secular, is without flaws. I saw the possibilities of what genuine community could be.

I am sure that there are many more examples of churches which, in their own context, exemplify ways in which we can see God's saving activity within those communities of faith. To what extent do we help members of our congregations perceive such glimpses of the kingdom in their midst? Those who claim to "love Jesus but not the church" and

---

37. Lash, "The Eucharist," 174.
38. Lash, "The Eucharist," 178.

some of the self-identified "spiritual but not religious" are unable to see that the journey of a richly fulfilled life in the Spirit will always need the discipline of the give-and-take of embodied life in community. What the growth of the religiously unaffiliated may be saying to us is that we may need to take a long, hard look at the extent to which we truly equip and prepare churchgoers to respond concretely to a world that is not only materially hungry but deeply spiritually hungry as well More so now than ever before, they are unlikely to come to us, no matter how welcoming we think we are. The church, the sacrament of Christ, must go to *them*. The church as a sacrament of Christ faces outwardly.

This means that our local churches are not isolated communities who attend only to the needs of those who "belong" to the church as members. Of course, the church does tend to its members but the church equips, strengthens, and encourages us to look around us, to be attentive to the welfare of our neighbors, to those marked as outcasts for one reason or another, to those around us who need to perceive the love and presence of God in the *world*. Our mission is not to make others conform to us, our ways and customs, our worldview; but rather, to be "channels" by which the Holy Spirit may draw them to Christ. Prayerfully, we can allow ourselves to be used as channels such that the world just might perceive Christ in us.

Because the church is the church of *Christ*, the presence of Christ there is significant for us, who profess to be a part of it, but also to the religiously unaffiliated. He is not just "up there" or at our local church on designated corners, but rather he is "out there." What has struck me as I see, hear, and read about the loss of the ones who were once religiously affiliated or the growth of the number of those who are unaffiliated, is the frantic search for those we hope will join us because we nice people or we have the kind of ministry programs that will attract families with youth and children. Is this lament about the numbers reflective a nostalgia for a bygone era in the United States when regular church attendance was a sign of social respectability and/or good citizenship practice? Is the fear based on a loss of the church's prestige in the community? Is the desperation prompted by the loss of revenue to secure the upkeep of property or the acquisition of more? I cannot say and certainly hope not. However, we live in an era in which church membership is in a fierce competition with a myriad of other things that people might like to do on Sunday morning or where they want to spend their disposable income if they have it.

My concern is less with the rise in the number of religiously unaffiliated but in how we perceive or interpret this trend. Is it a death knell or is it an unexpected opportunity? The church of Christ has its mission—to proclaim the gospel in season and out of season; to minister to the "least, the last, and the lost;" to bear witness against that which assaults the dignity of all human beings; and what does irreparable harm to the rest of creation. Our *raison d'etre* remains the same; however, we may well need to consider that God may be calling us to envision other ways of "doing" and "being" the church; rather than our stubbornly replicating what we have "always" done. I cannot predict the future of the church as we have known it. I do not know if we will ever see "large" numbers of churchgoers again. However, this time of waning influence and declining numbers is an opportunity to remember to Whom we belong and to seek with humility what it is we are being called to do *now*. When we are clearer as to Whom we serve; perceive more clearly the nature of our role as communities of faith; and understand that the church's very existence is a sacrament, insight may come to us as to where our focus should lie. This may be a time of great challenges but I see it as a season of hope, not despair. This is not because of who we think we are but who *God* is.

## Bibliography

Barna Group. "Meet the Spiritual but Not Religious." *Barna Group*, April 6, 2017. https://www.barna.com/research/meet-spiritual-not-religious/.

———. "They 'Love Jesus but Not the Church.'" *Barna Group*, March 30, 2017. https://www.barna.com/research/meet-love-jesus-not-church/.

Church of England. "The Articles of Religion in Modern English." Translated by the Church Society. https://static1.squarespace.com/static/5dd6f3ad8945682281fadd6f/t/60b19a2f8bd86139cf0459b0/1622252079565/39-Articles-Modern-English.pdf.

Dietrich Bonhoeffer. *Life Together*. Translated with an introduction by John W. Doberstein. San Francisco: Harper & Row, 1954.

Cross, Anthony, and Philip Thompson, eds. *Baptist Sacramentalism*. 3 vols. Eugene, OR: Pickwick, 2007–20.

The Episcopal Church. *The Book of Common Prayer*. https://www.episcopalchurch.org/wp-content/uploads/sites/2/2021/02/book-of-common-prayer-2006.pdf.

Grenz, Stanley J. "Baptism and the Lord's Supper as Community Acts: Toward a Sacramental Understanding of the Ordinances." In *Baptist Sacramentalism*, edited by Anthony Cross and Philip Thompson, 76–95. Eugene, OR: Pickwick, 2007.

Lash, Nicholas. "The Eucharist: Sacrament of Christ's Presence in the World." *New Blackfriars* 48.560 (1967) 172–85.

Love, Patrick G. "Differentiating Spirituality from Religion." https://characterclearinghouse.fsu.edu/article/differentiating-spirituality-religion.

Love, Patrick G., and Donna M. Talbot. "Defining Spiritual Development: A Missing Consideration for Student Affairs." Journal of Student Affairs Research and Practice 37 (1999) 361–75.

Parks, Sharon. *Big Questions, Worthy Dreams: Mentoring Young Adults in Their Search for Meaning, Purpose, and Faith.* San Francisco: Jossy-Bass, 2000.

3

# The Mysterion of God's Devotedness to Human Beings

Northern Realizations

G. Ronald Murphy

In his first letter of instructions to Timothy, St. Paul mentions the word many times: *eusebeia*, devotedness, loyalty to parents, reverence, faithfulness. In Latin, for those who remember Virgil's pious Aeneas carrying his elderly father on his shoulders from the burning city of Troy, it is understood as a son's *pietas*, a hero's filial devotion to his aged father. This piety or devotedness to parents, to older people, and to God as *theo-sebeia*, is something that Paul says Timothy should appropriately cultivate in himself and encourage in his flock (1 Tim 1:3). Once in the same letter, however, Paul says that loyal faithfulness is something truly great, and even a mystery, and the great mystery is that there is profound devotedness in the other direction as well: the mystery that God feels family devotedness, piety, toward us.

> Great is the mystery of devotedness [*to tes eusebeias mysterion*],
> Who [not which] was revealed in flesh,
> Vindicated in spirit,
> Seen by angels,
> proclaimed among Gentiles,

Believed in throughout the world,
Was taken up in glory. (1 Tim 3:16)[1]

Greatest mystery of all perhaps is that the divine devotedness to us, *eusebeia*, is a person, who (*hos*, in Greek) became a human being, was taken up in glory, and was proclaimed among the gentiles. Leaving aside the statement that God's devotedness is a person, let us concentrate here on the phrase "proclaimed among the Gentiles [*en ethnesin*]." After all, this great mystery was proclaimed among the Jews by constant reference to ancient predictive and enlightening poetic statements, especially from the prophet Isaiah and from the Psalms. The incident of the appearance of Christ talking to the two disciples on the road to Emmaus may be taken as a symbol of early Christian preaching among the Jews, "Oh, how foolish you are, and how slow of heart to believe all that the prophets have declared! Was it not necessary that the Messiah should suffer these things and then enter into his glory?" To which Luke adds significantly: "then beginning with Moses and all the prophets, he interpreted to them the things about himself in all the scriptures." After he left them, the reaction of the two shows the degree to which they were moved by this local method of explaining: "Were not our hearts burning within us while he was talking to us on the road, while he was opening the scriptures to us?" (Luke 24:25–32)

How does one use this method when one is not in the land of Israel and not among Jews? In lands where there is no knowledge of the Old Testament? As the Psalmist asked, how do you sing the songs of Zion, the songs of the Lord, in a foreign land (Ps 137)? If God was devoted to Gentile nations, however, as well as to Israel, then some of the mystery of God's devotion to them ought to show up in Gentile myth and poetry as well as it did in Hebrew. In some way, their stories and poetry too could show up as realizations which foreshadow, as myths which predict, and are possibly enlightening, to Gentiles about Christ.

Christian Gentiles should possibly be able to contemplate events of salvation in some of their own stories and poetry of divine rescue as being a foreshadowing, analogously foretelling in advance, and enabling their own hearts to be set burning within them as they realize that their ancient stories are coming true in Christ's story. For, as the Pentecost event shows, when the twelve Jewish apostles were gathered together and heard the sound of a mighty wind and received tongues of fire from

---

1. Unless otherwise noted, all biblical citations in this chapter are from the RSV.

heaven, they began to speak to the crowd assembled in Jerusalem from all over the world and "each one heard them speaking in his own native language" (Acts 2:8). It would not be too many decades thereafter before those who went home to Rome began drawing images of Christ in their catacombs as a beardless Roman shepherd carrying a sheep on his shoulders, wearing a Roman tunic with leather-strapped sandals; Christ envisioned in another wall drawing as the mythic Apollo riding across the sky in his solar chariot as he ascends the heavens to illuminate the whole world. Roman Christians were contemplating their own myths as predictive poetry.

Christians from Egypt as well now looked differently on their ancient ankh symbol of eternal life. Instead of having each of their immortal gods and the deceased Pharaohs holding the ankh symbol in their hands, now they drew the cross of Christ as an ankh with an oval above the crosspiece providing the space for the halo of Christ crucified depicted on the front of the ankh-cross. For Egyptian Christians their ancient symbol of eternal life alongside the gods became a forerunner of the function of the similarly shaped cross itself, to grant eternal life—with Christ.

The mystery is that the old stories of hope, of Passover and Exodus in Israel, of Yggdrasil's rescue of the last man and woman at Ragnarok in northern Europe, come true in the story of Jesus Christ, especially in his last supper and cross-tree. Artifacts still existing witness to this analogous, gradual poetic transition in Norway, England, and Denmark.

And so, what can be explored of the depiction of Christ in the Germanic North? Is there any viewable evidence, parallel to that from Rome and Egypt, for *eusebeia*, for Christ as devoted faithfulness on the part of the divine toward human beings, depicted in local Germanic art and artifact? That is the question addressed in this chapter.

In the North, the sacred symbol above all others is the Tree Yggdrasil (awesome + mount or ride, [or: the awesome one's mount]), Yggdrasil is the support of the whole cosmos]. This great evergreen ash[2] tree is at the center of the Germanic myth of the future rescue of the human race from annihilation at the end of the world. The Tree will perform this rescue out of loyal devotedness, worry and concern for human beings. When the end comes and ragnarok (the doom of the gods) is near, the Tree will tremble out of worry and concern over the doom of men and

---

2. Yggdrasil's mythic nature is unknown. No one knows where its roots come from. It is called an ash but is only known as an enormous evergreen tree that stands over the well of time and whose twigs supply the material on which the Norns carve the runes.

women on earth. Yggdrasil will then open up its trunk and let the last two human beings, a man and a woman called significantly Lif and Lifthrasir (life and life-thriver), enter in. The Tree will then protect and hide them until the end of the world is over. It will nourish them with the dew of the morning. When the end is over, it will release them to help start the world anew. This myth of the trembling Tree seems to have been used often in Northern poem and artifact as a foreshadowing of God's devotedness to his mortal human beings in Christ. We will look at "entering the Tree" in the stave church, in the Dream of the Rood, in the Externsteine relief, in the Middleton Viking grave crosses, and in the baptismal font at Aakirke, as a Germanic manner of explaining the same events that so concerned the two disciples as they walked on the road to Emmaus.

## The Stave Churches at Borgund and Urnes in Norway

View of the Borgund stave church. Photo by author.

Side view of the Borgund stave church showing carved serpents. Photo by author.

And so I began walking toward the dark stave church in Norway at Borgund. There was a French woman walking nearby and I overheard her say to a friend, "Il y'a une odeur" (There's a smell). And indeed there is a distinct smell of pine tar to the church although I could not detect it until I got closer. Stave churches are not painted but are regularly coated with pine tar which has acted as a sealant for the wooden building since it was built eight hundred years ago. Even the sense of smell informs you that the church is an evergreen tree! As you look up at the building the size of the roofs gets smaller and smaller, suggesting pine branches, as they move toward the top of the church, where the six roofs of the nave terminate in a vertical wooden spire like the top shoot of a spruce tree. Remarkably, the roofs and side walls have been completely covered with a protective coat of shingles for further weatherproofing. But if you look closer: each individual shingle has been given a lozenge-shape, making the covering of the stave church be that of a pinecone.

Stepping over the very high threshold, the visitor enters a space where there is wood on all sides and above one can see the ascending series of roofs going up to the small bell tower that rides saddle back on the fourth roof. Its sound must have been amplified by the structure as it descends from above. Also above at the tops of several staves[3] in the nave can be seen the heads of several of the old gods and animals, the one-eyed Woden[4] prominent in the church at Hegge. The central focus to which the eye is directed however is the large crucifix at the altar. Often, above the altar, the cross, the "rood," gave its name to the wooden doorway into the sanctuary area, the "rood screen" through which one must pass to be at the altar. Woden hanged himself on the tree Yggdrasil to learn the mystery of the future in the runes, which were later given to all; Christ was hanged on the cross, the rood, to open up the future of heaven for mankind in the Resurrection, given to all in the gospel and sacraments. The death on the tree was foretold in the North, as was the expectation that mysterious benefits would come from it.

Leaving the inside of the church, there are two more facets on the outside of this amazing artifact that become clearer and help give the identity of the stave church: the serpentine carvings on the roof and the elaborate carving of vines and animals on the doorway. There are snakes on the eaves of the upper roofs and their jaws are agape, they are ready to strike. This may seem shockingly inappropriate for a church, but it is not for the tree Yggdrasil. One may rush to claim this is perhaps an allusion to the bronze serpent lifted up in the desert, or to invoke apotropaic magic to give the serpents the function of frightening evil spirits away from a holy place, but this is too far afield and not necessary. The presence of snakes is indicative that the stave church is Yggdrasil. In the Elder Edda they are even named and described as ever biting on the tree:

> More serpents lie under the ash of Yggdrasil
> Than any fool can imagine:
> Goin and Moin, they are Grafvitner's sons,
> Grabak and Grafvollud,
> Ofnir and Svafnir I think for ever will bite on the tree's branches.[5]

---

3. The major staves, vertical pilings and planks are completely visible inside the church.

4. Woden, also Odin, is the head of the Germanic pantheon. He sacrificed one eye to acquire wisdom and the knowledge of the future. To the same end he later hanged himself on the tree Yggdrasil and seized the runes, the carved twigs of the tree that could foretell the future.

5. Larrington, *Poetic Edda*, 56. There are two Old Norse collections of Germanic myth and lore, written down in thirteenth-century Iceland. Some of the oldest material is in the *Elder* or *Poetic Edda* (author unknown), and the second, written by lawspeaker and chieftain Snorri Sturluson (1179–1241) is sometimes fuller and is called the *Younger* or *Prose Edda*, or also, *Snorri's Edda*. The word *Edda* itself seems to mean

The old portal of the Urnes stave church. Photo by author

When a native Norwegian of those twelfth-century days approached the tree-shaped stave church at Borgund, he would immediately recognize the mysterious nature of the tree with the snakes in its branches, and then would see the Christian crosses facing him on the lower eaves of the same church. On approaching the older portal of the stave church at Urnes in Sognefjord another surprising mythic image would be before him, a swirling twisting interweaving of plants and animals around the door, done realistically and yet elongated so fancifully that the observer can hardly tell where the tendril of a vine gives way to becoming the elongated leg of an animal. Even above the door itself, so masterfully has the carver been at work that several vines hang over the top of the doorway, while the door itself is covered with branches and vines in low relief. On the left-hand side a deer, peacefully combined with the vines, is chewing on the door frame as if it were bark, and the door itself a tree trunk. And so the poet-designer of the stave church has led the person who is about to pull the door handle to enter the church to the realization that he is at

---

"great-grandmother."

the same time entering the tree of life Yggdrasil, the tree that trembles out of concern for human beings in the face of their death, the tree that opens its trunk to let them in to save Life and Life-prosperer from annihilation. The church is that tree.[6]

## The Dream of the Rood

Some four hundred years earlier in about AD 700 an Anglo Saxon poet wrote the "Dream of the Rood." In this earliest of English poems the poet wondered how the wooden pole [rod or rood] which carried the crucified Savior, should be covered in precious metal and gems. In the poem the poet brings the cross to speak and he hears how the cross is really of wood. How it trembled (Yggdrasil!) when it saw the young warrior coming toward it and trembled again when the young warrior climbed up on it and embraced it. The rood tried to bow to him, but it could not, it was to stand erect even though the earth itself was trembling. The tree/cross then had dark shafts [arrowheads] driven through it as Christ was fastened to the wood. Like the dreamer we too forget that the nails had to be driven simultaneously both through Jesus and the cross. And then the cross tells how it was drenched in blood that poured from his side when he gave up his spirit. The blood-soaked cross wants all to realize that it shared intimately in Christ's Passion, in the crucifixion and rescue of mankind. Something that we might take perfectly for granted, a poet in the eight century, coming from a religion that honored the tree as the central and terminal savior of human beings, could not.

And so we cannot be surprised when in the midst of the poem the cross/tree asserts, "ic hælan maeg" (I can save!). In a gloriously ecumenical moment, the poet has realized that Jesus used the saving tree of the ancient religion and of his execution to be his co-worker in accomplishing the salvation of the human race. He has realized more than that. Looking at the saving role that the chieftain played in rescuing his people from death and bringing them home, the poet just barely mentions the resurrection and then rushes to the descent into hell to elaborate how Christ went immediately to help his people as a Dryhten/chieftain should: he went to hell to rescue his people from being dead and to bring them home.

---

6. For a fuller examination of the tree Yggdrasil and the stave church as well as other Northern artifacts, see my *Tree of Salvation, Yggdrasil, and the Cross in the North*, 1–65.

The ending of the poem becomes rhapsodic as author contemplates the joy of the angels and saints already in heaven as they welcome Jesus at the head of his long line of his people, leading them out of hell and entering with them into the bliss of his heavenly homeland/his eđel. Nothing could show the loyalty, the *eusebeia*, of God to his people more than that he would even die in order to go to the land of dead to find them and bring them back home. It is no wonder that the Harrowing of Hell became one of the most popular mysteries of the Middle Ages in the north.

## The Externsteine Relief of the Deposition from the Cross

LEFT | Externsteine relief, detail of Jospeh carrying Christ. Photo by author. RIGHT | Externsteine relief, lightly restored, showing the whole relief with Nidhogg. Drawing by Lawrence Selim.

For Germanic tribes then as today the idea of loyalty[7] was that it was reciprocal. A chieftain and his men were organized this way, the men

---

7. The Saxon word for personal loyalty was *triuwe*, also troth (once used in the marriage vows), and truth. The word is derived from tree. In this sense, Judas Iscariot is described in the Saxon *Heliand* as a *treulogo*, a "loyalty-liar."

staying with him in battle without deserting him, as he fought for glory and they fought for him, as was noted by the Roman historian Tacitus about the Germanic tribes two thousand years ago.[8] The next artifact, the relief of the deposition from the cross, possibly from the twelfth century shows this in a surprisingly direct and moving way.

When we approach the relief at Externsteine in North Rhine Westfalia it is immediately clear that the emotional center and focus of the complex composition is the figure of Joseph of Arimathea devoutly carrying the limp and lifeless body of his chieftain on his shoulder. Joseph's head is bowed and he is ready to carry the body of Christ to his grave. Jesus looks like a fallen soldier eerily similar to today's image of the wounded warrior being carried by his buddy. Had the poet of the "Dream of the Rood" lived some five hundred years later I think he would have liked the Externsteine sculptor's image of the loyal Joseph. Loyalty, piety, in this work of art is not just on God's side, however, but in the form of Joseph and Nicodemus as the chieftain's men being loyally devoted to him.

The other figure of devotedness in the relief is Nicodemus, looking exhausted with his hat pushed back by the cross, has just lowered the body of Christ onto the shoulder of Joseph. His position is unusual. He is not using a ladder as traditionally found in almost every depiction of this event, instead he is standing on a tree that has bent over to give him something to stand on. The tree has to be a representation of Yggdrasil, or of the Irminsul which stood for it and was near this spot, the faithful tree which is now helping one of Jesus's men reach up and take him down from the cross. Not only is the tree bent down, but all the human figures are as well, and all in the relief are weeping, including the sun and the moon. As was once told, or foretold, in the story of the death of the beautiful god Balder, that Hel said of him, if all creation weeps for him, I will release him from the dead.[9] All creation did not weep. One

---

8. The two outstanding duties of a chieftain to his people were help and protection. In his *Germania*, moreover, Tacitus noted that among the Germanic peoples it is a disgrace for his men to leave a fallen chieftain on the battlefield, and he then added the famous line: "*principes pro victoria pugnant, comites pro principe*" (chieftains fight for victory, the warrior-companions for the chieftain) (Tacitus, *Agricola and Germania*, 112–13).

9. Sturluson, *Edda*, 50–51.

god, Loki,[10] alone, had no devotedness to Balder and had arranged the accident that killed him; he did not weep. And so Balder had to remain among the dead. In the case of Jesus, however, "all creation wept." In both the Dream of the Rood and in the relief at Externsteine, all of creation is therefore shown doing what it did not do for Balder, weeping. Jesus will be released from Hel. Thus it would seem this work of art is speaking of the Resurrection of Jesus in full awareness of the mythic story of Balder. The sculptor has realized that the loyal and loving weeping of Christ's people, his sun and moon included, will accompany Jesus's rising from the dead. This could then account for the sculptor's depiction of Jesus as already rising on back left of the relief, at the very moment when all are weeping as they take him down from the cross and Joseph is carrying Jesus's body on his shoulder.

Jesus is shown invisibly rising with his life carried in his arm in the form of a child (badly eroded) together with his banner of victory. His right hand is raised in blessing over his mother who is holding his forehead and his men and their devotedness to him.

Down below the earthline, the dragon of death, the Nidhogg[11] (horrible + striker) seems also aware of Christ's return and is beginning to flee carrying two people in his coils. If the One who brings back the dead to life has come, it is time for death and annihilation to flee. It was fore-sung in the Seeress's Prophesy:

> Then the powerful, mighty one, he who rules over everything,
> will come from above, to the judgement-place of the gods.
> There comes the dark dragon flying,
> the shining serpent, up from the Dark-of-moon Hills;
> Nidhogg flies over the plain, in his wings
> he carries corpses; now she must sink down.[12]

There one phrase left to explore in connection with the Externsteine relief, that the one who rules over everything will come to the judgement-place of the gods. That place is at the foot of the tree Yggdrasil. And so with both the One who comes up above and the Nidhogg

---

10. Loki is the trickster god of deceit. He is the father of three monsters: Hel, half corpse, goddess of the dead and the Underworld; Jormungand, the Midgard Serpent of the encircling Ocean; and the Fenris wolf who at Ragnarok will devour Woden.

11. The Nidhogg is the underground serpent that lives at the root of the tree of all life, Yggdrasil. In Germanic mythology he sucks the blood of corpses and devours the bodies of the dead, reducing the dead to dirt. He is the force of annihilation.

12. Larrington, *Poetic Edda*, 12–13.

down below, we must be at the base of the tree. It is here that the sculptor has joined the base of the tree to the base of the cross with nailed foot of Jesus covering and joining them both. God's devotedness and human sympathy have met.

## The Viking Burial Cross at Middleton in North Yorkshire

LEFT | Viking Middleton cross showing warrior. RIGHT | Reverse side of Viking Middleton cross showing snake. Photos by T. Middlemass.

From the North of Germany to the North of England we travel to the next artifact, to the little village of Middleton near Pickering in north Yorkshire, in the Danelaw, firmly in Viking territory, to a graveyard cross of St. Andrew's church. There in the thousand-year-old parish church are stone crosses that date from the 900s, from the time of the Vikings both the Danes, and the Hiberno-Norse who had been defeated and driven out of Ireland to the north of England.

The cross that we are most interested in is known rather prosaically as "Cross B." But surprisingly it does not have a figure of Christ crucified on the front, but instead on the front of the cross shaft we find the person who is buried beneath the grave cross depicted as he must have been laid out in his casket. He and his casket are sculpted within Christ's cross. This is another way of imagining that the Christian who dies, like Lif and Lifthrasir, has entered the protective trunk of the great tree. He wears a pointed helmet with a metal nosepiece. Around his waist he has his long knife, a scramasax. On his right side there is his spear with its metal point at the top. Across from his spear, on his left side, is his shield, and below it, his long sword, and below that is his axe, with his left hand on the axehead.[13] The square box that the warrior is enclosed in is also the shaft of the cross. The warrior, in other words has been laid to rest within the cross and it was a Christian death that enabled him to enter the protective wood.

The cross head is detached somewhat from the shaft because it depicts light and life, its ring displays the radiance of the sun, the solar disc being carved at the very center of the cross head. The Viking warrior interred in the bipartite cross has thus really been buried into Christ's death and his resurrection.

I wanted to see the back of Cross B, but it was almost flush against the wall. With the help of a young German who was touring the Yorkshire moors we were to safely move Cross B a little bit forward, and on the back there it was! The underground serpent, the Nidhogg, was staring right at me. The artist had seen to it however that the horrible snake was no threat to me nor to the body of the buried warrior. Following Germanic mythic tradition, the Nidhogg was bound by unbreakable thread.[14] Not that any of the mythic fetters of the elves or dwarves could hold the snake of death back, but the thread of a caring Chieftain's resurrection could. The bipartite cross of Christ's death and resurrection had done out of devotion for a Viking warrior what no hero or god of Germanic myth had ever been

---

13. Throughout are small balls and other indistinct objects that are, I think, just fillers for the vacuum of an empty space. The remnant drawn below the dead person indicates the figure is male.

14. In the myths, evil is never destroyed but it can be bound. Fenrir, for example, had a special bond made by the black elves and dwarves so subtle that a monster like the wolf could not break it. Snorri says that it was made of six ingredients: "the sound of a cat's footfall and a woman's beard, the mountain's roots and the bear's sinews and the fish's breath and the bird's spittle" (Sturluson, *Edda*, 28–29).

imagined capable of doing: binding the Nidhogg, confining death, so that it cannot devour the helpless body of the buried Viking warrior.

## The Aakyrke Baptismal Font on Bornholm

Top | Aakirke Baptismal font. Bottom | Baptismal font detail with Wise Men returning. Photos by author.

Another journey in Germanic territory by plane or fast sailboat brings you to the Danish island of Bornholm in the Baltic Sea. It is a parallelogram in shape about twenty-five miles long by about nineteen miles in width, and is located in the Baltic between the southern coast of Sweden and the northern coast of Germany and Poland. Its island isolation has enabled it to preserve many medieval and earlier artifacts, as well as its own earlier form of Danish. Its climate is mild and brushed with a constant, gentle sea breeze from the west. On this island there exist four unique round churches built roughly at the same time at the stave church at Borgund. They are built around a large central pillar which expands at its top into a curved ceiling which stretches out to touch the surrounding wall at all points. Standing inside is like being under an open umbrella or under a large tree.

I went to study these churches as possibly modeled on Yggdrasil, but what I found as well was something I had not anticipated, a mysteriously intriguing baptismal font. The font is located in the church of St. John the Baptist in Aakyrkebu ('River church town') near the center of the island. We know the sculptor and the approximate date of the font because he carved his name in runes in one of the inscriptions on the font, and he is known to have lived between 1175 and 1210, Sigraf of Gotland.[15] When I walked accidentally into the church at Aakyrkebu (it was not a round church but had an interesting Carolingian front), a baptism was being performed. The priest was wearing a black cassock with the high white ruff of the sixteenth century. When the ceremony was finished and she and the family had left with the baby. I went forward down the aisle to examine the large font they had been using. It was like a more modern stone stoop and bore little resemblance to the hollowed out tree stumps of the same era that I had seen in Norway.

When I got close enough to see detail I found the font was a bit shocking. No cherubs and angels holding up the bowl, but rather the intertwined vines and animals that I had seen on the portals of the stave churches in Norway. More than that, four projecting heads were sculpted around the intertwined snakes and vines on the base: two lions, a ram and a man. Both the lions and the human being had a section of a long snake in their mouths which they are quite visibly biting. The serpent turns out to be more than one entwined snake, and at their tails the snakes transform into vines, leaves, and flowers. Once again we have a

---

15. Gotland is another island in the Baltic Sea, north of Bornholm and east of Sweden.

representation of Yggdrasil as the tree of life, of all living things, animal and vegetable, and eating one another to stay alive. It is in this form that we have seen Yggdrasil around the portals of the stave churches, and it is in this form that Yggdrasil is described in the Elder Edda. The tree is standing steady and suffering but teeming with the necessary violence of the cycle of life: deer gnawing at its side, the Nidhogg serpent biting at its roots, and innumerable snakes forever biting at its branches and striking at the deer that eat the branches.[16]

I decided to get down on the floor. (No one was in the church.) I wanted to see better what the artist had put under the baptismal bowl. It was an uplifting surprise: a complete absence of violence, a flourishing shower of blossoming flowers and fruit met my eyes. The baptismal bowl promises a kind of life that is more a blossoming than the tangle for survival. As the tree of life grows upward it promises a maturity and a fruitfulness of life to come. On the support of the bowl coming from the base the artist has even placed a rope as if to mark off the two levels of life. Then we come to the striking images that the artist has placed around the outside of the bowl as if they were the full blossom of life. They depict the life of Christ in eleven panels[17] from the annunciation to the crucifixion; the star performers in the panels, unexpectedly perhaps, are the three kings, the magi (Matt 2:1–12).[18] Fully eight of the eleven scenes are devoted to the nativity, the beginning of the blossoming of God's life among human beings, and five scenes of the eight are devoted to the magi.[19] (The shepherds are not represented.)

It is obvious that the coming and going of the three gentile kings is of major importance to the sculptor in establishing an interpretive context for the baptismal candidate's parallel approach to the font for baptism. The people approaching the font are also gentiles. Like the magi, being without Torah or prophets to guide them, they are following a star, a star whose message the kings have interpreted through the myth and astrology of their own religion. The Bornholmers have also come to the sacred place near the foot of the tree of life Yggdrasil where in their mythology there is a sacred spring which forms a pool of water called the

---

16. See Larrington, *Poetic Edda*, 56–57.

17. For a description and interpretation of each of the eleven scenes see my *Tree of Salvation*, 69–72.

18. In medieval times, it was accepted that the wise men were kings.

19. The *Heliand* is possibly a major influence in suggesting the importance magi in the North. Murphy, *The Heliand*, 21–26.

well of Becoming, wurd, from which the three Norns[20] scoop water every day to splash on the trunk of Yggdrasil so that it can always continue to be alive. Foreshadowed by the story of the Norns and the well they approach baptism, and from the baptismal font they will realize that it will be themselves that will be sprinkled with the water of eternal time, instead of the Norns it will be the priest. Their stories of Yggdrasil have led them, like the star, to the place where the gods meet, at the base of the tree, and where the waters of eternal time flow.

Now what of the archetypes, the magi? Germanic custom requires reciprocity from Christ and his mother for their gifts of gold, frankincense, and myrrh. Master Sigraf has thought of this too. And so in a masterful stroke he depicts the three kings not walking on foot, which is how he had them come, but astride horses that are happily prancing on their way back home. If you look carefully at the panels in which the kings are leaving Bethlehem, each one is holding a present in his hand which he received from Christ: a branch from the eternal tree of life. They can take it home with them so that all can hear the good news about the tree of life. And they can plant it.

## Conclusion

In Baptism and the Eucharist we are accepting our part in the great mystery of *eusebeia*, of God's concern for us and for our survival. In his sacraments He is putting the ankh of eternal life into our hands. He is asking us to let him be our shepherd. He is inviting us to enter the safety of the Tree. In his sacraments we are being led by a star to the waters of mystical life, where our gifts of gold, frankincense and myrrh are accepted and reciprocated by the gift of branches of the tree of life. And as we walk along the road, he helps us understand the religious stories of old in which, in many ways and in many different lands, the mystery of himself was all foretold. Then as evening comes on the road to Emmaus, he pretends to walk on until we invite him to stay with us and have supper. Then while eating supper he takes the bread, blesses it and breaks it, and hands it to us with the hope that we will remember and realize who this is.

---

20. The three Norns have names that indicate they are the flow of time: *Wurd*, "what came to pass"; *Verdanti*, "what is happening"; *Skuld*, "what shall come to pass." They are Shakespeare's *weird sisters*, and are also called the fates.

## Bibliography

Larrington, Caryolyne, trans. *The Poetic Edda*. Oxford: Oxford University Press, 2014.
Murphy, G. Ronald, trans. *The Heliand: The Saxon Gospel*. Oxford: Oxford University Press, 1992.
———. *Tree of Salvation, Yggdrasil, and the Cross in the North*. Oxford: Oxford University Press, 2013.
Tacitus. *Agricola and Germania*. Translated by H. Mattingly. New York: Penguin, 1970.
Sturluson, Snorri. *Edda*. Translated by Anthony Faulkes. London: Everyman, 1987.

Part 2

# Saving the Church as a Community

*So we, who are many, are one body in Christ, and individually we are members one of another.*

(ROMANS 12:5 NRSV)

4

# What Perfect Love Can Be

The Sacraments as Sites of Disunion and Hope in Christ

Brit Frazier

*So, Lord, at length when sacraments shall cease,*
*May we be one with all Thy Church above,*
*One with Thy saints in one unbroken peace,*
*One with Thy saints in one unbounded love;*
*More blessèd still, in peace and love to be*
*One with the Trinity in unity.[1]*

At the turn of the third century, Quintus Septimius Florens Tertullianus heralded the blessing of baptism: "Happy is our sacrament of water in that, by washing away the sins of our early blindness, we are set free and admitted into eternal life!"[2] Tertullian's graceful praise of baptism was no simple catechism or hymn to the Lord and source of every sacrament. Here was a declaration of spiritual warfare—a fevered counterpoint to

---

1. Stanza four of W. H. Turton's hymn, "Thou, Who at Thy First Eucharist Didst Pray."
2. Tertullian, *On Baptism*, ch. 1.

the Gnosticism of "a viper of the Cainite heresy" who was teaching in the same circles as Tertullian in Roman Carthage. In his first epistle to the Corinthians, St. Paul lamented an earlier disunion among the body of the faithful: "For, in the first place, when you assemble as a church, I hear that there are divisions among you. . . . When you meet together, it is not the Lord's supper that you eat. For in eating, each one goes ahead with his own meal, and one is hungry and another is drunk" (1 Cor 11:18, 20–21).[3] It was the Lord Jesus' good pleasure to nourish his Church with the sweetness of sign and sacrament, and from the beginning, it has been the Church's tricky inheritance to disagree about them.

The literature reviewing discrepancies between sacramental hermeneutics among streams of the Christian tradition is comprehensive and illuminating.[4] These divergences and deliberations are at the center of centuries of religious conflict and denominational reconstitution, and no serious student of church history can avoid their consequence. Indeed there is little challenge in filling an essay with recollection of the heresies and heartbreak that have burdened the divided body of Christ since the days of the first disciples, but the question at the heart of this collection invites us into a complementary reflection. If it is acknowledged that Christians have—historically and contemporarily—failed in our cooperation within a unitive and coherent sacramental vision, how, then, do we understand our life in Christ together? Can we dare to strive for harmony among our disparate theological commitments, and is this harmony desirable at all? What does the Bible teach us about God's relationship with and hope for his church? Where are the points of convergence between conflicting sacramental ontologies, and—most critically—how do the sacraments invite Christians of various inheritances into impassioned relationship with the true and living God? What follows gently aims to be an exploration animated by the hope in Christ that does not, as St. Paul writes, disappoint us (Rom 5:5).

The consideration and ultimate argument offered here will most decidedly not affirm that the differences between various apprehensions of sacramentality do not matter. It is of little service to contemplate the continued material involvement in creation of the triune God and to declare the insignificance of confessional differences among ecclesial communities. Rather than an artificial effort to reconcile differences into a false

---

3. Unless otherwise noted, all biblical citations in this chapter are from the RSV.

4. For an accessible introduction, see Holcomb and Johnson, *Christian Theologies of the Sacraments*.

universalism or a sort of "many paths up the mountain" approach, our time is more generatively spent looking closely at what is true: that God, in his fullness, has always longed for us. The incarnation of Jesus Christ, second person of the Trinity and Word of the Father, demonstrates the pure love of the creator for creation, and it is this love that continues to animate the substance and efficacy of the church's sacramental life. The theological variety that characterizes interdenominational friction is very real and often tragically burdensome, but within the unshakable reality of God's love and will for us, a sweeter certitude is laid bare. There is ultimately more that Christians celebrate in common than what divides us, and we are each—slowly, stumblingly—being knit with intimacy into the abundant life of Jesus Christ.

My own sacramental formation has been as a priest in the Anglo-Catholic tradition within the Anglican Communion. I teach my students about the Church's seven sacraments, pointing with particular emphasis toward the promises of baptism and the holy Eucharist as revealed in scripture. Even within my own tradition, conversations regarding the number and importance of sacraments and "sacramental rites" provoke disagreement, but I believe the sacramental encounter invites us into a holy capacity for surveying common ground. It is from this generous place of observation where we can begin to approach our best hopes for collective possibility. We will begin with what the Bible tells us (and does not tell us) about God's desires for Christian unity and sacramental order. Next, it will assist us to consider a brief survey of the distinctive existential conceptualizations of sacraments among Christian denominations. It will then serve our exploration to review, in brief, a few of the various efforts throughout history to look toward the sacraments as sites of interdenominational cooperation. We will then be prepared to dive into the heart of our invitation to think critically about what all (or nearly all) Christians can know about the sacraments and their constitution and potentiality. Instead of remaining with questions about how sacraments work, it will be a more fruitful exercise to consider what our participation in God's sacraments then demands of us. Finally, we will look forward in hope and humility toward what burdens might be ours to take up as disciples of Jesus and what burdens are ours to lay at his feet.

There is a tendency for Christians to drift toward one of two poles along a continuum of perceptions regarding the reality of the Church's *ontos*. At one end, there is the inclination to declare that only a singular iteration of the Church and its continuance is valid in faith and doctrine.

Within such views, alternative forms of Christian community are understood to be underdeveloped, at best, or even antithetical to what is perceived to be the purest iteration of the apostolic faith itself. At the other end of the continuum, any prioritization of unity among Christians is dismissed from being an admirable objective at all. In this view, the breadth of humanity's diversity precludes any possibility of substantive religious agreement, so why waste time considering it? In this view, it is better to tend one's own garden than to worry much about the gardens of the others down the street or on the other side of the world.

It is the Word of holy scripture that demands an alternative comprehension of Christian solidarity. The Bible insists upon a Church bound by responsibility, harmony, and accountability among its members, and the words of Jesus Christ himself become the scaffolding upon which scriptural mutuality and integrity are constructed throughout history. This call for unity among the faithful is most famously the marrow of Jesus' own high priestly prayer in the seventeenth chapter of the Gospel of St. John. Before his passion and crucifixion, Jesus prays to his Father regarding his disciples, "And now I am no more in the world, but they are in the world, and I am coming to thee. Holy Father, keep them in thy name, which thou hast given me, that they may be one, even as we are one" (John 17:11). He continues,

> I do not pray for these only, but also for those who believe in me through their word, that they may all be one. . . . The glory which thou hast given me I have given to them, that they may be one even as we are one, I in them and thou in me, that they may become perfectly one, so that the world may know that thou hast sent me and hast loved them even as thou hast loved me. (John 17:20–23)

In his *Homily 82 on the Gospel of John*, St. John Crysostom notes that this supplication recognizes the impossibility of human alignment with God's perfect congruence, and yet the prayers of Jesus firmly establish God's constituent oneness as the apostolic Church's ideal. However rudimentary the human capacities for perfect imitation of divine attributes might be, it is noteworthy that one of Christ's final petitions for his disciples' lives and ministry demanded a collective harmony. If this prayer were the only call for unity among the followers of Jesus, it would be enough for our continued contemplation and hopeful pursuit.

There is abundant scriptural attention to Christian unity beyond John 17. The Epistles of the New Testament, Pauline and otherwise, present plentiful exhortations to the earliest Christian communities regarding their tendencies toward disunion. To the Corinthians, St. Paul writes, "I appeal to you, brethren, by the name of our Lord Jesus Christ, that all of you agree and that there be no dissensions among you, but that you be united in the same mind and the same judgment" (1 Cor 1:10). To the Romans, we find the benediction, "May the God of steadfastness and encouragement grant you to live in such harmony with one another, in accord with Christ Jesus, that together you may with one voice glorify the God and Father of our Lord Jesus Christ" (Rom 15:5–6). As the fledgling churches stretched their wings along the shores of the Mediterranean and beyond, and as the gospel began to embrace a multiplicity of peoples, nations, and religious traditions, these very first letters of instruction shared a common refrain. Custom or origin notwithstanding, the first Christians were instructed to remain attentive to unity.[5] Integral to any community nourished by the gospel was a solidity of purpose and commitment to the pursuit of kindred peace. As St. Luke's depiction of the church in the Acts of the Apostles tells us, "the company of those who believed were of one heart and soul, and no one said that any of the things which he possessed was his own, but they had everything in common" (Acts 4:32). In matters both spiritual and material, the orientation toward harmony was heralded as ideal.

At the same time, however, scripture demonstrates that the church need not overly concern itself with certain more sublunary differences among Jesus Christ's followers. Diversity of gifts and habit need not unnecessarily distract the faithful from the more urgent and redemptive project of the gospel. The variety of human capacities comes from one Spirit, and distinctions in service and labor honor the same Lord (1 Cor 12:4–6). Indeed the famed "Jerusalem Counsel" of Acts 15 presents definitive testament to the church's blessing of certain pluralities. As apostles and elders gathered to consider whether and to what extent the Gentile believers should be required to adhere to the Law of Moses, St. Peter proclaims, "God who knows the heart bore witness to them, giving them the Holy Spirit just as he did to us; and he made no distinction between us and them, but cleansed their hearts by faith" (Acts 15:8–9).

---

5. See Rom 12:16; 2 Cor 13:11; Gal 3:28; Eph 2:19–22; 4:13; Phil 1:27; 2:1–3; Col 3:14; 1 Pet 3:8, for some among many scriptural injunctions regarding unity among Christ's first followers.

While certain matters of doctrine and praxis required general obedience, others were less pertinent to the thriving and expansion of the first Christian communities.

Scriptural calls for unity, it must be noted, are not offered in the singular interest of social cohesion. Prayers for peace and solidarity of spirit are not frameworks for a moral order or safeguards against the logistical dangers of schism. Rather, these urgent appeals for unity are appeals for the followers of Jesus to allow themselves to be knit into alignment with the irresistible unicity of God. God's own bright oneness animates the breadth of the Bible, Old Testament through the New, rooted in the *Shema Yisrael* of Deuteronomy 6 and echoed in the trinitarian murmurs of Father to Son in Mark 1 and Son to Father in John 17. As Katherine Sonderegger reminds us: "Divine Oneness, we must say, is a metaphysical predicate."[6] Furthermore, this vital unity is no mimetic human effort with objectives of divine imitation. A united church in heart, mind, and spirit does not just imitate an ontologically unified God, but indeed in its submission to divine unity, it comes to *participate* in the inner mechanisms of the trinitarian life. Baptized in the name of the Father, the Son, and the Holy Spirit (Matt 28:19), one is irrevocably incorporated into the dynamism of the heart of God. In this embrace by the "one Lord, one faith, one baptism," the individual and the community encounter nothing less than the living Trinity with freshness, intimacy, and peace. A spirit of common consecration and mutual love within the church is revealed not only as instruction, but as blessing.

Having explored the importance of Christian unity within holy scripture, we must now attend to the role of the sacraments and their place within this orientation toward or away from ecclesial harmony. It is necessary to point here toward the loosely gathered definition of "sacrament" that has undoubtedly been offered with thoughtful specificity in other chapters of this volume. For our purposes, we will understand sacraments as indeed those "outward and visible signs of inward and spiritual grace, given by Christ as sure and certain means by which we receive that grace."[7] While drawn from the 1979 Book of Common Prayer in the Episcopal Church, this Augustinian definition anchors the sacramental philosophy of an ecumenical variety of Christian traditions. It is generally the hermeneutic discrepancies (rather than the statement itself) that have ignited

---

6. Sonderegger, *The Doctrine of God*, 15.

7. "An Outline of the Faith, Commonly Called the Catechism," in Episcopal Church, *Book of Common Prayer*, 857.

disagreements within and between us. While my own Anglican Catholic location situates a constellation of biases, it is my prayer that the sacramental contemplation at the heart of this exercise calls forth a measure of charity should there be a perspective that I have missed.

History is generous with examples of how the substance, efficacy, significance, or necessity of sacraments have served as grounds for division between various Christian communities. From the concerns of St. Paul and Tertullian presented at the beginning of the chapter through the religious wars in Europe and the Holy Land throughout the second millennium after Christ and into the divergent commitments of Christian communities today regarding ritual participation, the sacraments have tragically served as sites of dissonance. Susan K. Wood helpfully locates the foundation of this dissonance in the rifts between ecclesial apprehensions of the relationship between the sacraments and the Church itself. Beyond differences between the mechanisms, purposes, and effects of the sacramental rite, Wood points toward a community's essential recognition of itself in relation to sacramental signs as the more insurmountable dissimilarity.

While denominational distinctions can run the risk of reductivism, Wood contends that three broader categories assist in illuminating the heart of ecumenical tensions. The Orthodox, Roman Catholics, and Anglicans, she offers, understand sacramental rites as constituting the church itself.[8] Baptism and the Eucharist (and, to a certain extent, the other five sacraments or sacramental rites) metaphysically incorporate the faithful into the earthly expression of the body of Christ. Baptism and the Eucharist are far more than mere signs of church membership or dues paid to be welcomed into a worshipping community, but rather serve as the primordial constitution of the church itself. As such, sacraments are effected by Christ via the church writ large, and they are not contingent upon the individual's initiative or receptivity. Thus such practices as infant baptism and the reception of the Eucharist by young children are embraced with little concern.

Traditions emerging more distinctly from the Reformation, Wood continues, locate sacramental praxis and teleology in the discernment of the Church not as sacramentally constituted, but as a *creatura verbi*—a creation of the Word.[9] Wood notes Martin Luther's specific and repeated

---

8. Wood, "The Sacramental Foundations of Ecclesial Identity," 455.
9. Wood, "The Sacramental Foundations of Ecclesial Identity," 463.

insistence that "the word of God builds the Church."[10] While sacraments serve in their own way to proclaim the fullness of the gospel, the signs themselves are generally subordinate to the preaching of the Word and the theological priority of encounter with the Jesus Christ of Scripture. Wood is careful to note throughout how any complete separation of word and sacrament presents a false dichotomy. Her reflections on the Christological center of doctrine regarding sacramental rites and the ontological reality of the church emphasize the work of Jesus at the heart of the efforts of variegated traditions.[11]

The third classification of sacramental interpretation is that of denominations that cohere among communities requiring a "believer's baptism." In these traditions, Wood clarifies: "the faith of an individual precedes in some fashion the formation of a faith community. God's action on an individual brings that individual to a profession of faith and this leads that person to affiliate with others with a similar experience to form a church which is congregationally defined."[12] Rather than an ontologically prior reality, the Church is that which becomes reality by the response of believers to the initiative of the Holy Spirit. Consequently, such sacramental rites as baptism and the Eucharist are not essentially constitutive of the church, but instead structure the attendant actions of the faithful in a reply of praise and thanksgiving. While ritual particularity varies among Baptist congregations and communities, there is general emphasis on an individual's commitment to Christ and resultant public proclamation of personal conversion than is typically found among Christians of other denominational affiliations.

Susan K. Wood's classification of these three models reveals a substructure at work beneath more prominent discussions between Christians regarding the sacraments. Conversations across associational lines cannot only consider the differences between what Christians believe about the substance of sacramental rites, but must also consider how disparate understandings of the nature of the church itself often undergird these questions. And yet—while the darker days of interdenominational conflict might appear to reveal little but tempests of disagreement all the way down, a closer look illuminates a bit of possibility. We will now turn to a brief review of some more formalized efforts to recognize the

10. Wood, "The Sacramental Foundations of Ecclesial Identity," 463, citing Martin Luther, *Martin Luthers Werke*, 596.

11. Wood, "The Sacramental Foundations of Ecclesial Identity," 465.

12. Wood, "The Sacramental Foundations of Ecclesial Identity," 472.

potentiality of sacramental agreement between Christians. Our focus will then shift to explore a few points of consensus that could strengthen ecclesial ties between followers of Jesus.

Formal commitments to interdenominational cooperation and reflection have themselves often served as a site of contention regarding their feasibility and beneficence. Certain traditions very much consider their own expression of Christianity to be the one true way of knowing and sharing the gospel of Jesus Christ. Their efforts in building relationships among Christians either recognize conversion to this articulation of the tradition as the optimal outcome or aim for collaboration with others in shared ethical or practical objectives that make no attempt to reconcile theological difference. Other traditions are less concerned with ecclesiological or doctrinal agreement. Some do not consider a singular affiliation to be necessary for incorporation into the body of Christ, and others are less interested in efforts to work toward a unity that seems beyond the capacities of human institutions that remain rife with divergence and contention. Many communities understandably dedicate their resources to what seems to be the more immediate work of preaching, worship, teaching, service, or another collective obligation within their own ranks. But the prayer of Christ himself in John's gospel compels Christians among every communion. Even within traditions that are more hesitant to explore interdenominational collaboration, there have been efforts throughout history to formally recognize common ground. A full review of the history of ecumenical agreements is beyond the vision of this chapter, but it is worth emphasizing that these agreements, while they may seem of minimal consequence beyond their immediate context, have material significance on the ground for many Christian people. Questions about marriage, economic and social commitments, military service, child-rearing, vocation, and other concerns related to the ordering of personal and family life are all intimately tied to religion. Agreements established between religious communions may mean the broadening of possibilities for individual and community affiliation.

Dialogue between Christian communities was no new revelation of the twentieth century, but the efforts of the Second Vatican Council in 1962–65 fomented a recommitment to charting the territories between disparate ecclesial theologies and observances. In his review of the post-conciliar ecumenical conversations regarding the sacraments, Jorge A. Scampini, OP, describes two varieties of inter-denominational discussion: the first, an assessment of a particular sacrament (i.e., baptism) and its constitutive parts and consequences. The second variety involves dialogue with respect to sacramental theology writ large.[13] Between traditions already embracing a shared philosophy of sacramentality (thus with little need for this second variety of discussion), deliberations often concern liturgical expression, practical considerations for the faithful, and nuanced interpretations of Christological and scriptural hermeneutics.[14] The Roman Catholic Church and the Eastern Orthodox Church, for example, recognize one another's shared sacramental inheritance such that concern regarding validity is less pronounced than it may be between other communions.

Among certain Protestant denominations, cooperative effort has contributed to mutual recognition of many common elements of sacramental theology. Scampini notes that "by allowing for greater confessional and ritual diversity, Protestant traditions do not regard differences among the respective positions as impeding the habitual practice of eucharistic hospitality, or even full Communion agreements among churches of different confessions."[15] Scampari's assessment does not take into prominent consideration the doctrinal commitments of Protestant communions like the Missouri and Wisconsin synods of the Lutheran Church whose concern for differences among theologies and praxis do indeed limit the habitual practices of worshippers unaffiliated with their particular expressions of the faith. In general, however, this assessment of Protestant traditions' more flexible terms for interdenominational agreement is reliable. Officially sanctioned agreements between Protestant churches vary by tradition, but they have notably included the Porvoo Communion between several northern European Anglican and Lutheran Churches[16] and the Leuenberg Agreement[17] uniting reformed churches in Europe since the latter half of the twentieth century.

Notable among the agreements aimed at nurturing ecumenical harmony vis-à-vis the sacraments is the 1982 document from the World Council of Churches titled, "Baptism, Eucharist, and Ministry." Comprised of over three-hundred member churches, the World Council of

---

13. Scampini, "The Sacraments in Ecumenical Dialogue," 677.

14. See Scampini, "The Sacraments in Ecumenical Dialogue," 678–79, for a helpful overview of sacramental agreement between the Roman Catholic and Orthodox Churches.

15. Scampini, "The Sacraments in Ecumenical Dialogue," 682.

16. See *The Porvoo Common Statement*.

17. See CPCE, *Leuenberg Agreement*.

Churches describes their mission not in terms of facilitating full communion across denominations, but as a collective of Christian organizational bodies "committed to close collaboration in Christian witness and service.... They are also striving together to realize the goal of visible Church unity."[18] The "Baptism, Eucharist, and Ministry" document cohered over fifty years of discernment and deliberation, beginning in 1927 in Lausanne, Switzerland and concluding in Lima, Peru in 1982.[19] The document does not purport to describe "consensus" between all contributors, but rather works to show the large degree of "significant theological convergence" between ecclesial communions.[20] Ultimately, "Baptism, Eucharist, and Ministry" points toward the origin of the church and its sacraments and ministries as fundamentally bound up within the life, death, and salvific resurrection of Jesus Christ, the Son of God—a truth that is at once so simple and of such great magnitude that its power for encouraging ecumenical dialogue is a noble foundation for the remainder of our exploration.

Beyond the questions of whether or not alignment regarding sacramental theology between Christian traditions is possible or desirable, there is a more enduring root of coherence and hope in five essential truths at the heart of Christian sacramental theology.[21] It will be these five points that I offer as solid ground for fostering respect and cooperation among the faithful. Each of these points are far from my own revelations of any novel theology, but are simply the pillars of the daily ministry of the gospel in which I share with my colleagues across denominational borderlines. They are offered from experience and illuminated by thinkers who have already taken to heart the prayers of Jesus in John 17. Notably, it is not necessary for a communion to even agree that sacramental validity is possible among other denominations for these points to serve as bridges between them. Whether certain church communities are concerned with sharing the fullness of the sacramental life with one another or whether

---

18. WCC, "Baptism, Eucharist, and Ministry," 5.
19. WCC, "Baptism, Eucharist, and Ministry," 6.
20. WCC, "Baptism, Eucharist, and Ministry," 7.
21. It may be that among the innumerable variety of Christian communities and individual interpretations of scripture there are outliers that may not fully embrace each of the four points I offer here. In general, I am confident that the majority of Orthodox, Catholic, and Protestant traditions would recognize the validity of these four basic truths in their essential forms.

this cooperation is not among their current interests, the following foundational principles can support mutuality, dialogue, and friendship.

The first principle of a unitive sacramental theology is the certitude that all sacraments come to us from God at his own initiative. It is the generous and generative agency of Jesus Christ, the Son of God, that bestows the graces of sacraments upon the Church writ large. In the sacramental life as in all creation, God is always making the first move. Whether a communion recognizes two sacraments, seven sacraments, or hundreds of sacraments, each sacrament meets the receptive heart of the beneficiary by no precipitating action of their own. This idea of God's initiative can be found in catechisms from Heidelberg to Rome, and it is aligned with holy scripture's revelations that "all things come from thee" (1 Chr 29:14). While various ecclesial communities may catechize differently regarding the importance of an individual's disposition for reception of the sacraments, the recognition of the divine initiative that begins and enlivens the sacramental possibility is present widely. Scampini notes that in historic disagreements between Catholics and Protestants that pertained to sacramental life, often what was missed was the reality that both share a common understanding: that the sacraments "effect grace by being a certain kind of 'instrument' in Christ's hands, their real minister.... Only Christ elevates the sacramental rites and gives them their instrumental power, as he acts through them."[22] While nuance and praxis may emphasize discrepancies between traditional teaching, there remains—at their foundation—a shared recognition of God's precipitating activity and irrepressible initiative.

The second point in which the vast majority of Christians can find fruitful hope for agreement as they contemplate sacramental theology is the fact that sacraments sanctify creation in their incarnational reality. Sacraments are a clear, physical manifestation of God's blessing of material creation, each a revelation of the promise of that creation's redemption assured in the incarnation of Jesus. The gift of the incarnation animates the sacraments, and the incarnation is solid theological footing for ecumenical reflection on the sacramental life. Lizette Larson-Miller insists that, "the historical event of the incarnation and its unfolding in all time and space is foundational for Christianity across the board as well as for ecumenical sacramental theology."[23] As Christians, our traditions and

---

22. Scampini, "The Sacraments in Ecumenical Dialogue," 688.
23. Larson-Miller, *Sacramentality Renewed*, 39.

faith—however they may differ in expression—extend from our belief in Jesus Christ, the incarnate Son of God. Indeed Edward Schillebeeckx names Christ as the "Primordial Sacrament," the true source of all human encounter with God.[24] The words of the Apostles' and Nicene Creeds give voice to the foundational theological commitments of the apostolic faith, and in them, we encounter the assurance of (or invitation to) belief in "Jesus Christ, his only Son, our Lord. He was conceived by the power of the Holy Spirit and born of the Virgin Mary" (in the Apostles' Creed) and Jesus who was "eternally begotten of the Father," the one who "by the power of the Holy Spirit . . . became incarnate from the Virgin Mary and was made man" (in the Nicene Creed).

In the incarnation, God sanctifies material creation anew as he comes among it in the person of Jesus. St. Athanasius tells us, "The Savior of us all, the Word of God, in His great love took to Himself a body and moved as Man among men. . . . He became Himself an object for the senses, so that those who were seeking God in sensible things might apprehend the Father through the words which He, the Word of God, did in the body."[25] When we affirm that sacraments come to us from God's initiative through Jesus Christ by the power of the Holy Spirit, we encounter the sacraments as sanctified creation twofold: both in the material substance through which Christ's presence is mediated and also as bodies who have become sanctified creation ourselves. We meet Jesus Christ himself—even if there is disagreement about precisely how—in such material substances as bread, wine, oil, and water. In the verity of the incarnation, all Christians know God intimately by the salvific life, work, death, and resurrection of God's Son, Jesus. It is this Jesus who sanctifies the created world in his use of its abundance for healing and blessing. It is this Jesus who draws each of us near through the sacramental life.

The third unifying truth undergirding sacramental theology is the cruciform character of the sacraments. In their constitution and efficacy, the sacraments call us back always to the paschal mystery: the life, passion, death, resurrection and glorification of Jesus Christ. The sacraments, as we have just explored, mediate encounter with the fullness of Christ whose incarnation points always toward the salvation accomplished upon the cross. Though certain Christian traditions emphasize particular dimensions of Christ's life in their doctrinal formation

---

24. Schillebeeckx, *Christ the Sacrament*, 13. See the entirety of the work. It is a blessing.

25. Athanasius, *On the Incarnation*, 43.

and liturgical praxis, again the historic creeds direct our hearts toward contemplation of the Lord who "for our sake was crucified" and "on the third day he rose again." The incarnation and Christ's messianic presence among us is always already bound up within his passion, and a sacramental encounter with Christ's life is therefore always already and also an encounter with Calvary. As Francesca Aran Murphy writes, interpreting St. Thomas Aquinas, "the grace the sacraments give overflows from the sacrifice of Christ at Calvary."[26] When Christians recover and nourish a sense of the sacraments' roots in salvation—that is, the fruits of the paschal mystery—there is planted a seed of the capacities for mutually beholding one another as belonging to the promises of that salvation.

The fourth principle that can stretch across denominational lines to inspire unity and partnership is the sacraments' inherent insistence upon the transformation of the Christian's perception of and participation in an ethical life. When an individual has received a sacrament by God's grace, the reality of the love made known between creator and cherished creation demands a turn outward on the part of the beloved to behold and affirm the dignity of all others who share this divinely created world. Indeed, when Jesus instructs his disciples before his departure in the final chapter of the Gospel of Matthew, he tells them, "go therefore and make disciples of all nations, baptizing them in the name of the Father and of the Son and of the Holy Spirit, teaching them to observe all that I have commanded you" (Matt 28:19–20). Baptism is intrinsically tied to Jesus' call to teach others all of the commands he has given to those who follow him, including commands to love the Lord their God "with all your heart, and with all your soul, and with all your mind" (Matt 22:37) and to "love your neighbor as yourself" (Matt 22:39).

These commands conceivably include, too, Jesus' other teachings throughout the Gospels, including the Sermon on the Mount in Matthew 5 and injunctions to care for the poor, the weak, and the sick in Matthew 25. Jesus himself tells us that the sacramental life, exemplified in baptism, precipitates and demands a unique recognition of God's love for creation. This recognition then inspires our response, opening our hearts to behold one another as God beholds us. Our confrontation with the incarnate and risen Lord in his sacraments necessitates our taking seriously his teachings regarding the ethical ordering of our lives and spirits, and we find within each sacrament or sacramental rite a re-ordering of

---

26. Murphy, "Christ, the Trinity, and the Sacraments," 618.

our more unsavory human desires. To receive the sacraments is to receive not only the person of Jesus, but also his teachings which—as we fully embrace them—illuminate even the darkest, most harrowing corners of the world.[27]

Our fifth and final point of departure for contemplating a foundation for sacramental mutuality is the truth that sacraments—in their substance and in their effect—nourish a unitive orientation within those who receive them. As the sacraments knit us firmly into the body of Christ, they call our attention to the truth that this body is not something we constitute on our own. We are not isolated recipients of grace nor insular participants in a private faith. Adrienne von Speyr writes:

> For there is no purely private sacrament in the Church. All the sacraments are a means and occasion for unity; each one unites all believers who are connected with it, whether they receive it directly or not. The sacraments are one of the most excellent powers of unification, since in a very mysterious way they guide all Christians into the unity of the Church . . . the unity of the Church, however, is absolute love.[28]

The last principle offered for consideration in this inquiry flows from the natural consequences of the previous four. At God's initiative, the sanctifier of all creation consecrates material reality by the power of the Holy Spirit, calling those who receive the sacraments into a cruciform life that then demands an attentiveness to the care and dignity of others. As that dignity is affirmed, and as the sacraments align the hearts of those who participate in them with the heart of Jesus Christ, any possibility of separation from the body is impossible. In each sacrament, the words of St. Paul to the Corinthians are rearticulated: "For just as the body is one and has many members, and all the members of the body, though many, are one body, so it is with Christ. For by one Spirit we were all baptized into one body—Jews or Greeks, slaves or free—and all were made to drink of one Spirit. For the body does not consist of one member but of many" (1 Cor 12:12–14). The sacraments—however our traditions have reckoned with them, whatever is within them that we can or cannot know—unite us in Christ Jesus. While pain and division may endure between communities of varying theological commitments so long as we

---

27. For more on ethics and the Eucharist, see Cavanaugh, *Torture and Eucharist*; Cavanaugh, *Field Hospital*; Hellwig, *Eucharist and the Hunger of the World*.

28. Speyr, *Confession*, 80.

remain this side of heaven, the sacraments insist that the multiplicity of the body beholds one another as fellow members, all called to the worship and service of one enduring and almighty God.

An orientation toward unity may feel far too burdensome for us to imagine much progress toward an earthly reconciliation, but we are not permitted to abandon hope. The Bible demonstrates that Jesus himself prays for the unity of his followers, and in this, we are offered a glimpse of what God has in store for us. Our ordinary efforts may seem minimal when compared with the tasks before us, but each one of us might play a part.

My daily prayer in ministry is that the Lord make clear which are the burdens that I am to take up and which are the burdens that he means for me to set aside (perhaps for later, or perhaps to leave for someone else). Some burdens are indeed mine for the unpacking—for the soothing or the unknotting, for patching up or taking down. Other burdens are too big for the day, or they will be better shepherded by another. A single day, ripe with a certain unmovable number of hours, is best spent with those burdens that God has appointed for the time, no more and no less. It is this prayer that enlivens, too, my prayer for the broader church in our diversity. Today, it may not be my burden to single-handedly reconcile centuries of interdenominational dissonance regarding sacramental substance and efficacy. But perhaps tomorrow it might be. Today, the magnitude of our grief as members of a divided body may be too impossible, too large for a single individual or community to repair. And yet tomorrow, by the mercies of God, we might be called to set out afresh—into another adventurous leap of faith in the One for whom nothing is beyond possibility.

Throughout this chapter, I have hoped to demonstrate that it is God himself who calls the church into unity, and that this unity cannot be considered apart from the church's sacramental life. We have taken seriously the divisions that remain among us, and we have not shied away from acknowledging the very real and immediate ways that sacramental theology and practice have separated us from one another. A brief review of historical efforts to assess points of convergence has revealed the importance of dialogue and a discerning spiritual imagination. Finally, we have explored five principles broadly common to the Christian faith that might serve as groundwork for our own prayers for the future of the church. Whatever our burdens might be to take up or to set aside, today or tomorrow, may our prayers continue for a body of Christ that ever more resembles the graceful wholeness of his Sacred Heart.

## Bibliography

Athanasius. *On the Incarnation*. Crestwood, NY: St. Vladimir's Seminary Press, 1996.
Cavanaugh, William T. *Field Hospital: The Church's Engagement with a Wounded World*. Grand Rapids: Eerdmans, 2016.
———. *Torture and Eucharist: Theology, Politics, and the Body of Christ*. Malden, MA: Blackwell, 1998.
Communion of Protestant Churches in Europe. *The Leuenberg Agreement*. https://www.leuenberg.eu/documents/.
Chrysostom, John. *Homily 82 on the Gospel of John*. http://www.newadvent.org/fathers/240182.htm.
The Episcopal Church. *The Book of Common Prayer, 1979*. New York: Church Publishing, 1986.
Hellwig, Monika K. *The Eucharist and the Hunger of the World*. 2nd ed. Kansas City, MO: Sheed & Ward, 1992.
Holcomb, Justin A., and David A. Johnson. *Christian Theologies of the Sacraments: A Comparative Introduction*. New York: New York University Press, 2017.
Larson-Miller, Lizette. *Sacramentality Renewed: Contemporary Conversations in Sacramental Theology*. Collegeville, MN: Liturgical, 2016.
Murphy, Francesca Aran. "Christ, the Trinity, and the Sacraments." In *The Oxford Handbook of Sacramental Theology*, edited by Hans Boersma and Matthew Levering, 616–30. Oxford: Oxford University Press, 2015.
*The Porvoo Common Statement*. https://www.anglicancommunion.org/media/102178/porvoo_common_statement.pdf.
Scampini, Jorge A. "The Sacraments in Ecumenical Dialogue." In *The Oxford Handbook of Sacramental Theology*, edited by Hans Boersma and Matthew Levering, 675–81. Oxford: Oxford University Press, 2015.
Schillebeeckx, Edward. *Christ the Sacrament of the Encounter with God*. Lanham, MD: Sheed & Ward, 1963.
Sonderegger, Katherine. *Systematic Theology*. Vol. 1, *The Doctrine of God*. Minneapolis: Fortress, 2015.
Speyr, Adrienne von. *Confession*. San Francisco: Ignatius, 2017.
Tertullian. *On Baptism*. https://www.newadvent.org/fathers/0321.htm.
Wood, Susan K. "The Sacramental Foundations of Ecclesial Identity: Barrier or Passageway to Ecumenical Unity?" In *Believing in Community: Ecumenical Reflections on the Church*, edited by Peter de Mey et al., 455–75. Leuven: Peeters, 2013.
World Council of Churches. "Baptism, Eucharist, and Ministry." https://www.oikoumene.org/sites/default/files/Document/FO1982_111_en.pdf.

5

# Sacramental and Liturgical Inclusivity through Understanding "Performativity" and "Tribalism"

JEREMY MEANS-KOSS

*Jesus himself, at the hour of his Passion, prayed "that they may all be one" (Jn 17:21). This unity, which the Lord has bestowed on his Church and in which he wishes to embrace all people, is not something added on, but stands at the very heart of Christ's mission. Nor is it some secondary attribute of the community of his disciples. Rather, it belongs to the very essence of this community. God wills the Church, because he wills unity, and unity is an expression of the whole depth of his agape. In effect, this unity bestowed by the Holy Spirit does not merely consist in the gathering of people as a collection of individuals. It is a unity constituted by the bonds of the profession of faith, the sacraments and hierarchical communion.*[1]

---

1. John Paul II, *Ut unum sint*, no. 9.

## Introduction

NOT MERELY A "GATHERING of people" or a "collection of individuals" as Pope John Paul II says, the church is a holy, catholic, and apostolic[2] community of believers called to follow Jesus Christ as his body (Rom 7:4; 1 Cor 12:12–27; Eph 3:6; 5:23), his bride (John 3:29), and his temple (2 Cor 6:16; 2 Thess 2:4); and yet it continues to suffer its most obvious and inescapable handicap—being comprised of fallible humans. In our zealous desire to create for Christ *his* church, we have time after time cast our fellow siblings—*our neighbors*—by the wayside or caused them to doubt if his church is indeed a place for them. In John Paul II's 1995 encyclical, *Ut unum sint* ("To Be One"), the pope poetically and definitively articulates that God desires his church to be unified by bonds of faith, sacrament, and a relationship with God as its head and great high priest.

Sadly, true to our human nature, what God decrees for good, man finds ways to pollute. We need not even look past moments in the early church to encounter moments where fallible human communities forgot God's desire for unity in favor of selfishness and tribalism. The apostle Paul recounts how the church in Corinth became so easily divided, even in something so universal as their sacrament of communion (1 Cor 11). Rather than a gathered and unified partaking of the Lord's Supper there was a subdivided sacramental practice; first, for the upper class, and then a second after the first for the servant class. It is that same sin that our global and universal church has managed to reproduce time and time again—trappings over transcendence—idolatry of identity over our shared identity as one community in Christ.

It has been in the midst of that suffering however where the church has managed to also adapt and even thrive. When the church was not a holy and transforming place for African-Americans, Richard Allen along with others began denominations such as the African Methodist Episcopal Church (AME). And when scholar priests like Martin Luther translated the holy scriptures from Latin into the native languages of the region, such as German, the Christian commoners were able to connect with God's word in a way they never had been able to do before. A casual glance at the plethora of churches around the United States—even within singular denominations—reveals that amongst Christ's body there are differential nuances that characterize each community. Every church *feels*

---

2. Cf. Nicene Creed, originally formulated at the Council of Nicea in 325 CE. A copy of the text can be found at USCCB, "Nicene Creed."

different because each has their own cultural identity and expression that make them both special and unique—they draw in potential disciples who need Christ but desire a community that taps into a part of their own identity—each church a tribal identity. But why?

If the church is to be a single unified body, why does each congregation need to feel so distinct? And if churches desire to open themselves up to our heavenly mandate of expressing the whole depth of God's limitless fatherly love to all of humanity, how can we authentically go about it? How do we create a shared experience of a "church home" without bulldozing or blanching the fellow needs of our siblings in Christ? And how do we fulfill our evangelistic obligations to God that create a liturgical space that invites the outsider into a relationship with Jesus without sacrificing Christ's ordinances or thousands of years of Christian wisdom?

In our ongoing quest to find God's love and acceptance not only in ourselves but in our neighbors we have created defined micro-communities, tribes, reinforcing human differentiation or our identities—identities that we perpetually perform—that intentionally includes and excludes for the purposes of group formation. And while we may desire to abhor such behaviors for their emotional and institutional segregation the reality is that we are also deeply complicit in this tribalism for its self-healing properties as well. In addition to its harms, Christian tribalism has provided a safe space for shared suffering, birthed innovative and evangelistic worship, and helped the invisible see themselves as part and parcel of the body of Christ. Yet in the midst of such diversity we cannot ignore Christ's clarion call for unity.

Evident by the historic exiles of the Israelites, the various house churches of the persecuted Christians, and the reformations of the second millennia, it is evident that spaces of ritual practice and worship were unable to be contained into one centralized location or even a single denomination. How then amidst such ritualized and geographical diversity can the church hope to honor such a lambasting truth that Paul set down upon the church in Corinth—that while difference will exist, there are some liturgical truths that cannot be altered? And how does that reality set forth a paradigm for our modern churches to practice evangelistic and inclusive fellowship while still remaining righteous? How do we "welcome the least of these" (Mark 9:37; Luke 9:48; cf. Matt 5), while remaining righteous?

Scripture mandates that if we desire to stem the further fracturing and hemorrhaging of Christ's disciples and in its stead efficaciously grow

Christ's church, both locally and globally, we must desire true Christian unity, empty of superfluousness and superficiality. By better understanding the "performance" and "tribalism" of identity beyond its tacit shell and see the necessary validation it can provide, the church can utilize sacramentality to effectively grow and build healthy communities for Christ.

## Scriptural Mandate

While it may not be popular or widely accepted, God through scripture does indeed place monumental priority on diverse human identities and the important task of encountering Christ's sacramentality as the great unifier of them.

An eisegitcal interpretation of Gal 3:28, "there is no longer Jew or Greek, there is no longer slave or free, there is no longer male and female; for all of you are one in Christ Jesus,"[3] might encourage a believer to conceive that as a Christian all of their other identities are moot save for their Christian one. Such is the overwhelming claim in churches that wish to sidestep issues of social identity politics. An exemplified parallel claim is made by people when they say things such as "I do not see color," when referring to someone's race. However, blindness of difference does not heal communities nor bring about unity. It instead merely creates vacuous silence around the pain of division.

In contrast however, an exegetical interpretation of that text in Galatians might consider that while Paul does indeed bestow Christological unity among disparate people, their former conceptions of themselves are not made invisible or moot but instead are enriched. While some may have been born Jewish and other Greek, they now share a unity in Christ. That does not abrogate certain cultural truths to their identity but instead creates a sacramental unifier which binds them together. A more exegetical translation of Gal 3:23 does not focus on the negation but on the universality it bestows. If we believe that Paul's words are blessed by God, words of God, then we can only understand them to be socially just and pure—without harm and malice; meant to unify and no traumatize. The Amplified Bible translation of the verse says, "There is [now no distinction in regard to salvation] neither Jew nor Greek . . . ." The translators aim being to accentuate the divine love of God revealing that Paul did not intended to destroy identity but rather include. Ignoring the

---

3. Unless otherwise noted, all biblical quotations are from the NRSV.

circumstances in peoples' lives is a pastorally inappropriate tactic—one Paul would never do. We must consider his words as pastorally and theologically synchronized.

To further assist us conceive of God's vision of diversity, scripture provides us the avatar of language. We encounter the diversity of language early on in scripture. In Genesis 11, newly after the horrific culling of humanity by the great flood, Noah's descendants begin to build the city of Babel. It is important to note that during this time "the whole earth had one language and the same words" (Gen 11:1). It's only then in verse four that we only get a hint as to why God decides to fracture humanity's language. In 11:4, we are told that the humans declared that they shall build a tower unto the heavens and "make a name for ourselves." One might see human arrogance and selfish desire as the sole cause for God's action, yet it is by the actions of Christ that we are invited into a more complex understanding of what God's motivations could have been.

The story of Babel is oft seen as punishment. But what if it weren't solely intended as so? What if the scriptural account of Babel is also God's clarion call for human cooperation and unity *in the midst of our differences*. Scripture tells us in Acts 2 of the miracle of Pentecost, when disparate tribes—people of noted differing language—continued to speak in their various languages yet were understood by one another.

> [5] Now there were devout Jews from every nation under heaven living in Jerusalem. [6] And at this sound the crowd gathered and was bewildered, because each one heard them speaking in the native language of each. [7] Amazed and astonished, they asked, "Are not all these who are speaking Galileans? [8] And how is it that we hear, each of us, in our own native language? [9] Parthians, Medes, Elamites, and residents of Mesopotamia, Judea and Cappadocia, Pontus and Asia, [10] Phrygia and Pamphylia, Egypt and the parts of Libya belonging to Cyrene, and visitors from Rome, both Jews and proselytes, [11] Cretans and Arabs—in our own languages we hear them speaking about God's deeds of power. (Acts 2:5–11)

If the division at Babel were only punishment, would not the miracle of Pentecost have created a permanent language reunification? Yet, they weren't. It was a sacramental moment of unity created by God in the understanding of diversity.

God's testimonial regarding difference is given repeatedly in both the Hebrew Bible and the New Testament. In the story of Adam and Eve, they encountered each others' differences yet were able to coexist united until they defied God. It was only after they ate of the forbidden fruit that Adam and Eve felt shame for their differences. While we may desire sameness, there is no reason we should believe God does not deeply value diversity in his disciples. In his Great Commission we are told Jesus said, "go therefore and make disciples of all nations, baptizing them in the name of the Father and of the Son and of the Holy Spirit" (Matt 28:19).

It is here that we are given God's parlay of diversity and sacramentalism. It is a point St. Peter delivers home in Acts chapter two after the Pentecostal miracle.

> [37] Now when they heard this, they were cut to the heart and said to Peter and to the other apostles, "Brothers, what should we do?" [38] Peter said to them, "Repent, and be baptized every one of you in the name of Jesus Christ so that your sins may be forgiven; and you will receive the gift of the Holy Spirit. [39] For the promise is for you, for your children, and for all who are far away, everyone whom the Lord our God calls to him." [40] And he testified with many other arguments and exhorted them, saying, "Save yourselves from this corrupt generation." [41] So those who welcomed his message were baptized, and that day about three thousand persons were added. [42] They devoted themselves to the apostles' teaching and fellowship, to the breaking of bread and the prayers. (Acts 2:37–41)

Diverse identities and God's sacraments seem to go hand-in-hand together. For as much as identity politics have divided Christians over the last two millennia, scriptural evidence points to diverse identities as being central to the Christian story. How then might we exegetically interpret Paul's words from Galatians through the lens of God's example of how he treats language? Perhaps rather than denying the singular identity of the person, Paul's words are meant to deny the bipolarity of examination itself—that is to say, the pitting of one identity oppositional to the other. No longer is there a comparison of Jew to Gentile or a comparison of slave to free or even a comparison of female to male. No longer are we permitted to propose division between such identities. Such a claim does not invalidate the identity itself, for the separate tribal languages were not negated, but instead proposed a new paradigm to their interaction. They share an overarching sacramental identity, of being one with Christ—to speak with individual performance yet act and understand through God's grace.

It seems apparent that God desires a Christian unity brought together by sacrament but is not dismissive of the individual identities that make up the whole. What is being rebuked instead is the desire itself to see identities *as* divisive. Human multiplicity is a necessary aspect of God's mission here on earth. God is deeply aware that humanity struggles with diversity and it is that inelasticity which threatens his mission of love. In blunt rebuking Jesus tells the people, "for if you love those who love you, what reward do you have? Do not even the tax collectors do the same? And if you greet only your brothers and sisters, what more are you doing than others? Do not even the Gentiles do the same?" (Matt 5:45–47). Making the arduous steps of working with those we despise is no easy task, yet it is such an important characteristic of God's people that Jesus rebukes his fellow countrymen for their hypocritical display of loving-kindness.

But it is Paul who helps us understand why God desires diversity—why he has designed it into our very fabric of being; and why our limited perspectives and judgement are only a hinderance to his mission. In 1 Corinthians 12, Paul openly declares that diverse identities bring with them valuable purposes.[4] And though Jesus tells us to not to judge each other quite plainly (Matt 7), Paul goes on further to explain that to those whom we have judged to be "weaker" or "less respectable" actually need

---

4. "[12] For just as the body is one and has many members, and all the members of the body, though many, are one body, so it is with Christ. [13] For in the one Spirit we were all baptized into one body—Jews or Greeks, slaves or free—and we were all made to drink of one Spirit. [14] Indeed, the body does not consist of one member but of many. [15] If the foot would say, 'Because I am not a hand, I do not belong to the body,' that would not make it any less a part of the body. [16] And if the ear would say, 'Because I am not an eye, I do not belong to the body,' that would not make it any less a part of the body. [17] If the whole body were an eye, where would the hearing be? If the whole body were hearing, where would the sense of smell be? [18] But as it is, God arranged the members in the body, each one of them, as he chose. [19] If all were a single member, where would the body be? [20] As it is, there are many members, yet one body. [21] The eye cannot say to the hand, 'I have no need of you,' nor again the head to the feet, 'I have no need of you.' [22] On the contrary, the members of the body that seem to be weaker are indispensable, [23] and those members of the body that we think less honorable we clothe with greater honor, and our less respectable members are treated with greater respect; [24] whereas our more respectable members do not need this. But God has so arranged the body, giving the greater honor to the inferior member, [25] that there may be no dissension within the body, but the members may have the same care for one another. [26] If one member suffers, all suffer together with it; if one member is honored, all rejoice together with it. [27] Now you are the body of Christ and individually members of it" (1 Cor 12:12–27).

be treated with greater respect and care. In contrast to our selfish desires for sameness, Paul instead regards differences as necessary for the church.

Over the course of Christian history we constantly find ourselves at odds with those whom we ought to call sibling. Yet if God through scripture mandates that the church be a place of diverse identities, not because of some genial nature or generosity but out of proper Christian theology, how do we invite and welcome diverse peoples together so that God's sacraments may unite us?

The powerfully and often overlooked aspect of Pentecost is that each different tribal member—each culturally different individual present—*heard* their own language being spoken, even though everyone was still speaking their own languages. There is deep opportunity it seems to model evangelism and welcoming hospitality on the miracle that Pentecost displayed. Church perhaps then can be experienced in such a way that visitors and new members might experience church as not only transformational but also as somehow deeply familiar.

*There is a powerful connection that occurs when we are seen and recognized by another. Over and over in scripture, God reminds us how important it is to be recognized; to be seen and understood.* As early as Genesis chapter one we hear how important it is to be seen. In the beginning, in the formless void, God created light. And after each day, God saw what he had created and called it good (Gen 1:1—2:4a). It is so necessary to be regarded, and regarded as good, that it is the very first story in all of scripture.

It is a lesson God continues to repeat through Jesus in the New Testament. Christ recognized the woman at the well, and though he may have told her to "sin no more" he never once rejected her. Jesus recognized the pharisees and he recognized the disciples. For positive or negative, Jesus saw others. And like his time in Emmaus after his resurrection, even Jesus himself was experienced through recognition. Most notably though is the annunciation of our Lord to the Virgin Mary.

But God does not just see us out in the world. Scripture tells us we have been seen and validated even before birth. The shared sentiment in both of God's validation of the prophet Jeremiah[5] and his validation of Jesus through the annunciation to the Virgin Mary[6] is the implicit

---

5. "Before I formed you in the womb I knew you, before you were born I set you apart; I appointed you as a prophet to the nations" (Jer 1:5).

6. "[26] In the sixth month the angel Gabriel was sent by God to a town in Galilee called Nazareth, [27] to a virgin engaged to a man whose name was Joseph, of the house

statement that even before the individual's identity was known to the world, God already had known the identity of this person and set them apart as special.

And once a person in scripture is born, they are named, as a further way we are told that a person's identity matters. Jacob is renamed to "wrestles with God," and the name Jesus means "God rescues." Names from the bible give insightful meanings to the characters of the stories. Lineages legitimize prophetic claims and as we see with prophets such as Jonah—who at first chose to run from his identity—that evading one's identity can only go so far before trouble befalls them.

The sharing of who we are, the performativity of our identities, is not something to be ignored nor to be lambasted. It is one of the most complex components that scripture uses to further God's mission.

## Performativity

Performativity is a term coined by sociologist and cultural theorist Judith Butler as she applied Foucauldian discourse analysis (concerning power and socialization) as she focused on gender and sexuality. Butler argued that our genders are communications; that they are component identities that do not exist in a vacuum but instead exist through the recognition and social and visible negotiations with others.

The "gendered body is performative," she writes describing to us that social identities have "no ontological status apart from the various acts which constitute its reality."[7] What Butler not only subsequently names but adds to the discourse through her book *Gender Trouble* is that

---

of David. The virgin's name was Mary. [28] And he came to her and said, 'Greetings, favored one! The Lord is with you.' [29] But she was much perplexed by his words and pondered what sort of greeting this might be. [30] The angel said to her, 'Do not be afraid, Mary, for you have found favor with God. [31] And now, you will conceive in your womb and bear a son, and you will name him Jesus. [32] He will be great, and will be called the Son of the Most High, and the Lord God will give to him the throne of his ancestor David. [33] He will reign over the house of Jacob forever, and of his kingdom there will be no end.' [34] Mary said to the angel, 'How can this be, since I am a virgin?' [35] The angel said to her, 'The Holy Spirit will come upon you, and the power of the Most High will overshadow you; therefore the child to be born will be holy; he will be called Son of God. [36] And now, your relative Elizabeth in her old age has also conceived a son; and this is the sixth month for her who was said to be barren. [37] For nothing will be impossible with God.' [38] Then Mary said, 'Here am I, the servant of the Lord; let it be with me according to your word.' Then the angel departed from her" (Luke 1:26–38).

7. Butler, *Gender Trouble*, 185.

this "public regulation of [this] fantasy through the surface politics of the body"[8] as she says it, is pivotal to the integrity of the individual's identity. The identity is thus a fabrication—a creation through enactments that are communicated—not to be taken as mere as ontological truths but as performances that create characterization, thus her use of such a nomenclature. We see validations of her theories in other various spheres such as race, national identity and citizenship, and really any type of identity that is only understood through an enacted participation.

While Butler's argument is positioned squarely in the field of gender and sexuality, her assertion is both foundational and paramount to the understanding of any conversation regarding identity. To her first point, that an identity is performative in an ontological sense, asserts that no identity exists in a vacuum nor is it absolute without the self and other to experience and/or name it. One is not knowingly any form of identity without another to create sameness or otherness to such performance. For Butler, one cannot be a woman without other women and non-women to measure and perform the gender with and against. Her argument holds true however for almost any ontological categorization and can be equally applied to a Christian context. Numerous scriptural examples recount for us that our identities as disciples of God (both in the Hebrew Bible and New Testament) are by direct relationship to YHWH/the Father. Discipleship cannot exist in a vacuum because even at its most primal, it would still be through our relationship with God. A close reading of the creation narratives in Genesis 1 and 2 reveal that we are named and known by God, even and especially at our formation—a theological tenet rekindled through scriptures like the Psalms, Jonah, Isaiah and Jeremiah.

In this regard, Butler's assertions are still true; that our identities, even our Christian ones, are ontologically established *through* relationship. Butler then goes on to argue that because identities exist in this relationship of performativity—of enacting or non-enacting to another—they then take on language germane to distinguish such enaction or non-enaction. This further navigation "pits 'I' against an 'Other.'" For Butler, there is a step-by-step process of identity differentiation, beginning with enactment and performativity but not ceasing there. Identities take on form because of what is then built around the identities. One of the most powerful examples in scripture is Christ himself. The name Jesus come from the Greek Ἰησοῦ from the original word Ἰησοῦς which comes from

---

8. Butler, *Gender Trouble*, 185.

the Hebrew יְהוֹשֻׁעַ which means "YHWH saves/the Lord is salvation." To Butler's original statement, Jesus' very name describes his identity. He *is* salvation and is described as such. The critical point being, identities and the language surrounding them, everything from how they are described to what they are named, are important aspects that cannot and should not be overlooked or relegated.

> If identity is asserted through a process of signification, if identity is always already signified, and yet continues to signify as it circulates within various interlocking discourses, then the question of agency is not to be answered through recourse to an "I" that preexists signification. . . . The language of appropriation, instrumentality, and distanciation germane to the epistemological mode also belong to a strategy of domination that pits the "I" against an "Other" and, once that separation is effected, created an artificial set of questions about the knowability and recoverability of that Other. . . . Paradoxically, the reconceptualization of identity as an *effect*, that is as *produced* or *generated*, opens up possibilities of "agency" that are insidiously foreclosed by positions that take identity categories as foundational and fixed. For an identity to be an effect means that it is neither fatally determined nor fully artificial and arbitrary. . . . The critical task is, rather, to locate strategies of subversive repetition enabled by those constructions, to affirm the local possibilities of intervention through participating in precisely those practices of repetition that constitute identity and, therefore, present the immanent possibility of contesting them[9]

What Butler offers after this assertion is to discuss what it means for an individual to become trapped by an identity. It is a point that author, theologian, and sociologist W. E. B. Du Bois made almost a century earlier in his book *the Souls of Black Folk*. In one of the most poignant writings of the modern era, Du Bois depicts the harsh reality of being trapped by an identity. Born into "a world which yields him no true self-consciousness, but only lets him see himself through the revelation of the other. . . . One ever feels his two-ness,—an American, a Negro; two souls, two thoughts, two unreconciled strivings; two warring ideals in one dark body, whose dogged strength alone keeps it from being torn asunder."[10]

---

9. Butler, *Gender Trouble*, 201.
10. Du Bois, *Souls of Black Folk*, 10.

Du Bois' poetic words argue that even if one wishes to exist as a different identity, if the "other" only sees you as one identity, then it doesn't matter how much you may wish to exist as a different identity, you are trapped through merely being in that relationship. It is such a powerful and hurtful experience that Jesus preaches to it in his beatitudes and Paul sermonizes it pastorally in his letters.

Du Bois' words and Butler's conceptualizations allow us to glimpse the reality that all our identities relationally exist like a script for a play where the actors either consciously or subliminally understand their roles to either perform or not perform based on their charactered identities. This harsh reality may not be something that one is always conscious of, as Butler points out, or maybe painfully obvious, as Du Bois points out, but its presence is absolute. And while the Bible may constantly point out the relational and performative parameters of our Christian identity, humans exist with multiple identities and intersectionality. In addition to scripture's insistence that our identities are brought into one united fold of Christendom, it is clear from the field of history that human intersectionality and multiple identities have played a deep role in the division and fracturing among Christians. To ignore such division would not yield any differing results than previously experienced over the past two thousand years.

What Butler offers however, as she discusses agency and subversion, is a strategy for moving towards common unicity—though not total unity or conformity but instead a third way, a *via media*, that offers the individual to exist as both within the reality of society but also gain self-actualizations towards a more self-differentiated[11] life. In her own way, gender and sexual sociologist Judith Butler's argument parallels similar arguments made by Jesus and Saints Peter and Paul in scripture. As Christ says, "to give what belongs to Caesar to Caesar" (Mark 12:17), Jesus is not denying human realities of borders and tribes. He is instead presenting a third space where being a citizen of Rome and a disciple of Christ are not mutually exclusive. We cannot escape what society has already signified us to be, but what we can do is redefine through our own behaviors and re-naming what those identities mean through performing and enacting a new reality. Jesus says at his sermon on the mount, "let your light shine before others, so that they may see your good works and give glory to your

---

11. Self-differentiation is an individual's ability to function for the betterment of both the self and the social settings for which they are part. It is a simultaneous awareness of group dynamics as well as their own sense of self without causing harm to either.

Father in heaven.... For I tell you, unless your righteousness exceeds that of the scribes and Pharisees, you will never enter the kingdom of heaven" (Matt 5:16).

Christ's directive is strong. Your identity as a disciple is shown through action. It is not meant to be conflated with the Pelagian heresy of "salvation by works alone" but is instead a real affirmation that performativity of the discipleship identity involves enactment. How does this relate to church membership and unicity? How does validation or understanding "caesarian" identities in God's churches provide a path to group cohesion? In order to understand how best to create unicity, we must then ponder how performed identities form connections.

## Post-Modern Tribalism and Unicity

Around the same time that Pope John Paul II published *Ut unum sint* a different cultural commentor, French sociologist Michael Maffesoli, published his work entitled *the Time of the Tribes*, in which he posits a postmodern conception of group social dynamism. Maffesoli proposes that individuals no longer "participate in or correspond to" identity groups solely through what he calls "Contracted groups"—whereby individuals voluntarily adhere to a group membership (contractually or mechanically). Instead, he proposes that they primarily exist through "Affective tribes"—whereby individuals emotionally adhere to a collective common grouping (sentimentally and organically).[12] Though Maffesoli admits that it may also be deemed "emotional community," he finds the more precise phrasing to be affective tribalism because of its "'cohesive' aspect of the social sharing of values, places or ideals which are entirely circumscribed (localism) and which can be found, in varied forms, at the heart of numerous social experiences."[13]

It is here we find overlaps of Butler's performative identities and group social dynamism. To synthesize these two sociologists' arguments, we see that as individuals exist in their performative identity, they find emotional tribes of those identities. While this may seem like common sense to suggest that like people find each other, what is critical to the conversation is how Maffesoli understood that these emotional communities—these affectual tribes—replace or sublimate the original

---

12. Maffesoli, *Time of the Tribes*, 18.
13. Maffesoli, *Time of the Tribes*, 19.

# Sacramental and Liturgical Inclusivity—MEANS-KOSS

contractual groups of which individuals might be part. Such is a phenomenon Christians experience first-hand over and over again; for even though Christ may have established one holy and apostolic church, there is no doubt that the Jesus Movement is not united.

As we begin to understand the sociological underpinnings of this social fracturing, we can also perhaps use this same insight to help it heal and create unicity. Interestingly enough, Maffesoli does offer to us that unity can be achieved not without regard to differentiation but rather perhaps even through the tensions amongst them.

> It is possible to imagine that the bond holding a given entity together might in fact be constituted of that which divides (cf. the conjugal polemic). The tension between heterogeneities could be said to guarantee the solidity of the whole. The master craftsmen of the Middle Ages knew a thing or two about this, and built our cathedrals on this principle. This is the *order of the mass*. Thus, lifestyles which are foreign to each other can sketch the outline of a way of living together. And this occurs while remaining curiously faithful to the specificity of each. From this arose the richness of the great cultural moments, at their very founding.[14]

For Maffesoli, it is the attenuation of multiple identities within the larger mass of people that produces a cohesiveness for the larger group. No longer must churches cater to specific political ideologies or fandoms, they can perhaps use the tension of differentiation to reinforce the various affectual tribal groups' larger membership in the church. To do so however takes an honest recognition of the various affectual tribes present, not ignore them.

We seem here to be reconfronted by Peter's Pentecostal miracle of multiple languages, tribes, and yet a reinforced centralized ecclesiological structure—one baptized church. Where we go from there however to achieve that larger unity is also offered by Maffesoli.

> Thus, succeeding the dream of unity is a sort of *unicity*: the adjustment of diverse elements. In the image of the coenesthesia which is able to integrate, within the framework of conflictual harmony, bodily functions and dysfunctions, the notion of the outsider emphasizes the founding aspect of difference. What is more, this is not due to the unanimist perspective of tolerance, but is caused by what might be called the organicity of opposites; the famous *coincidentia oppositorum* of ancient wisdom

---

14. Maffesoli, *Time of the Tribes*, 100.

that, from medieval alchemists to Far Eastern Taoists, has given birth to many organizations and many social representations. Especially for Taoism, in its description of the "interior country," the field of cinnabar, the root of man is situated "*three* inches above the navel in order to express the *trinity* of Heaven, Earth and Man." To highlight its richness still further, the Tao sees the three as that which gives birth to the "Ten thousand ones."[15]

It cannot be escaped that in the midst of such discussion a trinitarian visualization persists as a unifying force among community of difference. With great poetry Maffesoli writes, "Infinity begins with the third person."[16] While he directs the reader to understanding how cacophonous social perception is developed, we as Christians can apply our own trinitarian understandings to Maffesoli's insight.

In Maffesoli's example of the Taoist conceptions of Heaven, Earth and Man, there is an interplay between the divine realm, the material world and humanity. Such a similarity also exists within Christian wisdom. The exceptional wisdom that seems to permeate even beyond Maffesoli's understanding is within his own admission that from this Taoist trinity, "the ten thousand ones"—from God's trinity all of creation comes forth. From Adam, all humanity is born (Gen 1–2), from Abraham all nations will be blessed (Gen 18), and from Jesus all creation is reconciled (Matt 28:20; Mark 10:45; John 12:23–24; Col 1:20). What Maffesoli admits, is already present in scripture. God redeems.

Just as Maffesoli argues for a unicity produced by dissimilarity, St. Paul too echoes such wisdom. "For just as the body is one and has many members, and all the members of the body, though many, are one body, so it is with Christ. For in the one Spirit we were all baptized into one body—Jews or Greeks, slaves or free, and we were all made to drink of one Spirit" (1 Cor 12:12–13). Paul does not deny difference but rather offer that the Spirit is what binds.

Maffesoli offers that *successive sedimentations* create a *special ambience* or "diffused union."

> Through successive sedimentations, create a special ambience—what I have called a diffuse union. I would like to suggest an image to help us in our reflections: at its beginnings, the Christian world was a nebula of entities scattered throughout the Roman Empire. This proliferation secreted that lovely theory of the

---

15. Maffesoli, *Time of the Tribes*, 105.
16. Maffesoli, *Time of the Tribes*, 105.

"communion of the saints." This link was at once firm and flexible, but for all that, it ensured the solidity of the ecclesiastical body. It is this group effervescence and its precise ethos which was to give rise to the civilization of today. It is possible to imagine that we are face to face today with a sort of "communion of the saints." Electronic mail, sexual networks, various solidarities including sporting and musical gatherings are so many signs of an ethos in gestation. Such trends are the framework of this new spirit of the times which we call sociality.[17]

What Maffesoli offers us is a sociological foundation that undergirds Peter's declaration to the people in Acts two, that they repent, be baptized in the name of Jesus, receive the Holy Spirit, and know that God's promise is for them, their children and "all who are far from, everyone whom the Lord our God calls to him. . . . [The people] devoted themselves to the apostles teaching, fellowship, and breaking of bread and the prayers" (Acts 2:38–42).

Put differently, Maffesoli writes, "it is critical to bring out the fact that there is a refractory social foundation to unity: refractory to any representational or organizational one-dimensionality. This foundation seems to be functionally manifest at moments in which massification occurs together with an explosion of the values underlying this mass."[18]

Through various examples including the early church, the Reformations of Europe and the Renaissance, Maffesoli articulates that social cohesion exists through an overarching emotional connection of values. To attempt to suggest our own values is foolhardy with regards to Christian idealism, especially when scripture already provides—a repenting, a baptism, a breaking of the bread and the prayers. Scripture thus gives us the ingredients for the recipes for unicity that Maffesoli describes as possible: *sacramentality*. How then do we create a Christian liturgical and cultural local church experience that takes all these points into account?

## Conclusion: Creating an Inclusive and Truly Welcoming Sacramental Tribe for Christ

It is by meditating on Du Bois' words that we emotionally understand part of why God chose to enact his Pentecostal miracle in the way he did.

---

17. Maffesoli, *Time of the Tribes*, 73.
18. Maffesoli, *Time of the Tribes*, 158.

Division is something we can all conceptually understand but as Du Bois, Butler, and Maffesoli have explained, it is that emotional connection regarding identity that guides group social dynamism. One does not read the miracle of Pentecost and find any hint of the darkness or loneliness that is echoed in Du Bois question, "why did God make me an outcast and a stranger in mine own house?"[19]

The miracle of Pentecost, of Christian unity, is that it does not impose the sobering truth of double consciousness that Du Bois describes in his writings. In Pentecost, God re-engineers affective tribalism. Christian unity becomes a miracle of multiplicity rather than a homogenization.

It is no wonder why churches strain to retain members when Christian identity is tied deeply to other emotional identities such as economics, politics, cultural values, sexual behaviors, and gender politics. Both Butler and Maffesoli have already described for us why individuals only search for church communities that look and sound like them. They desire emotional security and fellowship. For better or worse—people emotionally desire those who suffer or succeed like them. Those are their affective tribes.

The church that seeks to only cater to affective tribalism produced an eventual erosion of the sense of self described by Du Bois, and carries with it a violation of God's decree that we are to know that we are his beloved children (Eph 5:1). The sensitivity to identity performance is then not only something important to understand but critical to ensuring that we don't create oppressive Christian communities that breed harm and exclusion at our fellow siblings in Christ—even if we think we are creating safe spaces.

In the first dozen pages of his book *Between the World and Me*, Ta-Nehisi Coates artfully repaints a narrative that though for some may be new, for many is not unfamiliar. Countless examples abound of artists replaying for humanity the categorization and sufferings of people and Coates book is merely one of the most recent examples of such an artistic endeavor. The point here is not to diminish his or any other work that does such critical work. It is instead, however, to illuminate that the work of creating a truly welcoming goes beyond surface level performed identities. The pains and beauties that each person experiences cannot be simply replicated by visual que or even plain acknowledgement. Until someone can see themselves within a community, no matter how

---

19. Du Bois, *Souls of Black Folk*, 10.

much they feel appreciated and accepted in a space, it is still not theirs. A guest is still a guest. Home ownership and renting aren't even the same. The subtleties of inclusion are not easy to navigate and even less easy to achieve in an exponential bell curve towards involvement.

If we continue along this same line of reasoning and wish to build a unicity within church communities fortified with sacramental unity we must reconsider what unicity looks like as we attempt to attract members of disparate cultural tribes that can all coexist unified under the same sacramental banner of Christ. And while there may be sufficient desire from a church to welcome diverse members and create space for different people and tribes to come together, there is sufficient scriptural and historical evidence to suggest that belief in Christ alone is insufficient to create lasting church community to attract or retain such diversities together. Even as churches on all sides of the social and political spectrums tout their church with words like "welcome home," "all are welcome," "black lives matter," "love is love," and many others—and while they may truly mean it—it is with boldness that we must admit that welcomeness and inclusion are not the same thing—welcomingness is not the same as sameness.

How then we create this amazing welcoming church that is universal and perfect? We don't. We can't. As I have already stated early on, anything that God creates for good, we humans can find a way to pollute and destroy with our brokenness. To image that we can "fix" God's church is a denial of that very real truth. But we *do* have direct access to God's grace in the matter—visible signs of God's invisible grace. If we surrender to the fact that we cannot fix the church or create the church, we can also surrender to God's help in our desire to do that. The sacraments are thus the most logical and immediate access to such miraculous assistance.

Looking at the sacraments as miraculous examples of how to guide church, we must regularly confess our sins, wash the feet of our neighbors, pronounce and live out our baptismal covenant, be sealed as confirmands into our metaphorical identities as our priesthood and marital covenant to Christ, find healing from extreme unction, and take on—and ingest—the broken body of Christ.

If this above statement feels deeply figurative and hard to place, good. It shouldn't be something easy to understand and should be a deeply prayerful and discerning undertaking for each community. But measuring up these sacramental—grace-filled—opportunity compared with anything we could hope to imagine or construct, would be foolhardy and doomed to failure.

The sacraments at their core are about Christ and God doing the hard work that we know we are unable to do. Peter did not act as linguistics teacher or interpreter. God did that work. Peter merely created the space for God to act. Peter gave intension and God did the rest.

To rescue our fracturing body, we must do likewise.

## Bibliography

Butler, Judith. *Gender Trouble*. London: Routledge, 2006.
Coates, Ta-Nehsis. *Between the World and Me*. New York: Spiegel & Grau, 2015.
Du Bois, W. E. B. *The Souls of Black Folk*. Digireads.com, 2016.
John Paul II. *Ut unum sint*. https://www.vatican.va/content/john-paul-ii/en/encyclicals/documents/hf_jp-ii_enc_25051995_ut-unum-sint.html.
Maffesoli, Michel. *The Time of the Tribes: The Decline of Individualism in Mass Society*. London: Sage, 2000.
United States Conference of Catholic Bishops. "The Nicene Creed." https://www.usccb.org/beliefs-and-teachings/what-we-believe.

6

# Wrapped in Paradox

The Impact of the Church and Its Sacrament of
Reconciliation on Political and Social Life

CATHERINE MEEKS

> We embark on the spiritual journey in hopes of achieving wholeness, but long before we get there, the journey only sharpens and magnifies our sense of contradictions. The truth of the Spirit contradicts the lies that we are living. The light of the Spirit contradicts our shadow-life. The unity of the Spirit contradicts our brokenness.[1]

I HAVE SPENT MANY sleepless nights thinking about this essay and vacillating between rescinding my agreement to write it and attempting to fasten myself to the keyboard and getting it done. As I observed my behavior, I had to spend a bit of time interrogating myself about the root of the issue that was causing me such angst. Finally, I realized that I was debating with myself about the lens through which I view the church and wondering if my conclusions would be helpful in advancing a conversation that might contribute to generating new energy and aliveness in the church.

---

1. Palmer, *The Promise of Paradox*, 5.

## Part 2: Saving the Church as a Community

The lens through which I view the church was shaped by my long search for freedom and a place that would allow me to have a sense of belonging. My Arkansas sharecropping farm girl history coupled with racism and poverty did not offer me alternatives. Hope was the most precious resource for my family and me. And that hope was grounded in the absolute belief that God existed and that we would be blessed at some point if we kept trying to move forward without giving in or giving up when times were hard. Times were always hard, but they did not prevent me from searching for truth under every rock. It was very difficult to find adults who were able to be supportive because my questions seem to be unsettling to them.

My life long search for truth and freedom continued into and through college as I participated in worship with folks in house churches and various denominations. Finally, I was led to the Episcopal Church where I have been for the past four decades. The quest has been organized around seeking to find a place where the gathered community was truly seeking to follow Jesus while trying to become free of the cultural threads that are quite challenging to that intention. This essay refers mostly to the Episcopal Church though one can make a similar case regarding many other denominations. My search continues.

My relationship to the church is fractured at the moment. This fracture has nothing to do with Jesus nor my commitment to the journey of faith. It has to do with the institution that has laid claim to Jesus and his teachings as its reason for existence and as its badge of identity, but is totally separated in multiple ways from living into the truth of that claim. It has not spoken up when it needed to do so about so many of the atrocities that have plagued us both historically and in the present moment. One only needs to take a look at the weak responses from most church leaders regarding racial oppression and violence, political polarization, poverty and the many other forms of dehumanization of our siblings to see numerous examples of the deficit of courage that exists in our leaders.

Lack of courage makes prophetic witness impossible. Perhaps this is the greatest problem facing the church at the moment. While it has a container that represents faith and hope, its cowardice continues to undermine what it claims to be. It is not very difficult to understand some of the fear held by those who are in leadership because they seem to believe that they are responsible for keeping the church doors open. However, when keeping the doors open becomes more important than bearing witness to the journey with Jesus in ways that will lead those who hear about him desire to be on that path as well, then it is time for serious reevaluation of what that community understands its mission to be. Also, it is possible that if the leaders could turn their focus to the prophetic message of Jesus, it might become easier to keep the doors open.

Of course, the lack of courage is not new to the church. Our historical records that depict the Sunday morning services that were framed by the noonday lynchings and celebratory picnics create vivid images to hold as we reflect upon what the church can say to those in the midst of political polarization. Actually, it can say nothing until it owns its complicity! In spite of this, there are many who are hungering and thirsting for someone to have a courageous word for them and the church has the structure and can gain the authority to speak if it would turn itself around and engage with those hungry souls.

Thus, we meet one of the great contradictions that faces the church. It can speak, it is expected to speak but it is not speaking with the prophetic voice that it claims as a part of its identity.

What is to be done with this contradiction? How is it to be navigated. What is the remedy for this failing? Church leaders across all major denominations find themselves confronting this question, but seem to be losing the struggle to hear answers that really relate to the question in a manner that provides the energy that can help to change the narrative. Since the main issue lies in the lack of courage, any attempt to answer the remedy question has to address that state of being. It is not a simple matter to determine how one goes about finding courage.

The capacity to be courageous enough to do the work of speaking as a prophetic witness can not be developed from external sources. It comes from the inner core of one's being. Thus, personal and careful interrogation of that core is essential in order to catch glimpses of what hinders the birth of courage and to create the desire to allow the light of the Spirit to shine into one's life in a manner that will help to shift the energy of fear and help courage to emerge.

The work of C. G. Jung and others can help in this exploration because that work addresses the make-up of the inner life especially in regards to the Shadow/Persona construct.[2] Unfortunately, there is little to no understanding about this dynamic in most churches because there is an unwillingness to embrace this type of psychological excavation and to seek ways to understand its importance. While individuals, who are

2. Whitmont, *The Symbolic Quest*, 156.

in communities called churches, may be engaged in this work, it is not a widespread part of the collective conversation in the church community. There is not enough focus about the best way to engage one's journey. Folks are more likely to be given prescriptions from the pulpit and in classes or forums that are designed to reinforce what they are to think and how they should behave. This does not generate aliveness.

Jung helps us to understand that this lack of aliveness comes from immobilizing conflicts in the psyche. The church has to come to terms with the shadow/persona issue as an institution just as individuals have to do. The persona represents the role that an individual or institution wishes to hold on the worldly stage and the shadow holds the material that is repressed to help facilitate the ego ideal.[3] This dynamic is more commonly recognized in individuals, but when trying to understand an institution's behavior it is very helpful to use this model.

Most thoughtful reflection will lead to understanding that the church has an idea of what role it wishes to play on the worldly stage. It is this desire that has created its success to whatever extent it exists and its failures. Of course, we are talking about a collection of human beings who constructed this institution and are overseeing its functioning, thus the inner community exploration has to happen both individually and collectively.

As individuals within the churches begin to explore their inner landscape and allow their hidden personality elements to emerge and become more integrated into their overall way of being thus enlarging their view how to present themselves to the world, change in the institution will happen. As individuals do their inner community work they will be far less interested in the status quo and its prescribed behavior plans. The new energy which is released by developing this sense of self creates an aliveness that wishes to live in a new way. The new possibilities will require leaders in the churches to shift their energy as well and if they are doing their own work and supporting or leading this collective inner community work, that will be good news for the institution. But, if there is not a collective effort, there will be stalemates at the best and chaos at the worst because of the contrary energies competing to be acknowledged.

As long as the church continues to hold a vision of itself that fits nicely into the cultural constructs of materialism, patriarchy, racism, sexism and basically operating as a small business with similar success to

---

3. Whitmont, *The Symbolic Quest*, 160.

a business, it will not be enjoying the fruits of prophetic witness and its shadow side will be quite satisfied with that state of affairs. This way of being in the world does not leave any space for demonstrating that the church and its sacraments have anything to do with the culture, because it looks as if it is a mirrored image of the culture. The shift will come when there is transformation within the institution.

An investigation into the way in which the church has stood in the world hoping to maintain status and control but not coming to terms with how real power comes into being presents the world with the current institution. The truth is that it is caught in its own paradoxical energy. It preaches peace and practices violence. There are many churches who do not find any problem with parishioners bringing weapons into the buildings because it is necessary for them to feel secure. What is such a church's understanding of itself as entity in the world that makes it possible to believe that it needs weapons to defend itself during its times of worship? How is the power for transformative thought going to be created if the gathered body holds such a fear filled image of itself? Unlike the holding of genuine paradoxes, holding this type of contradictory energy is immobilizing and not liberating. Until, there is a willingness to go into the inner recesses of the heart and soul to explore the reasons that folks believe that showing up for worship with a gun is necessary and working to see what that means for their overall way of being in the world, nothing will change. This is only one small example of how the shadow can control the energy flow and render the institution incapable of speaking a word of hope and healing beyond its walls.

The Spirit does contradict this way of being held in the energy of the shadow and invites transformation. But, the invitation has to be accepted. Thus far, the church has been very clear about being unsure about such invitations and one of the results is the loss of membership which is a part of almost every conversation about Christianity these days. Perhaps when it gets even worse, the invitation to transformation will be more attractive. In order to say "yes" there has to be a willingness to embrace the unknown and that might require a shift in power and thus less ability to control. More than likely, it will indeed require many shifts in power and shifts in the perception that the church holds of itself on the worldly stage.

It is interesting to reflect upon the fact that Christianity is based upon following a person who was crucified and yet, so much effort is put into avoiding suffering. But it is in the willingness to embrace suffering that true transformation is made possible. Suffering pushes us to move away from the status quo which is causing the pain and to seek a remedy. Transformation is made possible when the broken hearted bring themselves to the place of seeking healing from the God who teaches us that God's strength is made perfect in weakness.

Of course, this behavior requires leaving behind the church's image of itself as self-sufficient. The resources of money, education, good programs, respect in the community and all of the other ways that the persona is being constructed get in the front line on the path that leads to declaring that weakness in the human being provides for the expression of God's strength. There is usually less interest in this paradigm than the one that demonstrates what the culture understands as success and being on the cutting edge of all that is involved in achieving such status.

The fear of losing this position helps to create prophetic voicelessness. The prophetic witness listens to hear the word that God is trying to deliver to the people and the church claims to be the container for that work. But this entire discussion is about the way that it is not currently embracing that fact, but could if it would . While there are many reasons why this has not been done, deep fear is the basic reason.

Of course the problem that remains is that the institution cannot thrive unless its people become free. If the people cannot see themselves with power and thriving then, they cannot present that image to the world outside of their circle. Therefore, one can see why prophetic witnesses who do not count the cost of suffering and are only interested in bringing the message that has been given for the people to the people are not welcome in places where there is a lack of freedom individually and collectively.

The word that the Spirit brings is one of hope that bears witness to the possibility that life does not have to be lived in brokenness. The Spirit can help in revealing that healing and wholeness are possible and there is a path through the church and the sacrament of reconciliation that can be helpful in leading to political and social solidarity with those folks who hold diverse ideas about the way to make sense of the world.

It is important to acknowledge the tension that is created by having a clear view of the ways in which the church has fallen extremely short in stepping up to the plate to speak a prophetic word and that it holds a vast amount of power and capacity to impact the way in which society engages with one another. In an earlier portion of the conversation, the need to address the shadow was presented. While no one would presume to speak about how a sacrament actually does its work, it is clear that working with the shadow contributes to helping all of the human interactions designed to create the possibility for Beloved Community to be born and to have a better chance of sustainability.

The sacrament of reconciliation is an outward ritual that involves contrition, confession, penance and absolution and is to be engaged when believers are interested in restoring their relationships with God and one another. But, it is important to note that relationships between two or more persons that have been fractured in some manner represent inner brokenness in each of the persons involved. The earlier discussion about the inner community was included in this essay to highlight the idea that while one will never know how the Spirit does its work, there are parts of the healing journey that individuals can engage which will help in facilitating the journey to healing.

When inner work is deemed unnecessary because someone has been told to pray, this represents a misunderstanding of the healing process. Persons seeking to be reconciled with their fellow humans can spend time reflecting upon the state of affairs in their inner community and work to discover in what ways they have broken relationship with themselves. An honest time of silence and reflective questioning can yield much rich material that will be helpful in the process of participating in the sacramental ritual of reconciliation.

The accompanying inner work helps to strengthen the resolve to become more open to a new way to see. In order to develop that new way of seeing one has to relinquish old ways and those ways are generally connected to the narratives around which people's lives have been organized. There is no magic prescription for shifting those narratives and creating new ones. The work can be done successfully, but it is a process and the denial of that fact has caused undue suffering. The suffering comes when the mystical is mistaken for magical. God is not magical, thus processes make sense and understanding that reality can be liberating.

One of the ways this knowledge helps to liberate believers is in creating an understanding that it may take time for change to manifest itself. It cannot be stressed enough that no one can tell the Spirit how to work or explain how the work is done. But, when there are issues that resist the efforts that seem to be more geared to magic than mystery, it is good to pay attention to what is happening and to ask questions about what else the Spirit might be attempting to teach about the issue.

When conflicts arise in our social and political realms, they have the potential to escalate into irresolvable encounters or to be modulated and resolved. The outcomes depend upon the people who are involved and whether or not they have turned their intentions toward managing such encounters. When one is grounded in a perspective that helps to reinforce a particular resolve then conflict has less of a derailing effect. Thus, the sacrament of reconciliation and the connection to the church itself can help in that grounding process and in creating alternatives for behaving.

The formation classes of the church should engage the issue of inner community, inner dialogue and inner healing as well as the work around the shadow and its projection. So much of the conflict in the world could be managed in a better manner if all parties involved knew how to move beyond projection of their personal feelings and preferences onto others while seeking solutions. This type of behavior change can be taught. But, the church does not address it in the central manner that could lead to a reduction of struggle for its members and help to relieve some of the troubles in the wider community.

In this present moment as we recover from COVID-19, the racial unrest caused primarily by the murder of George Floyd and the turmoil in the climate, it is clear that the polarization in our country needs multiple remedies. The church has a grand opportunity to say "yes" to these invitations to enter into this milieu at some point and offer its best remedy. While it has all of the challenges that were spoken about earlier, it still has the ability to shift the energy if it can find the will to do so.

Jesus is still standing at the door waiting to see whether or not it will open wider for him to enter with the particular call that he wishes to make. The call to authenticity that requires the church to confront its shadow and to reimagine the way forward for itself as the follower of a Guide that made it clear what the way ahead demands everything. Jesus, the Guide, "Who, being in very nature God, did not consider equality with God something to be grasped, but made himself nothing, taking the very nature of a servant being made in human likeness. And being found in appearance as a man, he humbled himself and became obedient to death, even death on a cross" (Phil 2:6–8 NIV)· is the one calling the church to follow him.

If the church wants to have a reliable voice, it will need to take a new look at who its leader happens to be. Clearly there is a need for the church to reconcile itself to Jesus' leadership in a new way which will bring new energy that is capable of meeting the needs that are before us in the twenty-first century. Just as the old wineskins will not do for the new wine that is being stored, neither will old solutions work for the new problems that are before us. As we pay attention to the issues that arose in 2020 with COVID-19, the racial tensions and the climate, we have a chance to witness that our old ways are not going to suffice any longer.

But the critical question to be asked and answered in every corner of Christendom is: Do we have the courage? Do we have the courage to take up our cross and follow Jesus into the polarized neighborhoods across our land? Do we have the courage to engage across the political divides that are keeping us at the door of danger all of the time? Do we have the courage? The sacrament of reconciliation can help us with this issue also. But it needs to be partnered with an awaken consciousness about the nature of the psychological landscape and the manner in which that inner terrain impacts outer reality. Without the benefit of making such connections, the use of the sacrament becomes much akin to a person suffering with arthritis refusing to eat properly, exercise or manage their stress levels and who simply take extra doses of their prescription without supporting their medication by their behavior. This type of behavior can work for a short while but it is not sustainable. Thus engaging in the practice of any ritual needs to be supported by one's inner community where the intention to see in a new way becomes invited to the altar of one's heart.

The head and the heart have to be engaged in the work of transforming the political and social realms of life because those who accept the invitation to engage in this work will be asked to bring the spirit of vulnerability to the encounter. When there is an attempt to get someone to see an issue from another point of view, there is a requirement to bring reconciling energy into the engagement. This is made possible when there is someone who can with authenticity and compassion invite others to allow them to walk in their shoes. The reconciling energy will manifest itself because such an invitation requires that the inviter be willing to take off their shoes first. Thus, when one is in the presence of this type of energy it is more difficult to stay rigidly fixed in whatever positions one is holding. Of course, there are exceptions to this and in those cases where someone is not open to accepting the invitation to engage in dialogue or to consider that someone might really want to walk in their shoes in order to understand them, it will be more difficult to engage in this manner.

Dr. Howard Thurman encourages us to consider keeping our hearts as swinging doors so that others can come and go because it is in the hearts of one another that we find refuge.[4] The ability to offer refuge to another in one's heart is directly related to the work of exploring the

---

4. Boling, "The Hunger of the Heart."

inner community and engaging with the energies that reside internally that help us to invite others in or to push them away. This work enlarges our hearts. The heart work invites those inner community members who will continue to reside in the shadow and become undermining forces as long as they can go unacknowledged to become incorporated in the persona. When this happens they become a resource and can be of assistance when conflicts arise in the outer lives of all who are walking on this path.

This is the type of work that will offer much needed support to all of the rituals of the church so that they can begin to demonstrate the capacity that they have to transform participants and to make the creation of a new way to see a reality. The Spirit longs for the work to be done because it continuously bears witness to the fact that the brokenness is not what God had intended for God's people. The intention for unity is verified in the sacrament of reconciliation and it is clear that there has to be internal unity if there is going to be external unity. The inner turmoil of a chaotic inner community is powerful enough to continuously destabilize all attempts at creating an alternative to the chaos in the outer realm.

Since, it is difficult to argue that there is no connection between the inner landscape of believers and the outer world that they find themselves embracing, how should the church support their journey in trying to embrace this reality with integrity? What is the model that Jesus presented to all who are willing to embrace it? What needs to happen in order for that model to become the central factor in what the church is doing?

The poet Rilke reminds us that we have worked very hard to organize life around the easy but that holding to the difficult is what must be done. What is the relationship of holding to the difficult, following Jesus Christ and trying to be a voice in the world for political and social relationships that reflect love and offer invitations to all come into the heart? It is difficult to imagine that there is any person among us who does not wish to have sanctuary somewhere, but the fear and the many wounding forces in the culture have tried to teach that no such thing is possible. Jesus speaks against that analysis and the church is mandated to join Jesus' voice if it plans to continue to claim him as the leader of it.

Jesus stands in front of the church with an uncompromising message of invitation to all to come unto him with all the burdens and woundedness that are being carried and to expect to find rest. Thus, the church has to find its way to make that invitation alive in the world that it is engaging. There is a necessity for the church to reconstruct its persona to include making space for the "least of these" in ways that allow folks to see that it means to have an open heart and that the " all are welcome" signs on the lawns are genuine invitations to come as you are. The invitation has to be supported by sustaining energy that is grounded in the inviters having done their inner work so that they have the capacity to relinquish expectations for rewards of any sort except the grand reward of having been able to hold onto the difficult intention of keeping an open heart.

The church has to reimagine itself as an entity who, like Jesus, is about the business of God instead of so many of the other businesses that it has allowed to determine its way of being in the world. The church's only business is to help the world to realize that all of the folks on the planet are God's beloved children and that our most important work is seeking to embrace the liberation of the spirit which will enable us to live here together while affirming the dignity of all. The business involves being a light, being the salt of the earth, being the force in the world that shows that there is another way to engage with one another that moves beyond transactions based upon power and control.

The idea of the truth setting one free needs to be affirmed by the church as it provides teaching that helps all who engage with it to learn all that they can about what Jesus' invitation entails. Actually, Jesus models a way of being engaged with life that requires being willing to be moved through many transformations during a lifetime. It is this part of the call that requires the inner work that has been discussed and if the church embraced that work in an intentional manner much healing will result from it.

It would be helpful to have more attention given to the manner in which spiritual formation is presented. Those offerings need to be carefully crafted to provide ways for the heart and head to be engaged. It is not enough to provide numerous opportunities for gathering more information in one's head unless there is attention being given to helping to make sure that it becomes a part of the heart. The participants in the spiritual formation processes need to have ways to experience the truth of the knowledge being gained and the experience of living a life with Jesus at the center. One cannot expect to be transformed by truth alone which is not accompanied by experience. The truth needs to be partnered with the search for meaning and experience in order for it to become the guiding energy that is needed to navigate the paths that will be given for Jesus' followers to travel. Though classes are given, knowledge and experiences gained, there has to be space made for the Spirit to engage in the process as well. Paul reminds us, "These are the very things that God revealed through the Spirit, for the Spirit reaches the depth of everything, even the depths of God. After all the depths of man can only be known by his own spirit, not by any other man and in the same way the depths of God can only be known by the Spirit of God" (2 Cor 2:10–11 NIV).

If the church intends to embrace its sordid history, creating Jesus in its own image, its many contradictions and all other brokenness, the Spirit will have to be allowed to enter into the conversation that the church claims to want to have with those who are in it and the ones that it seeks to bring into it. It is being called again in this present moment to engage the invitations that are clearly before it. The work of interrogating itself to see whether or not it can find the courage to go beyond its levels of comfort and become willing to be led wherever the Spirit is trying to lead it remains to be discerned as the future continues to unfold.

While there are courageous voices that are standing up to bear prophetic witness and declaring that the message of Jesus continues to be sufficient to address the challenges of the twenty-first century, the institution has to catch up with that handful of prophetic voices. The polarization that exists in the United States at the moment is serious enough to make all who have any allegiance to a faith perspective hold onto the hope that the church will say yes to the present moment's invitation and become a force for creating a new way to see. The hope is that the church will open itself to the energy of courage and accept the invitations that are being presented to it, which can help it to become the leader that it can be in forming the path to healing and a new way to see and engage in all facets of life.

## Bibliography

Boling, Landrum. "Conversations with Howard Thurman: The Hunger of the Heart." https://www.youtube.com/watch?v=NPsZBS-20eU.

Palmer, Parker. *The Promise of Paradox: A Celebration of Contradictions in the Christian Life*. San Francisco: Jossey-Bass, 2008.

Whitmont, Edward C. *The Symbolic Quest: Basics Concepts of Analytical Psychology*. Princeton: Princeton University Press, 1978.

# 7

# Addressing Polarization and Apathy through Sacramental Preaching

CRYSTAL J. HARDIN

*Grace is God's favor toward us, unearned and undeserved;*
*by grace God forgives our sins, enlightens our minds,*
*stirs our hearts, and strengthens our wills.*[1]

FLEMING RUTLEDGE NOTES THAT every Christian, lay or ordained, has an enormous stake in preaching; indeed, a life-or-death stake.[2] Extend that thought for a moment to every person, Christian or not, who finds themselves on the receiving end of a sermon. Extend it even further to consider the climate as it is potentially shaped by the preaching moment and, well, our potential impact as preachers of the gospel is far greater than most would be willing to admit.

My context is the Episcopal Church, and the perception of the Episcopal pulpit is that, putting it simply, not much happens there. And this

---

1. Episcopal Church, *Book of Common Prayer*, "The Catechism," 858.
2. Rutledge, "By the Word Worked."

perception is not limited to us but extends to many of our liturgically inclined neighbors. Most of our sermons are well-meaning, certainly, but there is little expectation that they will be life changing. And yet, in corporate worship, we celebrate the sacraments, those "outward and visible signs of inward and spiritual grace, given by Christ as sure and certain means by which we receive that grace."[3] We gather around them in heart and mind as sacramental community, a community oriented around the belief in a God who is *with* us, really *present* to us, still *speaking*, permeating physical realities with the hope and promise of something even more real and fantastic: grace.

Shouldn't our preaching both embody and provoke our sacramental orientation? And if sacramentality, sacramental thinking, and the sacramental ordinances of the church are the key, our offering to the body of Christ in crisis, could the preaching event cultivate a climate of sacramental imagination, a communal receptivity to the dependability and depth of God's grace and the variations in its form? Could it address the passions of the polarized and the indifference of the apathetic?

## The Problem

This book seeks to address the various ills that plague us in a so-called post-Christian landscape by suggesting that participation in sacramental community is necessary for our corporate survival. Let me be clear what I mean by saying it is necessary for our corporate survival. I write in terms of our corporate personhood as the body of Christ rather than in the more limited sense of our survival as any particular denomination or church writ small. And yet, I also write knowing full well that there is no true death of corporate personhood with Jesus Christ at the head; it is very much his life and work that sustains his church, not ours. Apart from him, we can do nothing. That is why it is, in a sense, our life as the body which is at stake. When we no longer acknowledge Jesus as the source and subject of all of our verbs, when we give ourselves to other narratives of meaning, when we no longer seek him as our source—our life, corporate and individual, withers.[4] He is the vine. We are the branches. Any theology of preaching, any preached word, should start and end with this understanding.

3. Episcopal Church, *Book of Common Prayer*, "The Catechism," 857.
4. Rutledge, "The True Vine."

In this chapter, I am particularly interested in two phenomena, the passions of the polarized and the indifference of the religiously apathetic, and how sacramental preaching might address them. As a preacher in the Episcopal tradition who grew up Southern Baptist, I am particularly interested in the connection between pulpit and people, pulpit and liturgy, and pulpit and sacraments. How might grace be cultivated and claimed in the preaching moment across traditions? And how might sacramental preaching act as a balm for much of what ails us? These are my questions. Let me be clear that, by looking more closely at these questions and subject areas, I do not intend to narrow the scope of the pulpits' witness, nor do I mean to suggest that the pulpit is the only effective tool. In fact, it is not a tool at all, as that would suggest that it is we, the preacher, who wield it with a particular goal in mind. Instead, the pulpit, the preacher, the spoken word, it is God's, and it should never be a means to an end that is anything other than communicating the good news known in the blessed Trinity: Father, Son, and Holy Spirit.

With that out of the way, let us turn briefly to the passions of the polarized and the indifference of the religiously apathetic. To say that we are, as a society, increasingly polarized would surprise no one. Fifty years ago, only a smattering of Americans expressed anger when asked their feelings about their child(ren) potentially marrying someone from a different political party. After the 2016 U.S. presidential election, the Harvard Business Review and Pew Research Center reported that "a third of Democrats—and nearly half of Republicans—would be deeply upset [if their child(ren) married someone from a different political party]. Americans not only disagree on the issues, they increasingly personally dislike those from the other party."[5] This shouldn't be surprising, given that "45% of Republicans and 41% of Democrats think that the other party is so dangerous that it is a threat to the health of the nation."[6] More recent polls and studies suggest that this is getting worse and not better.[7]

Partisanship is not new, and yet the nature of its polarization is shifting. The Stanford Center on Philanthropy and Civil Society notes that "polarization isn't a single, monolithic phenomenon. There are two types: the kind we express in wonky disagreements over laws and policies, and the kind we *feel*—that visceral red vs. blue passion that fuels partisan

---

5. McConnell et al., "Research: Political Polarization."
6. McConnell et al., "Research: Political Polarization."
7. Pew Research Center, "Partisan Antipathy."

acrimony and take-no-prisoners elections."[8] The latter is on the rise and has been coined *affective polarization* by those who study it, and it has very real and lasting consequences for the ways we govern, communicate, engage in truth-telling (or not), compromise, and relate to one another. Various studies show that this kind of polarization increasingly bleeds into and shapes our lives on fundamental levels, as people grow more passionate in their positions, which are too often articulated in terms of what they are against vis-à-vis their "opponent(s)." To put it simply, partisanship has become for many a passionate matter of social identity and a measure for evaluating others with a broad brush, with implications for behavior across the board, from economic exchanges to church attendance.[9]

At the same time, another phenomenon is on the rise: religious apathy. Lack of religious conviction coupled with superficial adherence to a religious affiliation is widespread in the industrialized West.[10] We have all heard about the "nones," or the religiously unaffiliated, but there is a distinction between that group and the religiously apathetic. The latter might be quite content to identify themselves as religiously affiliated, while the former is defined by their lack of religious affiliation. Of course, it would be a mistake to assume that any group is monolithic in its rationale or static in its composition. What can be said is that religious apathy is less about what you believe and more about how you believe. Pew Research reports that 63 percent of atheists, 40 percent of agnostics, and 26 percent of adults with "no particular religion" cite irrelevance as an important factor in their religious identity.[11] They are not believing or disbelieving *per se*, they are simply indifferent.

Apatheists are not skeptical, nor is it fair to say that they are dismissive. They simply do not believe the debate worth having, the question worth asking, the premise at all necessary. In an article for *The Atlantic*, self-professed apatheist Jonathan Rauch writes:

> Apatheism concerns not what you believe but how. In that respect it differs from the standard concepts used to describe religious views and people. Atheism, for instance, is not at all like

---

8. Voelkel, "The Nature of Polarization Is Changing."
9. Pew Research Center, "Partisan Antipathy."
10. Union of International Associations, "Religious Apathy."
11. Pew Research Center, "Why America's 'Nones' Don't Identify." Note that among U.S. adults whose religious identity is atheist, agnostic, or "nothing in particular," 36 percent cite irrelevance as a very important reason why they are unaffiliated.

apatheism; the hot-blooded atheist cares as much about religion as does the evangelical Christian, but in the opposite direction. "Secularism" can refer to a simple absence of devoutness, but it more accurately refers to an ACLU-style disapproval of any profession of religion in public life—a disapproval that seems puritanical and quaint to apatheists. Tolerance is a magnificent concept, John Locke's inestimable gift to all mankind; but it assumes, as Locke did, that everyone brims with religious passions that everyone else must work hard to put up with. And agnostics? True, most of them are apatheists, but most apatheists are not agnostics. Because—and this is an essential point—many apatheists are believers.[12]

Many apatheists are unaffiliated with a particular faith tradition or church, but still claim a belief in God. Still others sit in our pews on occasion, and yet are unconvinced of the relevancy of what we profess. For those of us who steward parishes, this is probably not shocking information. And, given current trends, many who sit in our pews, most especially young people who have not yet claimed a religious affiliation for themselves as adults, will soon be unaffiliated, many claiming religious apathy as the reason.[13]

The increasing and ever-more passionate polarization in our society considered alongside a growing indifference towards religion should concern and provoke deep discernment on the part of those who act as stewards of word and sacrament. People are not short on passion, and yet their passion is woefully and, in some cases, harmfully misdirected.

## A Theology of Preaching

*I preached as never sure to preach again,
and as a dying man to dying men.*[14]

---

12. Rauch, "Let It Be."

13. Jones et al., "Exodus." "Nearly four in ten young adults (ages 18–29) are religiously unaffiliated . . . nearly four times as likely as young adults a generation ago to identify as religiously unaffiliated" (Jones et al., "Exodus," 3). Note that "the growth of the unaffiliated has been fed by an exodus of those who grew up with a religious identity" (Jones et al., "Exodus," 4).

14. Baxter, *Poetical Fragments*, 35.

We are a broken people in a broken world grasping for something real, something true, something with the power to save us. As W. H. Auden so beautifully captures, "Nothing can save us that is possible; we who must die demand a miracle."[15] As Christians, we profess a uniquely singular and perfectly healing miracle for all manner of human brokenness: Christ Jesus, our Redeemer. As sacramentalists, we hold firm to an understanding that the sacred can be known in the ordinary, that the material world can truly and efficaciously communicate spiritual realities, that, indeed, the sacred penetrates reality relentlessly. How often, how much, and whose doing may still be up for some debate. But what can be said is that the sacramental church bears Holy witness to a God *in pursuit* of us, first and always in the form of Jesus, the primordial sacrament, Word made flesh.

As N. T. Wright notes, "sacramental theology is all about discovering, 'in fear and trembling,' how to allow that Word to go on becoming flesh."[16] It is unfortunate that in many Christian traditions word and sacrament have come to be held at arm's length from one another, two sides of the same coin made competitors to no one's gain. Instead, they are both necessary to form disciples that are sacramentally attuned and to bear witness to the fullness of God's grace. And yet, to reclaim the significance of preaching, preachers must first flesh out, and submit themselves to, a robust theology of preaching, one that takes seriously God's continual, apocalyptic revelation in and through Christ Jesus and the preacher's vocation in relationship with that revelation.

What is your theology of preaching? What happens in the preaching act? What is the point of preaching anyhow? What is the relationship of preaching to the liturgy? To the sacraments? This is not necessarily seminary fodder, but it should be. Any who would take on the vocation of preacher should understand what they are getting themselves into—and not just the week in and week out writing of sermons, but the call and commission to preach the word of God. Preachers should be well-rooted in a theology of preaching that guides, nourishes, challenges, and equips, one that stands in firm, purposeful relationship with the sacraments. If we treat preaching as little more than weekly meditations where we share some personal thoughts, some biblical suggestions for a life well-lived, a funny story or two, or some commentary on secular happenings coupled with a few things Jesus would most certainly do, then why bother? If

---

15. Auden, "For the Time Being," in Auden, *Collected Poetry*, 353.
16. Wright, "Word and Sacraments."

preaching lacks power and the preacher lacks conviction, what's the point? Flannery O'Connor once wrote about the Eucharist, "If it's a symbol, to hell with it," and I'd extend that sentiment to preaching. If nothing is at stake in the act of preaching other than, perhaps, our own egos, to hell with it.

Entire books are written on theologies of preaching and these are more nuanced and in-depth than this chapter allows for or requires. Needless to say, there are many dimensions to this issue, including the form and function of the sermon, role of the preacher and the congregation, understandings of authority and tradition, and, last but not least, context (which rightfully shapes both the why and the how of the preaching act). Further, developing a life-giving, vocation-sustaining theology of preaching is as much in doing the work as it is in arriving at the conclusion. With that said, let us briefly turn to a few broad considerations before moving on.

First, God has spoken, and God continues to speak. This is foundational. And it is on this foundation that a robust theology of preaching must rest. By preaching, I simply mean public proclamation of the truth to God's people there gathered—a specific part of a larger ministry of the word, one that rests on the premise that God has spoken and continues to speak words that are "powerful, effective, and creative of reality. The God who *speaks* is the God who *acts* through his words."[17]

> God's revelation begins with a sermon; God preaches and the world is made. "God said, 'Let there be light,' and there was light." Six sermons are preached in a wonderful sequence; the Word of God is proclaimed in heaven's pulpit and all comes to pass; the preaching forms the universe . . . the Word preached is no empty word; it accomplishes what it pleases and never returns void to him who speaks.[18]

As Fleming Rutledge notes, "Everything we believe about God is predicated on three words: 'and God said.' . . . Preaching is always a re-enactment of [this] primal miracle."[19] And, of course, the grace of God's abundantly generous, self-revelation can be seen ultimately in the Son himself, the Word made flesh.

---

17. Adam, *Speaking God's Words*, 15.
18. Adam, *Speaking God's Words*, 15 (quoting William Temple).
19. Rutledge, "By the Word Worked."

God has spoken and speaks an effective and powerful word preserved in Scripture and still active in our midst. To preach is to allow God working in us and through us to bring into being God's intention through our God-gifted words. Our role "is not to make God's words powerful through our speaking, but to help people recognize the power and significance of those words."[20] After all, we are not the effective agent; God is "the animating agency inhabiting the written text as the preacher is led by the Holy Spirit, speaking words that effect, that bring into being, what God intends."[21] God is present in the faithful preaching act, both in its preparation and its delivery, in the person of the preacher and in those who would listen. Powerful, efficacious, convicting, and apocalyptic is the Word of God the preacher is tasked with communicating. We must preach as if we believe it.

## Sacramental Preaching

In my own context, as in many traditions, preaching is nestled within a larger liturgical and sacramental drama, one that takes seriously word and symbol and the real presence of Christ in both. As Ruthanna Hooke writes:

> Word and sacrament are balanced in a relationship of equality that few other branches of the Christian tradition sustain as fully. For Anglicans, preaching and Eucharist are a counterpoint to each other; each are doing the same thing in a different way, in that each is a means of encountering God. The Eucharist is, therefore, a form of proclamation, and preaching is sacramental.[22]

The sermon should point to and elucidate the liturgical movement, with the Eucharist at its fulcrum, and vice versa. The relationship should be complementary, rather than adversarial or disjointed. As N. T. Wright notes, "The sacraments not only do not displace the Word, but the higher a sacramental theology you have, the more you need a high theology of the Word to flesh it out. The precise point of the sacraments is that these are the moments when the story comes to life."[23] In and through the sacraments, God reveals himself to us and works his good will within us.

---

20. Adam, *Speaking God's Words*, 55.
21. Rutledge, "By the Word Worked."
22. Hooke, "Prophetic Preaching as Sacrament," 97.
23. Wright, "Word and Sacraments."

As a growing chorus questions the very nature and value of preaching, especially in light of the continued decline and, frankly, disinterest in church attendance, we would do well to consider (or reconsider) the preaching moment's relationship to sacramental theology and the sacraments themselves.

What is meant by sacramental preaching? Well, like so many things, it depends upon whom you ask. First and foremost, sacramental preaching does not hold as necessary the premise that the preached word is (or even could be) a sacrament in and of itself. Of course, there are proponents of this belief, but, for the purposes of this chapter, we will move away from this point of contention. Too often it acts as a straw man. Another potential point of distortion and disruption when talking about preaching generally, and sacramental preaching specifically, is the person of the preacher. Their beliefs, intention, motivation, skill, and faithfulness brought under the microscope and too often derailing conversations about the preaching act. The person of the preacher matters, of course, as does the personhood of the would-be recipient. Martin Luther would remind us that we would be "mistaken if we tried to 'cut away' the human property of the sermon in order to obtain its divinity, without anything human mixed with it. Such an effort presumes that God is better found or grasped in a realm beyond the human."[24] Instead, in and through Jesus Christ, we know the truth of God Emmanuel, the truth that "from human mouths are heard the voice and tones of God, 'not the voice that speaks from heaven above, but that which is down in the midst of men.'"[25] And yet, the person of the preacher is a second level consideration in many respects (one that will be further discussed in a moment). God is the efficacious provider and authority and any preacher merely the instrument. To speak about sacramental preaching is first to remember that.

Sacramental preaching holds that Christ is really present in, with, and through the proclaimed Word. God is *still speaking*. Just as the Eucharist is an encounter with the real presence of Christ, the preaching moment can also be such an encounter. Martin Luther held this view, that "'in the sermon one actually encounters God.' However, instead of receiving Christ through eating and drinking, we receive him through speaking and listening. What is common in both cases is that the receiving is through physical acts. Likewise, both are means of grace and involve

---

24. Beach, "The Real Presence of Christ," 89.
25. Beach, "The Real Presence of Christ," 89.

the presence of Christ himself."[26] Dietrich Bonhoeffer likewise urges that "the proclaimed word is not a medium of expression for something else, something which lies behind it, but rather it is the Christ himself walking through the congregation as the Word."[27] John Calvin believed similarly, that preaching is the very Word of God, albeit derivative in nature.[28]

On the other hand, theologians like Peter Adam shy away from claiming preaching as the very Word of God, instead offering the view that it is the "work of the Spirit in the preacher as well as the hearer that God uses to bring his Spirit-inspired Word to effect in human lives."[29] In either case, the sacramental character of the preaching moment lies in God's gracious propensity to show up, to sow grace in unexpected places through frail means, and to work in us and through us to effectuate God's purposes. Whether God's very Word for the hearer or our words effectuated by the presence of Christ in our midst, the preaching moment should be considered and approached as sacramental in character.

For a moment, let us return the person of the preacher. I have a theory that the person of the preacher becomes a quick issue of contention because of our own reservations and insecurities about stepping forward and claiming the authority of the pulpit (or, allowing another to make that claim). Perhaps, in some ways, this is meet and right. The grace that is the preaching moment should not be taken lightly. And yet, as Ruthanna Hooke suggests, a "'high' view of preaching need not lead to a 'high' view of the preacher."[30]

> Karl Barth, who insists that preaching is the Word of God no less than scripture and Jesus Christ, on whom the preached word depends, argues that this exalted view of preaching actually requires the humility of the preacher, since the fact that preaching is the Word of God is entirely due to God's grace, rather than anything inherent in the preacher.[31]

It is the power and authority of God that is at work, not the preacher's own. Thus, to claim the authority of the pulpit and to stand in that authority is to humble oneself to God's use in the preaching moment. Preachers

---

26. Beach, "The Real Presence of Christ," 89.
27. Bonhoeffer, *Worldly Preaching*, 126.
28. Bonhoeffer, *Worldly Preaching*, 126.
29. Adam, "Speaking God's Words," 119.
30. Hooke, "Prophetic Preaching as Sacrament," 97–98.
31. Hooke, "Prophetic Preaching as Sacrament," 98.

must trust God to do what God will do, with or without their submission. Klaas Runia acknowledges the inner tension within the concept of sacramental preaching. Maintaining the power of the preached word while recognizing that the human element can be less than ideal is a delicate balance. Giving up on one end distorts the other and vice versa. To hold the two in tension is to acknowledge the sacramental coupling of human frailty and divine agency, impossible and yet, by grace, granted. Excavating and articulating that grace is at the heart of sacramental preaching.

Of course, there is a sacred responsibility inherent in the preaching act, especially where it takes seriously a sacramental orientation. Ellen Davis proposes that "the preacher's first and most important responsibility is to educate the imaginations of her hearers so that they have the linguistic skills to enter into the world that Scripture discloses."[32] The preaching event as a continual cultivation of biblical imagination within the gathered community in many ways parallels the eucharistic action. We break open the word together before we break the bread and these actions are not singular, are not a single moment in time, but are continual, connected, and complementary. The preaching event should invite and cultivate a biblical and sacramental imagination that honors holy Scripture as a unique revelation, God's own self-disclosing, in sacramental form—inviting, even insisting upon, our participation.[33] And, what's more, participation in a posture of curiosity, wonder, and exploration, rather than one of power, control, and problem-solving. Participation that is truly radical and culturally subversive.

## Addressing Polarization and Apathy through Sacramental Preaching

Political polarization is an increasingly defining aspect of American society in contrast to the religious landscape, which continues to change markedly in the other direction. Not only can religious observance no longer be assumed, but the depth of that observance even amongst "believers" is arguably anemic. As people, we are increasingly lonely, dissatisfied, fearful, and mentally and emotionally taxed. And our relationships with God, creation, the church, our fellow man, and ourselves remain strained. While it is beyond the scope of this chapter to attempt to explain the complex

---

32. Davis, *Preaching the Luminous Word*, 93.
33. Eugene Peterson, "Foreword," in Boersma, *Sacramental Preaching*, viii.

relationship between political polarization and individual and communal piety, what appears obvious is that the church is losing market share to partisanship in the hearts of God's sin-sick and weary people.

There is good news. God, our physician, is faithful, and the dependability, depth, and healing nature of God's grace is evidenced in the variations in its form. This is exemplified in the sacraments, particularly in the holy Eucharist, where the church is invited to journey into a different, truer, reality: "Our entrance into the presence of Christ is an entrance into a fourth dimension which allows us to see the ultimate reality of life. It is not an escape . . . rather it is the arrival at a vantage point from which we can see more deeply into the reality of the world."[34] In submitting ourselves—our bodies and souls—to sacramental truth through the practice of communal sacramentality, we submit ourselves to another world, a truer world, loosening our grasp on *our individual way* as we reorient ourselves around God's way. In the sacrament, we come home. Our preaching should embody and provoke this encounter, just as it should cultivate a climate of sacramental imagination that identifies, nurtures, equips, and empowers the people of God to recognize grace in their lives.

## Storytelling and the Power of Shared Narrative

*Stories invite us into a world other than ourselves, and if they are good and true stories, a world larger than ourselves.*[35]

The power of stories—those we tell about ourselves, the world, and others—cannot be denied. Reynolds Price writes that human beings have an inherent "narrative hunger," a "need to hear and tell stories . . . the sound of story is the dominant sound of our lives."[36] The current state of political partisanship and increasing polarization has its roots in narrative, and the power of narrative to influence emotional reactions to the benefit of political machinations.[37] Narrative as a political tool galvanizes polariza-

---

34. Schmemann, *For the Life of the World*, 27.
35. Peterson, "Forward: Sacramental Theology," viii.
36. Peterson, "Forward: Sacramental Theology," ix. In "The Storytelling Animal: How Stories Make Us Human," Jonathan Gottschall writes that our "inborn thirst for narrative means that story—its power, purpose and relevance—will endure as long as the human animal does. See Eagleman, "The Moral of the Story."
37. D'Adamo, "How Storytelling Explains World Politics"; Hawkins and Flint, "Two Stories, One America."

tion because it tells a story of "us" versus "them," of scarcity rather than abundance, and of might and power as saviors. These narratives, when successful, often offer simple solutions to complex problems while, and this is important, constructing or reconstructing the identity of those whom they seek to win, urging an identity reliant upon the political leader or party and directly adverse to those on the "wrong" side of the narrative. These narratives promote affective polarization and become critical to our identity, so much so that we continually posture to promote or to defend that narrative at the cost of others. Civil conversations and constructive dialogue fall victim to the need to win, rather than a desire to be in mutual, affirming relationship. Without a "willingness to understand other points of view . . . and to continue a dialogue" we are unable "to integrate the varying perspectives into a [shared] story" toward a "truly common good."[38]

Political narratives are a corruption of our longing for God, wherein we place our trust in another narrative altogether, a narrative that does not reconcile nor heal, but leads to increased social fracture and communal disease. That narrative is of a world we have created, wherein we willfully, or at the very least negligently, forego the charge to abide in God and the world God has created for us as a collective. Instead, as individuals, we create our own worlds. The church and her sacraments offer a powerful counter-narrative, or perhaps it is more rightly called an overwhelming primordial narrative. Eugene Peterson reminds us that

> the story that is Holy Scripture invites us into a world of God's creation and salvation and blessing, God in human form in action on the very ground on which we also live, an incarnational *story*, that is, a flesh and blood story, a story worked out in actual lives and places . . . , a Jesus *story* in which we recognize the action of God in the everydayness of a local history in our stories, a *sacramental* story.[39]

This shared story is what our hearts long for, is what our souls crave. Our individual reaching for narrative is rooted in this collective origin story. Human beings are structured from creation to seek that story as "hearers of the Word" and to participate in that ongoing story.[40] Poet Christian Winman writes, "Christ speaks in stories as a way of preparing

---

38. Edwards, "What Is the Common Good?," 94.
39. Peterson, "Forward: Sacramental Thinking," viii.
40. Hilkert, *Naming Grace*, 33.

his followers to stake their lives on a story, because existence is not a puzzle to be solved, but a narrative to be inherited and undergone and transformed person by person."[41] The primary role of the preacher, argues Karl Rahner, is to tell the sacred story such that it awakens and makes explicit "what is already there in the depths of [the person], not by nature but by grace."[42] To do so effectively, preachers must resist the urge to preach from within the political (and/or societally assumed) narrative and instead claim the one, true narrative as made flesh in Christ Jesus and evidenced sacramentally. Preachers must trust the power of God working through human language to evoke the sacred reality at the center of our collective lives.

## Calling Home

*The story of hope in human history is a narrative that must be told ultimately with human lives if it is to be heard as credible.*[43]

The Christian story is a living story, a path marred by sin and yet marked by the still stronger force of grace. Preachers are guides, walking that path while also inviting and equipping God's people to consider this path their own. It is less about pronouncing the truth from on high, and more about entering into the sacred story alongside our hearers in a manner that "articulate[s] the text's multiple voices, over weeks and years, so that these voices may gradually become the background against which the voices within the community are heard and their differences adjudicated."[44] Preaching that names grace calls God's people home when it takes seriously the complexity of the lived experience while opening up a truer, more spacious reality. In this way, "the mystery of preaching is at once a proclamation of God's word and the naming of grace in the human experience."[45]

In Jesus, God has spoken "God's own self-expression. Jesus, the Word made flesh, became the primordial sacrament of God in the midst

---

41. Peterson, "Forward: Sacramental Thinking," ix.
42. Peterson, "Forward: Sacramental Thinking," ix.
43. Hilkert, *Naming Grace*, 37.
44. Davis, *Preaching the Luminous Word*, 98.
45. Hilkert, *Naming Grace*, 49.

of human history."[46] The church, as the body of Christ, is called to participate in Christ, the abiding sacrament, and the preacher stands in an interesting space, between people's lived experiences and the eternal presence of God. Naming grace acts to bridge that perceived gap, excavating the gathered community to reveal the continued workings of the Holy Spirit in and through that community and the world. In turn, this cultivates a sacramental imagination among God's people, a way of looking at the world that is fundamentally different than the political narrative, or any other narrative for that matter short of God's narrative, which is all in all. Preaching should "draw the hearers of the word into a deeper relationship with God that is at the same time a deeper experience of their everyday human life and relationships as graced."[47] It is through a living narrative of grace—the mystery of a God in pursuit of us—told and retold that God's people re-member and are called home to their collective origin story, bringing "a deeper dimension of human life to awareness and conscious responsibility."[48] This has radical implications for those who know "the power of words as symbols to bring about or to deepen what they signify,"[49] especially vis a vie the deeply polarized cultural narrative that hangs its hat on principles in contradiction to the gospel. Preachers must then speak with authority and faith in the sacramental promise that "God's word of salvation, hope, healing, and liberation is being spoken in new ways today in people's daily lives"[50] and that this word was, is, and will continue to be the only story worth staking our lives on.

## Jesus the Christ, Always Relevant

*Is there any word?*[51]

The question of relevancy is an important one as it is a question, if not *the* question, people bring to liturgy. More than twenty years ago, Mary Catherine Hilkert named this truth, a truth that the preacher in particular must confront.

46. Hilkert, *Naming Grace*, 34.
47. Hilkert, *Naming Grace*, 34.
48. Hilkert, *Naming Grace*, 47.
49. Hilkert, *Naming Grace*, 47.
50. Hilkert, *Naming Grace*, 48.
51. Hilkert, *Naming Grace*, 65.

> Contemporary believers remember the stories from the past precisely so that they might claim them as their own stories. This gathered assembly also wanders in its own deserts. These believers, too, are faced with storms at sea when they are not at all sure whether Jesus is in their midst. . . . Contemporary Christians continue to question whether God speaks and acts in their lives—and if so, where? They come to the Eucharist and wonder: Is there any word from our God?[52]

As the political narrative gains prominence and increasing numbers cite irrelevancy as fuel for religious apathy, preachers would do well to consider how the question of relevancy influences how and why they preach. In our attempts to "be relevant" are we subjugating the gospel to the headlines? In our attempts to be "apolitical," are we ignoring the very real concerns of our people by avoiding the headlines altogether? Are we conforming to and reinforcing our secular context of divisiveness and toxicity in what we preach and how we preach it? Or are we recharacterizing the world as we see it by encouraging a communal, sacramental imagination and a hunger for the world as it should be? Are we moving beyond simply responding to the world as it is into a deeper dimension? Of course, there are many ways that preachers attempt to be relevant that do not engage the question of politics and what we will or will not preach from the pulpit on that topic. However, for purposes of this chapter, the focus will be on how the intersection between the passions of the politically polarized and the religiously apathetic shape the preachers' search for relevancy. A strength of the sacraments is their failure to conform to the worlds of our creating. Instead, they always reveal a world that is fundamentally different. Our preaching should stand on similarly firm foundation.

"God is the subject of the verb," urges Fleming Rutledge, whether we like or not, "my calling and your calling is to attend to what the Bible says about God."[53] This God speaks, remains active in the world, and is always, as a matter of fact, relevant. It is this that should convict the preacher. The temptation to succumb to the narrative that the church must meet the world where it is at by offering commentary on the events of the day is understandable. And yet, too often, the result is sermons that lack depth in the surface level pursuit of relevance. Our liturgy and our sacramental orientation demand a different approach and the people whom we serve deserve a different approach. Yes, people are necessarily engaged in the

---

52. Hilkert, *Naming Grace*, 65.
53. Rutledge, "By the Word Worked."

cultural moment. It is on their minds and their hearts. And yes, polls show that people increasingly view the church as irrelevant. This does not mean, however, that what people need or want is for the church to become an echo chamber of the cultural moment. This is little more than superficial or cheap relevance. And, cheap relevance is as good as cheap grace, which is worth nothing. Instead, people are in search of connection and depth. They are hungry for the radical extravagance of God's saving grace, as known in history *and* experienced in the present day. The question, "Is there any word?" begs a response to the conditions of humanity that is fundamentally different than what any other narrative, political or otherwise, has to offer. It is the preachers' task to make those connections and to make them with conviction. It is not the preachers' task to make God relevant on our terms, be they political or otherwise. To do so is to make ourselves (never God) irrelevant.

For the preaching event to be truly relevant, it must enter into the human experience and seek to name the vulnerability and shame that we would rather not speak of—vulnerability and shame that, when left unnamed and untended, lead us to seek love, belonging, and healing in all the wrong places (including polarizing political narratives). Not individually, of course. The pulpit should never be about individual exhortation or condemnation. Instead, the preacher must look deeply at the human condition and face the realities of sin, death, and yes, even evil, head on. If we are to profess that God has, in Christ, redeemed humanity, then we must contend with what appears to be evidence to the contrary.[54] Some of this evidence is located in our cultural moment, including our political polarization and religious apathy, and yet these are mere symptoms of deeper realities. If we stay on the surface, giving religious flavor to what people are already hearing on the news or through social media, then people will (and should) find what we have to offer to be ultimately irrelevant. The sacramental witness is the conviction "that in spite of all that is broken or contradictory, the power of God's grace is stronger than the power of human sin."[55] To preach that, we must be willing to confront the power of human sin and to wonder about God's apparent absence, even as we point to moments of grace, resurrection, and redemption in the very lives of our people. When we preach in this way, we preach a word that is eternally relevant. When we do so within the context of eucharistic

---

54. Hilkert, *Naming Grace*, 50.
55. Hilkert, *Naming Grace*, 191.

worship, we respond at an appropriate depth dimension to the truth as found in Christ Jesus—a truth made present in and through the liturgy, as heaven and earth unite.[56]

## Conclusion

Where the church gathers in eucharistic worship it gathers as the promise and hope of the greatest commandments: love God, love people.[57] Rooted in the filial relationship of Son to Father and the trinitarian relationship in which God encounters us, our individual church communities are, at their best, familial and sacramental. They require acknowledgment of our belongedness to God and, thus, to one another. They insist upon a recognition of our brokenness and intense need for Jesus. Together as church we do the hard work of living the Christian life, which is imperfect and messy. The joy and challenge presented in such a familial bond awakens us to a profound oneness, a shared human condition whose help is always and ultimately in the name of the Lord. In one another we see ourselves, sin and all. In our oneness, we glimpse the kingdom yet to come. This is, of course, in direct confrontation with political narratives that urge an "us" versus "them" mentality and rely on an anthropology insistent upon our ability to save ourselves.

When we preach to surface level concerns in an attempt to be relevant, we not only miss the opportunity to join the larger eucharistic action and gathering in proclaiming the good news, but we undermine the potential depth of the familial bond and strength of the sacramental community. Preaching to issues raised by a political narrative risks creating an echo chamber, where those who agree with the politics of the preacher are comfortable and those who do not leave. And yet, completely removing the preached word from the concerns of the world to alleviate any possibility of offense is equally problematic. The preacher must attend at a deeper level to the ills of which political concerns (and others) are merely symptoms. The preacher must seek a relevancy that is hard-earned through faithful relationship with the blessed Trinity, holy Scripture, and God's people—a relevancy that probes deeper and speaks the good news of Christ Jesus into the very lives of God's people. In doing

---

56. Schmemann, *For the Life of the World*.
57. Hardin, *Preaching Politics*, 5.

so, we help to equip those who would hear to preach with their own lives the gospel truth.

As a gathered sacramental community, we orient ourselves around the belief in a God who is *with* us, really *present* to us, still *speaking*, permeating physical realities with the hope and promise of grace. Our preaching should both embody and provoke our sacramental orientation, while cultivating a climate of sacramental imagination among God's people. By preaching to the depth dimension into which the liturgy processes, the preaching event shares the good news of Christ Jesus that is eternally relevant. To do so effectively, the preacher does not shy away from controversy, conflict, or the concerns of their community, but confronts those things head on—by excavating and naming sin *and* grace as they exist underneath the surface. Political polarization is a symptom of a greater ill. To ignore the latter in engagement with the former not only risks "irrelevancy" but undermines the strength of our sacramentality.

## Bibliography

Adam, Peter. *Speaking God's Words: A Practical Theology of Preaching*. Vancouver: Regent College Publishing, 1996.

Auden, W. H. *The Collected Poetry of W. H. Auden*. New York: Vintage, 1991.

Baxter, Richard. *The Poetical Fragments of Richard Baxter*. 4th ed. London: Pickering, 1821.

Beach, J. Mark. "The Real Presence of Christ in the Preaching of the Gospel: Luther and Calvin on the Nature of Preaching." *Mid-America Journal of Theology* 10 (1999) 77–134.

Boersma, Hans. *Sacramental Preaching: Sermons on the Hidden Presence of Christ*. Grand Rapids: Baker, 2016.

Bonhoeffer, Dietrich. *Bonhoeffer: Worldly Preaching*. Translated by Clyde E. Fant. Nashville: Nelson, 1975.

D'Adamo, Orlando. "How Storytelling Explains World Politics, from Spain to the US." *The Conversation*, February 6, 2017. https://theconversation.com/how-storytelling-explains-world-politics-from-spain-to-the-us-71142.

Davis, Ellen, with Austin McIver Dennis. *Preaching the Luminous Word: Biblical Sermons and Homiletical Essays*. Grand Rapids: Eerdmans, 2016.

Eagleman, David. "The Moral of the Story." *New York Times*, August 3, 2012. https://www.nytimes.com/2012/08/05/books/review/the-storytelling-animal-by-jonathan-gottschall.html.

Edwards, Mickey H. "What Is the Common Good? The Case for Transcending Partisanship." *Daedalus* 142 (2013) 84–94.

The Episcopal Church. *The Book of Common Prayer and Administration of the Sacraments and Other Rites and Ceremonies of the Church: Together with the Psalter or Psalms of David according to the Use of the Episcopal Church*. New York: Seabury, 1979.

Hardin, Crystal J. "Preaching Politics: Not Yes or No, but How." In *Prophetic Preaching: The Hope or the Curse of the Church?*, edited by Ian S. Markham and Crystal J. Hardin, 91–108. New York: Church Publishing, 2020.

Hawkins, Stephen, and Tommy Flint. "Two Stories, One America: How Political Narratives Shape Our Understanding of Reality." *Kennedy School Review*, July 20, 2016. https://ksr.hkspublications.org/2016/07/20/two-stories-one-america-how-political-narratives-shape-our-understanding-of-reality.

Hilkert, Mary Catherine. *Naming Grace: Preaching and the Sacramental Imagine*. New York: Continuum, 1997.

Hooke, Ruthanna. "Prophetic Preaching as Sacrament: Finding and Using a Political Voice." In *Prophetic Preaching: The Hope or the Curse of the Church?*, edited by Ian S. Markham and Crystal J. Hardin, 91–108. New York: Church Publishing, 2020.

Jones, Robert P., et al. "Exodus: Why Americans Are Leaving Religion and Why They're Unlikely to Come Back." Washington, DC: Public Religion Research Institute, 2016. https://www.prri.org/wp-content/uploads/2016/09/PRRI-RNS-Unaffiliated-Report.pdf.

McConnell, Christopher, et al. "Research: Political Polarization Is Changing How Americans Work and Shop." *Harvard Business Review*, May 19, 2017. https://hbr.org/2017/05/research-political-polarization-is-changing-how-americans-work-and-shop.

Pew Research Center, "Partisan Antipathy: More Intense, More Personal." *Pew Research Center*, October 10, 2019. https://www.pewresearch.org/politics/2019/10/10/partisan-antipathy-more-intense-more-personal.

———. "Why America's 'Nones' Don't Identify with a Religion." *Pew Research Center*, August 8, 2018. https://www.pewresearch.org/fact-tank/2018/08/08/why-americas-nones-dont-identify-with-a-religion.

Rauch, Jonathan. "Let It Be." *The Atlantic*, May 2003. https://www.theatlantic.com/magazine/archive/2003/05/let-it-be/302726.

Rutledge, Fleming. "By the Word Worked: The Unique Power of Biblical Preaching." Lecture delivered at the Parchman Endowed Lectures, George W. Truett Theological Seminary, Waco, TX, September 2019.

———. "The True Vine." Sermon delivered at the Cathedral Basilica of Saint John the Baptist, Savannah, GA, 2017. https://generousorthodoxy.org/sermons/the-true-vine.

Schmemann, Alexander. *For the Life of the World: Sacraments and Orthodoxy*. New York: St. Vladimir's Seminary Press, 2004.

Union of International Associations. "Religious Apathy." http://encyclopedia.uia.org/en/problem/138219.

Voelkel, Jan Gerrit. "The Nature of Polarization Is Changing." *Stanford PACS Blog*, December 7, 2020. https://pacscenter.stanford.edu/pacs-blog/the-nature-of-polarization-is-changing.

Wright, N. T. "N. T. Wright on Word and Sacraments: We Need Both." *Reformed Worship*, September 2008. https://www.reformedworship.org/article/september-2008/nt-wright-word-and-sacraments-we-need-both.

8

# Intergenerational Worship
## The Sacrament of Radical Belonging as the Body of Christ

Sarah Bentley Allred

### Introduction

During the Q&A section of an adult forum presentation I offered on intergenerational worship for a mid-size church in a college town in Ohio, an older gentleman bluntly informed me that when he hears babies crying in church, he tells the parents where to find the nursery. Slightly shocked, I asked him if he might consider engaging the parents in conversation. "In my experience," I said, "some parents do not want to use a nursery because Sunday is one of the only days they have for family time. It is very important for them to worship with their children. Would you consider getting to know the parents and perhaps engaging them in conversation about why it is important to them to worship together as a family?" He did not budge one bit. "No one can hear with those kids crying!" he stated emphatically.

He was not wrong. Crying infants can be extremely distracting during worship. The challenge we face in creating vibrant intergenerational worship is right there: the attempt to equally value the experience of the parents who want to worship with their sound-making children and the adults who want to hear the music, prayers, readings, and sermon without interruption. Neither desire is wrong, although they are sometimes in conflict. Intergenerational worship is about finding ways to praise God together without forcing anyone out—be it the choir, the member with hearing loss, the child who does not want to go to the nursery, or the individual who uses a wheelchair.

All worship can be sacramental, even in the absence of a sacrament such as Baptism or Eucharist. When individuals draw together around sacred objects in song and prayer, their actions are outward and visible signs of God's presence in their lives guiding and drawing them into Christian community.

Intentionally intergenerational worship can also be sacramental. In the body of Christ, we all belong in the fullest sense. Our work as Christians is to draw closer and closer to the kingdom of God, where all are embraced and valued. Churches have the difficult and holy opportunity to cultivate spaces that move towards this reality of deep belonging that has not yet come to fulfillment on earth. At best, intergenerational worship leads us to practice embodying unconditional, radical belonging. A reality that is both already and also not yet. Often, this requires sacrificing personal preference in order to make space for other members of the body of Christ. This is the self-giving, sacrificial love modeled for us by Jesus, the sacrifice of putting the good of the whole ahead of one's own desires. The words and actions of age inclusivity are outward and visible signs of the inward and spiritual truth: through God, we all belong in the fullest sense.

## Who Is This Liturgy For?

My Mother was ordained to the priesthood when I was just a year old, so I've been a "preacher's kid" my entire life. As a teenager, I sometimes resented the large amount of time I was required to spend in church. We even went to church during family vacations. But now, as an adult that has worked in multiple congregations over the last decade, I delight in the opportunity to be a visitor. Of course, I cannot help but show up as someone passionate about intergenerational ministry. And I'm always wondering, who is this liturgy prepared for? What does the space, the bulletin, the things said and the things left unsaid tell me about who is intended or assumed to be participating in this worship service?

Often, church leaders prepare worship that is primarily designed to actively engage adults. While I am most familiar with how this plays out in my own denominational context, the Episcopal Church, I do not believe it to be a unique phenomenon. I hear similar concerns from my colleagues across the denominational spectrum.

While worship is designed to actively engage adults, churches may offer children worship bags, nursery care, Children's Chapel, a children's message, or a children's space. None of these offerings are inherently bad. Worship bags have the potential to engage children in deeper participation with the liturgy. Nursery care can offer exhausted parents much needed time for undistracted spiritual renewal. Children's Chapel can prepare young children for full participation in the worshiping life of the community. A children's message can bring the gospel to life and draw young people closer to God. And a children's space can offer families a place to belong and worship together within the larger body of the faithful.

This can be good ministry that draws us towards love of God and neighbor. But let's call it what it is. When we prepare for worship in these age segregated ways, we have a multi-generational worship service rather than an intergenerational one. We have a worship service where people of many ages are present, but not necessarily a worship service where people of many ages are equally engaged, equally valued, or equal participants. Intergenerational worship, worship for all ages, requires intentional preparation that seeks to equally value the gifts and needs of each generation and to prepare an environment where people of different ages can actively participate.

When I visit new places of worship, my lens is generally one of age inclusivity. But of course, we can interrogate these experiences further. Is the worship service intended for English speakers? White bodies? Literate folks? Gender non-binary bodies? Differently-abled bodies? Neurotypical individuals? The point here is not that every church should be offering services in multiple languages. The point is that worship is the heart of who we are as Christian faith communities. Our liturgies send explicit and implicit messages about who belongs. Offering all members of the worshiping community equal access to active engagement and participation in liturgy provides a sacramental foretaste of the kingdom of God, where all belong in the fullest sense.

### Worship Can Be "Both/And"

Most church leaders are used to planning age specific worship, whether we realize it or not. We plan preschool chapel time, worship for a youth retreat, or a Sunday morning worship service with a distinct age group in mind. When we imagine these different services, the characteristics of each might be very different. Our default, what we consider "normal Sunday worship," is generally adult-centered. During workshops on worship for all ages I often asked participants to help me create two lists: a list of characteristics of child-centered worship and one for adult-centered worship. Here are the lists one group of participants came up with. These are representative of the typical responses I receive.

## Child-Centered Worship

- Children's sermon
- Simple music
- Short
- Interactive
- Object lessons
- Kids choir
- Loud
- Children have roles in liturgy
- Storytelling
- Donuts
- Not much silence
- Repetition
- Shallow (so often)
- Puppets
- Action songs
- Adults watching the kids
- Multi-sensory

## Adult-Centered Worship

- Reflective
- Quiet
- More formal music
- Longer songs
- Preaching
- Adults in leadership roles
- Solemn
- Contemplative
- Meditative
- Praise
- "Normal"
- Organs, chants, litany, confession
- Liturgical
- Serious
- Passive engagement
- Long
- Stuffy
- Boring
- Very didactic

Reading through these lists provides a picture of two very different worship services. It also provides insight into our often unchallenged assumptions about how people of different ages experience God in worship. We assume that adults experience God through silence, intellectual preaching, listening to scripture, formal music, and internal reflection. The images of adult worship provoked by this list are quite passive. On the other hand, we assume that children experience God through their senses, through movement, storytelling, upbeat music, and active engagement.

There is certainly some truth in these lists. Many adults, myself included, find anthems sung by a professional church choir to be a spiritual experience. Likewise, when I have led children in reflecting upon where they experience God in worship, they often mention things like the sound of the bell and having an active role such as acolyting.

However, these unchallenged assumptions can also be detrimental to people of all ages. Children can experience God in silence and in listening to organ music as well as through active participation. Adults can experience God through movement and taste as well as listening. Furthermore, upon close examination we can see that many things from each list are, in fact, ways that people of all ages come close to God. Storytelling, interaction, serving a role in liturgy, repetition, preaching, and reflection can all be intergenerational. Examining these assumptions helps us move from a binary, either/or framework where worship is primarily for adults or for children, to an expansive, both/and framework where the needs, desires, and gifts of all ages are considered.

There is no standard formula, no ideal intergenerational liturgy. Vibrant worship for all ages looks different in every context. Rather than a pin-point in the middle of the Venn diagram, there is a large overlapping space. What makes worship *intergenerational* rather than *multi-generational* is the intentional move towards the middle, intentionally considering the needs and gifts of different generations and actively wondering, "How can the ways we prepare and perform liturgy extend a sense of kingdom belonging to as much of the body of Christ as possible?"

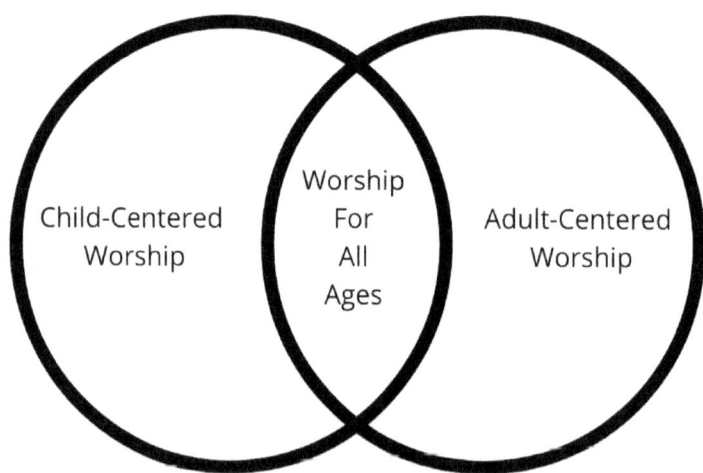

## Something for Everyone, Not Everything for Everyone

When church leaders seek to equally value the needs, desires, and gifts of all ages while preparing for worship (attempt to move towards the center of the diagram), it is inevitable that each individual element of the worship service will not be meaningful for each person present. It is fairly easy to tailor all elements of a worship service in a way that values the needs, desires, and gifts of every person present when you are preparing a 7:30 a.m. Sunday service for ten older adults or a chapel service for twelve three-year-olds. But this would be a nearly impossible task for a worship service with all ages.

The hard truth is that when a more full representation of the body of Christ gathers together in worship, we all have to sacrifice a little bit. Not everything can be for everyone. This requires each of us to release some amount of personal preference in order to honor the gifts, needs, or desires of other members of the congregation. Preparing an environment where people can catch a glimpse of the unconditional, radical belonging of the kingdom of God is the responsibility of the entire community.

As a co-leader of an intentionally intergenerational worship service, I learned what this looks like in practice through trial and error. For example, during the early days of this specific service our leadership team got very excited about simple, repetitive music that can be easily learned by heart without the use of sheet music. This style of music is sometimes called oral tradition music or paperless music. Taize music falls into this genre. We were excited about this style of music because it seemed so intergenerational. It was accessible to pre-readers, older members of the congregation whose eyesight was failing, and everyone in between. But after using paperless music exclusively for a few weeks, we realized something was off. In a reflection session, members of the congregation shared how they were missing familiar hymns. Based on this feedback, we shifted to a model for music that included the use of a hymn for the opening procession, paperless music during communion, and a hymn for the closing procession. While the pre-readers were not able to engage in singing the hymns as easily, they were able to fully participate in the music during communion. Likewise, not all of the adult members enjoyed the new paperless music we were introducing, but they appreciated the opportunity to sing familiar hymns as worship began and concluded. Something for everyone, not everything for everyone.

As this example demonstrates, balance is an important value of worship for all ages. Within the full scope of the liturgy there can be something that actively engages and values each generation, and we also have the freedom to include elements that are meaningful to a particular subset of worshipers. Striving to offer balance is not the same as trying to be all things to all people. Balance acknowledges the vast array of gifts and needs within the body of Christ and offers a diversity of ways to experience God in worship. This approach recognizes that someone will likely not connect with some aspects of the service. It requires members of the worshiping body to practice sacrificing some amount of personal preference, to practice the self-giving love Jesus modeled. In contrast, the attempt to be all things to all people is rooted in a desire to please people or avoid conflict or keep the pews filled. It is anxiety driven, not Christ-centered.

Preaching is another area ripe for engaging the worship for all ages principle "something for everyone, not everything for everyone." Most preachers are already well aware that not every example they use in a particular sermon will connect with each member of the listening community. For this very reason, many preachers choose one focus point for their sermon and expand upon that point with a variety of stories and examples. We can use the exact same principle to preach in a way that engages a wider age range of listeners by offering a mix of images, metaphors, stories, and examples that speak to a variety of ages and life stages. If a sermon includes a story about driving or grocery shopping or taxes, we can balance that with examples that younger listeners connect with such as playgrounds, rivers, or classrooms. This is not just about keeping the full congregation's attention during the sermon, when we hear our lives reflected in preaching, we feel seen. Sermon illustrations can be outward and visible signs of that unconditional, radical belonging.

A third area of liturgy to which this principle can easily be applied is worship leadership. The typical worship service offers a wide range of leadership opportunities from ushering to singing in the choir. Often these roles are filled by adults with the exception of youth acolytes. Reexamining our process for inviting the congregation into shared leadership of worship with an eye towards age inclusivity can open up new possibilities for diversifying these leadership roles. With appropriate training and support, children as young as two-years-old can carry an offering plate or hand out a bulletin. Older children are quite capable of ushering, carrying bread and wine to the altar, or lighting candles. Middle and high school students can do all of this as well as lectoring, playing instruments, serving on the altar and flower guilds, and running audio visual equipment for live streaming. Not every role is appropriate for every age (or every person). I would not suggest that five-year-olds be trained as chalice bearers. But intentionally engaging people of all ages in worship leadership offers opportunities to experience a deep sense of belonging.

During my time co-leading the aforementioned intergenerational worship service I had the privilege of participating in multiple training sessions for young worship leaders, approximately grades second through seventh. The excitement and enthusiasm these young people brought to the training was contagious. After a session that focused on preparation of lay readers, one parent told me that for the first time ever her children asked to read the Bible before bed rather than another book. During another session, we trained the group to ring sanctus bells. As part of the training we asked, "Why do you think we use these bells during worship?" The children answered right away, "To remind us to pay attention." "To tell us something important is happening." Then, when we looked up the eucharistic prayer together and asked the group when specifically they thought the bells would be rung, they named all three moments.

What I know to be true in my own life, and what I have witnessed in my work with children and adults, is that we humans are more invested in the things we are actively participating in and contributing to. Vibrant liturgy is not created and performed by clergy while a congregation passively observes. Vibrant liturgy is created by the whole congregation through singing, call and response, shared leadership, giving and receiving. We are formed as the body of Christ as we practice being the body of Christ together in worship.[1]

When worship is led by a small number of highly trained adults it usually runs fairly smoothly. When we widen the circle of leadership, we can almost guarantee that occasionally something will not go as planned. An acolyte will turn up just as the service is about to begin, still wriggling into vestments. Money will slide out of the offering plate onto the floor. Someone will read the wrong lesson. The service may be less pristine, less excellent, less perfect. But rather than lamenting this imperfection, this can be an opportunity for trust. As a friend and co-leader of worship for all ages often reminded me, "Nothing, nothing, nothing, not even a liturgical misstep can separate us from the love of God." God is not *more* present when everything goes to plan. But perhaps God is more present when we, as leaders, release control. Let go of our own desire for perfection and trust that liturgy planned and carried out with intentionality is, somehow, mysteriously, constituting us more and more deeply as the body of Christ.

1. Fischbeck, *Behold What You Are*, 4.

## Moving beyond Performative Inclusion

Sometimes our well intentioned efforts to include more age diversity in worship are performative rather than inclusive. For example, during a children's sermon a preacher might invite all the children to come forward to listen to a brief message and engage in conversation. When the preacher asks the children questions their earnest answers elicit laughter from the adult members of the congregation who are watching. On the surface, a weekly children's sermon seems intergenerational. It offers a way for children to be included in worship. But when children are drawn apart and put on display for the rest of the congregation, it is more like a performance or exhibit than an expression of valuing the gifts, needs, and desires of the young people.[2] It is generally not the best way to make space for children to experience radical, unconditional belonging.

A similar performative inclusion can happen with children's choirs. While adult choir members often sing from the choir loft, the back of the congregation, or the choir pews, the children's choir often sings from the front of the congregation using hand motions and perhaps even holding handmade artwork that relates to the song. Rather than learning that singing is an important form of worship leadership, children often learn that singing in church is a performance that elicits photos and applause.

Including and involving children in worship in some way is preferable to ignoring them all together, but with more intentionality we can find ways of engaging them in worship that not only values their needs and desires but allows them to offer their gifts to the community just like people of other ages. Rather than offering a children's sermon, a preacher can move towards an intergenerational style of preaching. If this is too big a shift to start with, consider having children stay in the pew with their parents during the children's sermon. At the end, offer a few questions for discussion. Likewise, rather than having the children's choir perform for the congregation, choir directors can teach the children and the congregation about the importance of leading music for worship. The children can be invited to sing pieces with the adult choir throughout the year or, if they sing separately, they can sing from the same location as the adult choir would and be dressed in a similar manner. If the adult choir wears vestments, the children could wear vestments as well. As we consider children's participation in worship, we must actively wonder not

---

2. Mercer, *Welcoming Children*, 214–16.

just "How can we include children?" but "How can we extend a sense of kingdom belonging to children?"

## Change Can Stir Up Conflict

Most of us are naturally somewhat resistant to change. When you begin to talk about making changes to worship, something so emotional, personal, and synonymous with tradition, people can become very upset very quickly. It's no wonder that many congregations are worshiping almost the same way they did ten, twenty, or fifty years ago (or at least they were before the COVID-19 pandemic).

Change within Christian community can be particularly challenging. As Joyce Ann Mercer writes, "difficulties inhere when persons who differ from one another join together in a shared activity and space seeking to encounter God."[3] Making changes to a communities worship service to bring it more in line with worship for all ages practices, often elicits some push back. The church musician may be opposed to including more accessible music. The priest may not want to shorten the length of their sermons. Older adults might be concerned about being distracted by the sounds and movements of children. Parents will, perhaps, see no reason to get rid of Children's Chapel because it offers them a more focused experience of worship. These concerns are real and reasonable. And these conversations will require significant effort, deep listening, attention to emotions, patience, grace, and trust in the slow work of God.

So why bother? First, regardless of what you "accomplish" through these efforts in terms of changes to worship, you will be following the Gospel directive to serve "the least of these" (Matt 25:40 NRSV). Children are unable to advocate for their own full inclusion in the worshiping life of a community. In promoting worship for all ages, we engage in a process of valuing, serving, and advocating for members of the congregation with very little power.

Second, the attempt to shift towards practices of intergenerational worship is the attempt to draw closer to the kingdom of God. In the kingdom of God, we are all embraced and valued. We belong in the very fullest sense. It is the counter-cultural work of choosing self-giving, agape love over individualism and of recognizing our interdependence. In the body of Christ, "if one member suffers, all suffer together with it; if one

---

3. Mercer, *Welcoming Children*, 234.

member is honored, all rejoice together with it" (1 Cor 12:26). This is radical, unconditional belonging.

Third, research shows that intergenerational relationships and participation in worship with the full church community are two important factors in the spiritual development of young people. To grow in their own faith development, "children need frequent, regular, ongoing opportunities to interact with people of faith."[4] These relationships provide a sense of belonging in the body of Christ and model what it means to live a Christian life. Research by Kara E. Powell, Brad M. Griffin, and Cheryl A. Crawford offers similar findings on the importance of intergenerational relationships for teenagers. Furthermore, their research finds that "high school and college students who experience more intergenerational worship tend to have higher faith maturity."[5]

Change not only *can* stir up conflict, it often does. Some, even those who find the rationale for worship for all ages compelling, will use this as an excuse to avoid engaging in this work. But those able and willing to offer to God the time and energy required for this work will find the process of shifting towards intergenerational worship practices an incredible opportunity for community building and formation.

## Addressing Personal Preference

Perhaps the biggest barrier to vibrant worship for all ages, worship that actively engages and equally values the gifts and needs of every generation, is personal preference. We live in a consumerist society that places a high value on individuals. Often, we find ourselves feeling that what is important or good for us as individuals (or as a household) is more important than what is good for the greater community. But, as Katherine Turpin writes, "basic Christian theological claims such as the love of God and neighbor, care for the alien and the orphan, reverence and stewardship of creation, and justice for the poor and oppressed fundamentally come into conflict with the basic meaning claims of consumer capitalism."[6]

All of us, church leaders included, are immersed in consumer capitalism throughout our daily lives. And we bring these ways of thinking and being to church. Christian community, and worship in particular,

---

4. Allen and Ross, *Intergenerational Christian Formation*, 53.
5. Powell et al., *Sticky Faith*, 75.
6. Turpin, *Branded*, 17.

models and invites us to embrace a different set of values: agape (self-giving love), belonging, gratitude, trust in God, and truth, to name a few. Growing into this different set of values and counter-cultural way of being in the world is the work of a lifetime. Inviting members of the congregation to set aside their personal liturgical likes and dislikes in order to create a greater sense of belonging for other members of the community is part of this work.

This is tough work and often our efforts are ineffective. I've seen two successful methods for helping people shift from an individual, personal preference mentality to the counter-cultural values of agape, gratitude, trust, and truth. The first is group discernment, engaging in processes of collective prayerful listening for the movement of the Holy Spirit. The second is intentional relationship building and tending.

## Discernment, Not Problem Solving

When we see a problem, it is natural to move into the mode of fixing and solving. The problem solving model focuses on solutions, which often leads to conversations where people offer strong opinions and feel their personal preferences should be taken into consideration above the personal preferences of others. Opportunities for conflict and hurt feelings abound. There is a different model for approaching concerns from the sounds that children make in worship to the location of the annual parish picnic. This model, discernment, is grounded in mission/purpose and the movement of the Holy Spirit. Discernment can lead groups into a space beyond personal preference, a space of agape (self-giving love) that is aligned with God's desire for the community.

For example, a problem solving approach to replacing Children's Chapel with children's participation in the entire worship service might look something like this: At the end of the COVID-19 pandemic you begin to consider how you will rebuild the children's ministry program at your church. You decide that the research and lack of volunteer capacity make this the perfect opportunity to stop offering Children's Chapel and instead have children in the sanctuary for the full worship service. Desiring buy-in for this change, you hold a parent meeting to build support. During the meeting, you explain the post-pandemic lack of volunteer capacity as well as the research around the importance of full-church worship in the faith development of children. After this brief presentation, you open the floor for discussion. You'll likely have a few folks who agree. Perhaps both parents work and Sunday is one of the only days they have to be together as a family, and they like worshiping together. But you'll likely have other parents who argue emotionally for keeping Children's Chapel. Maybe they find it difficult and distracting to worship with their children, their children complain about worship being boring, or they believe children don't understand what is happening in the Eucharist. These parents might move into problem solving mode and volunteer to help with Children's Chapel or suggest that it should be available for those who want it and each family should have a choice. By the end of the meeting, you have gathered a lot of opinions and heard a lot of personal preferences, many of which conflict, and other than the opening prayer you've barely touched on how God is part of any of this.

A group discernment approach to replacing Children's Chapel with children's participation in the entire worship service can invite parents to move past their personal preferences and consider what shifts or changes God might be calling you to make in your children's ministry. In this approach, it is important to start by reminding those gathered of the purpose of your children's ministry (for example, our children's ministry creates an environment that allows young people the opportunity to experience God, grow in loving relationships, and serve). Then, you could engage in a period of reflection on how parents have seen this purpose in action over the last year. You might also ask, "What challenges prevent your family from engaging more fully in our church's children's ministry?" and "What are your hopes and dreams for our children's ministry in the coming year?" At this point, you could engage in some noticing and reflection on how Children's Chapel does and does not accomplish the stated purpose of your children's ministry. Or, you might say, "Given all that we have just reflected upon, I'm wondering if Children's Chapel is the best way to accomplish the purpose of our ministry." You might close with a prayer for guidance and ask the group to be in prayer around what programs fit the purpose of your ministry most closely.

In the discernment approach outlined above, members of the community are invited into engagement and interaction around an area of concern, but the conversation is anchored in the (hopefully) agreed upon purpose of the ministry and how God is already present and at work through the ministry. People are still invited to share their experience, but questions such as "Where are you experiencing God in worship?" and "What have you noticed that distracts you from experiencing God in worship?" move the focus away from preference and opinion and towards the movement of the Holy Spirit.

Discernment does not guarantee any particular outcome. In the example above, the group may end up discerning that indeed, Children's Chapel does align closely with the purpose of the ministry and should not be replaced. Discernment is not outcome oriented. Rather, it opens opportunities for respect and deep spiritual connection between members of a faith community. Although this type of discernment takes place outside of worship, it builds a sense of belonging by engaging people as equals in the process of listening for God's guidance. In my experience, when people hear other members of their community reflect on their experience of God, it is often moving and hard to argue with.

## Staying in Relationship

A second method for addressing the personal preference barrier to vibrant worship for all ages is relationship. We all know that ministry is relational, but sometimes we forget how powerful intentional relationship tending can be. This is not the same as people pleasing or trying to be all things to all people. It is about being rooted in your purpose and values and staying committed to remaining in relationship even when disagreement arises.

The best examples I can give of the relational work needed to move towards vibrant worship for all ages come from the intergenerational worship service I co-led. One of my roles was to schedule oblation bearers. I often invited parents to serve in this role with their young children. One week I invited a two-year-old and his father to bring up the bread and wine by email, but never heard back. I did not think much of this, knowing the father was a busy graduate student, but about a week later I ran into the parent and he asked if I had a moment to talk. He explained that he had not replied to my email because he was so embarrassed to tell me that the service was not working for his family. He felt like his young child was too disruptive and other worshipers were looking at him critically. He wanted to participate but just didn't feel like there was a place for his family at the service, it was not child-centered enough for his two-year-old. Around that same time, another member of our worship leadership team spoke with someone else who did not feel like there was a place for her at the service. She felt that the children were too disruptive, the service was too child-centered. It felt like a service for families.

Each of us listened carefully and affirmed the experience of the worshiper. We spoke about the core value of the service, intergenerationality, and explained how we were, imperfectly, trying to find a middle ground where worship was not adult-centered or child-centered. We acknowledged that the service could not be all things to all people and that those who participated would likely be uncomfortable in one way or another as together we tried to make space for people of every age. And, most importantly, we assured them that we would have no hard feelings if they did not feel called to participate in the service.

These were just two of the uncomfortable conversations we had while trying to shift our communities' mental model from worship that fulfills my personal piety and feeds me spiritually to worship as an enactment of the world as it should be: a place where people of all ages praise God together. After each of these tough conversations, we sent a hand-written note reiterating our assurance that the person was always welcome at the service and that there would be no hard feelings if they chose not to participate.

A few months passed. The parent from my first conversation returned to the service as a faithful participant and eventually joined the worship leadership team. The person who found it distracting to worship with so many children also returned to worship many times and even asked for our help in writing an Easter sermon that would engage people of all ages. After Easter this person sent us a recording of the sermon with this note, "Thank you for all you all have taught me and brought to our community this year . . . You all amaze me. It is because of you that I stepped out and was intentional about making this sermon intergenerational."

These are just two stories. But they illustrate well how the process of preparing for intergenerational worship, as well as the actual service, leads us towards the kingdom of God, where all people are fully embraced and valued. The culture of the service made people feel comfortable sharing honestly why they stopped participating. The leadership team did the hard work of listening with open hearts and staying in relationship without hard feelings. The worshipers felt welcome to return and, over time, grew into a different relationship with this style of worship and their presence brought the whole service closer to radically embracing all members of the body of Christ.

## Permission to Start Small

Shifting a traditional, adult-centered Sunday morning service towards a worship service for all ages is no small task. It is the work of years, not months. It is less a destination than a process that draws us closer to one another and to God. So, consider this your permission to start small. You could start with a season of personal prayer and discernment. You could start by reading more about intergenerational worship. You could engage some other members of your church community in conversation about intergenerational worship or you could start by offering some intergenerational programs outside of worship.

Your starting point will be impacted by your context and your role within your faith community. If you are a liturgical decision maker in your context, you will have a wider range of possible starting points and, quite frankly, a lot more power to move this process forward. If you are not a liturgical decision maker, the permission to start small is even more important. You do not have the same kind of power, but do not underestimate the impact of small, incremental changes over time. It's not about the specific outcome, it's about the process. The process of respecting the dignity of every human being, from the youngest infants to the oldest adults. The process of empowering each other to offer our God-given gifts to the community and to the glory of God during the Eucharist. The process of embodying the kingdom of God, where all are embraced and valued.

It is this process, this work, not a specific outcome, that forms us as the body of Christ. We are formed in worship and in worship we practice a counter-cultural way of being. It is good and right and a joyful thing to embody kingdom values at church or during worship. But the goodness does not stop there. Our liturgy concludes with the dismissal which is a sending forth. We are sent "in peace to love and serve the Lord."[7] The vision of worship for all ages is one that extends beyond the confines of Sunday liturgy as well. It dreams of a worship service that prepares people of all ages to value the gifts and needs of each person they encounter in daily life. It hopes to help people practice the gospel values of agape (self-giving love), gratitude, trust in God, and truth so that they can live these values all week long. It is a vision of building God's kingdom on earth, one conversation, one new song, one reflection session at a time.

---

7. Episcopal Church, *Book of Common Prayer*, 366.

## Conclusion

Worship is sacramental even when the service does not include healing or Eucharist or Baptism. When individuals draw together in song and prayer, their actions are outward and visible signs of God's presence. Intentional worship for all ages is also sacramental. Using images that resonate for different generations in a sermon, inviting a child to share their gifts as a lay reader, selecting music that people of every age can sing, these are outward and visible signs of an inward and spiritual grace: the grace of full belonging. The grace of God-given gifts to offer. The grace of worthiness. Intergenerational worship is the sacramental practice of the radical, unconditional belonging that exists only in the body of Christ through the grace of God. It is not a destination. It is not something we achieve in this lifetime. It is something we practice knowing that somehow, mysteriously, in the kingdom of God it is already true.

## Bibliography

Allen, Holly C., and Christine L. Ross. *Intergenerational Christian Formation: Bringing the Whole Church Together in Ministry, Community, and Worship*. Downers Grove, IL: IVP Academic, 2012.

The Episcopal Church. *The Book of Common Prayer and Administration of the Sacraments and Other Rites and Ceremonies of the Church: Together with the Psalter or Psalms of David*. New York: Church Publishing, 2007.

Fischbeck, Lisa G. *Behold What You Are: Becoming the Body of Christ*. New York: Church Publishing, 2021.

Mercer, Joyce A. *Welcoming Children: A Practical Theology of Childhood*. St. Louis: Chalice, 2009.

Powell, Kara E., et al. *Sticky Faith: Practical Ideas to Nurture Long-Term Faith in Teenagers*. Grand Rapids: Zondervan, 2011.

Turpin, Katherine. *Branded: Adolescents Converting from Consumer Faith*. Cleveland: Pilgrim, 2006.

Part 3

# Saving Ourselves

Truly I tell you, just as you did it to one of the least of these who are members of my family, you did it to me.

*(MATT 25:40 NRSV)*

# 9

# Ethical Formation through the Liturgy and Sacraments

*Ian S. Markham*

The author of Ephesians writes: "Put away from you all bitterness and wrath and anger and wrangling and slander, together with all malice, and be kind to one another, tenderhearted, forgiving one another, as God in Christ has forgiven you" (Eph 4:31–32).[1]

As the early church worked out her identity in letters collected together in the New Testament, there are many moments when Paul, in particular, along with other authors issue an exhortation to the church to learn to live in relationships of love with each other. And we find such attempts moving. We all love Paul's extraordinary hymn to love, where he writes: "Love is patient; love is kind; love is not envious or boastful or arrogant or rude. It does not insist on its own way; it is not irritable or resentful; it does not rejoice in wrongdoing, but rejoices in the truth. It bears all things, believes all things, hopes all things, endures all things" (1 Cor 13:4–7).

While we find such passages moving, if we are honest with ourselves, they are also challenging. The invitation to love is difficult. We actually quite like stewing in our bitterness, wrath, and anger. On the individual,

---

1. Unless otherwise noted, all biblical citations in this chapter are from the NRSV.

social, and perhaps especially the political levels, we actually quite enjoy slander. Too often, we don't even try to embody Paul's vision of love. A little envy, a little arrogance, and being irritable or resentful are much more fun than an attempt to not do these things. Too many Christians ignore the challenge of sin; they ignore the attractiveness of sin; and they ignore the level at which change will come. It won't be conscious assent because we all intellectually assent to the value of love. It needs to be at the level of the subconscious—at the level of habits, reactions, and gut reactions. This is where we need to work because the love project needs to go deep inside.

In this article, we will explore the predicament of sin—its attractive nature, yet our ostensible desire to resist sin. Then the case will be made that true transformation requires the careful work of "formation," which happens both at the conscious and, more importantly, the subconscious level. This work of formation is the work of regular participation in the liturgy and the act of receiving the sacrament. To be ethical—to be loving—one needs to allow God to use the liturgy and sacraments to make a difference.

## The Predicament of Sin

Talk about sin has gone out of fashion. We prefer to "understand" rather than to judge. Sin, as a category, feels like it is an oversimplification of the complexity of being human. In addition, both traditional theologians and more progressive theologians provide good reasons to distance ourselves from the concept of sin. On the one hand, we have the traditionalists too bound to "original sin" and to the Adam and Eve narratives; on the other hand, we have the progressives, such as the feminist critique, who find the language destructive.

Starting with the arch-traditionalist, Augustine of Hippo is often viewed as problematic. In *The City of God*, he seems to link the fall with sexual sin. There is compelling evidence for this reading of Augustine. After all, there is a sustained reflection on whether it was possible for Adam and Eve, before the fall, to be sexual intimate. The problem explains Augustine is "lust." So he writes.

> We see then that there are lusts for many things, and yet when lust is mentioned without the specification of its object the only thing that normally occurs to the mind is the lust that excites

the indecent parts of the body. This lust assumes power not only over the whole body, and not only from the outside, but also internally; it disturbs the whole man, when the mental emotion combines and mingles with the physical craving, resulting in a pleasure surpassing all physical delights. So intense is the pleasure that when it reaches its climax there is an almost total extinction of mental alertness; the intellectual sentries, as it were, are overwhelmed.[2]

So how can you have sexual intimacy without the sin of lust in the garden of Eden? The answer he gives is extraordinary. It is possible, explains Augustine, however, the act will be without passion. "Instead, the sexual organs would have been brought into activity by the same bidding of the will as controlled the other organs."[3] In other words, everything would be under the cool gift of reason: there would be sex, but it would be without the sexual passion. Augustine has solved the problem of "lust"—concupiscence—which is clearly condemned in Scripture, by creating a "lust free" form of sexual intimacy.

In so doing, Augustine created this deep link between sin and sexual desire. Many are the evangelical Christians who have agonized over their desire to masturbate in their teenage years. Desire for the Xbox was nothing compared to the desire for the girl at school. To covet was acceptable (or at least appeared less serious as sin), to lust was not. From teenage desire to the politician who has an affair, sexual sin has been central to the Christian sense of sin.

It is not surprising that feminist theologians have pointed out how unhelpful this is. A good illustration of this is Rachel Sophia Baard. In her *Sexism and Sin-Talk*, she argues that too often the Christian account of sin has been damaging to women. In her discussion of Augustine, she writes:

> Moreover, concupiscence—that is, distorted desire as a result of humanity's loss of God-directedness—whilst not necessarily a sexual concept, was often understood primarily in sexual terms. This added to the negative associations attached to the body and sexuality, which had negative consequences for women, due to the classical Western dualistic framework that associated women with the body.[4]

---

2. Augustine, *City of God*, 14.16 (p. 577).
3. Augustine, *City of God*, 14.26 (p. 591).
4. Baard, *Sexism and Sin-Talk*, 87–88.

This critique points out how the fall leads to a negative attitude to our body, which in turn leads to a denigration of women. The stereotypes then follow: it is the women who use their charms to tempt men; women therefore must be controlled by a father before marriage and a husband within marriage. Bodily desires are to be resisted; celibacy is celebrated; and women cannot be front and central in a holy place. Against all this, Baard wants a prophetic account of sin-talk, which challenge systems and power dynamics. Interestingly, she points out certain dangers in some of the traditional feminist treatments of sin. And the heart of her argument is that she certainly wants the word "sin" not to be identified with the behavior of women.

In many ways this is one of those debates where everyone is right. As we learned later from Freud, Augustine is in many ways right. Freud offered a critique that suggested that sexual dynamics from a very early age are shaping our human identity at a subconscious level. It is a complex realm that is central to our sense of self and our comfort with our bodies. In addition, as we learned from #metoo, an uncontrolled sexual desire can be deeply destructive and express itself in inappropriate remarks or inappropriate touching.

Meanwhile, Baard is also right. A disordered life focused on self can involve many different malfunctioning appetites. Consumerism, indifference to human suffering, and ignoring the many ways in which we participate in an unjust economic system are all sins; many of which have significant impact on human lives.

The invitation of the gospel is to allow God to work on our lives. The goal is holiness—a life focused on God, where our appetites are properly ordered, and where the other is honored. The promise of the gospel is that this is where fulfilment is found. This is where life can be lived constructively rather than destructively. Instead of spiraling down into a life of loneliness and uncontrolled and inappropriate passion, joy is found—joy in God and joy in love of others. But what is the vehicle of this divine transformation of a human life? This is the work of formation.

## The Work of Formation

The great prophet of the exile, Jeremiah, introduced the famous image of God as the potter. In Jeremiah 18, we read:

> The word that came to Jeremiah from the Lord: "Come, go down to the potter's house, and there I will let you hear my words." So I went down to the potter's house, and there he was working at his wheel. The vessel he was making of clay was spoiled in the potter's hand, and he reworked it into another vessel, as seemed good to him. Then the word of the Lord came to me: Can I not do with you, O house of Israel, just as this potter has done? says the Lord. Just like the clay in the potter's hand, so are you in my hand, O house of Israel? (Jer 18:1–6)

Paul in the epistle to Romans picks up this image. He is agonizing over the status of Israel in God's providential plans and uses the image to stress God's sovereignty. Paul writes, "Has the potter no right over the clay, to make out of the same lump one object for special use and another for ordinary use" (Rom 9:21). From both Jeremiah and Romans, a theme emerges. God is working on human lives; God will mold us in ways that God wants us to be.

The image is rich. Watching a potter work on clay is fascinating. It is hard and patient work. It takes time to get the process just right. The clay does not always cooperate. Many is the moment, when the potter finds the emerging glass or vase suddenly going wrong right towards the end of the process. At the same time, the potter is sovereign. Potters will ultimately get their way. The beautiful creation will emerge. The clay will be transformed from a lump into an object of usefulness and beauty.

In Christian theology, we are invited into a process, where the Holy Spirit aspires to be the hands of God on our lives. God wants to take the clay of our lives and transform the clay into a beautiful gift for God that can transform the world. God stands ready to take time that is needed to work on our egoism, selfishness, preoccupation with the trivial, and our wickedness. It is a work that touches all our assumptions and prejudices. So, God wants to delve down to the arena of unconscious bias where we relate differently and inappropriately to persons of color. God wants to challenge our attitudes to LGBT+ persons. God wants us to recognize the evil of patriarchy. And God wants us to affirm the *imago Dei* in persons with special needs.

The clay is formed by the potter into the beautiful object. So, we come to the key concept of formation. Formation is the act of being formed; it is a work within the church, where God can use many players to shift our focus from self to God. It is worth remembering that Jeremiah saw the Babylonians as a tool that God was using to mold the clay of the

Israelites. So, it is not simply fellow Christians who can play a key role in formation but also those outside the Church.

In all cases, our propensities to sinfulness will be challenged. Sin goes deep; so, the task of formation is a demanding and constant work. It requires the capacity to be constantly reflective on our ways of being and relating to others. From decisions about purchases to decisions around the use of time, formation is an invitation to prayerfully invite God into every aspect of our lives.

As noted above, some of the hardest areas of formation are at the level of subconscious acts and decisions. In this place, our reason cannot go. Why do some people feel uncomfortable with a woman as a boss? Why do some people greet the white person who is passing us but cross the road to avoid talking to the black person? Formation must reach these places. This can be hard. So, the act of God in this key part of formation wants to work on our defensiveness as we are confronted or challenged by others.

From time to time, the Christian tradition has flirted with the concept that if you just do this single act (for example, give your life to the saving power of Jesus), then you are suddenly changed from the ways of sinfulness to the way of holiness. However, the heart of the tradition has stressed the centrality of the "process of sanctification." It is not instantaneous. Instead, it is a long grueling process of gradual change; sometimes there are seasons when certain sinful habits reassert themselves and once again we have to refocus on allowing God's grace to forgive us and then with the aid of the Holy Spirit grow afresh into holiness.

It is this process to holiness that makes the liturgy central. Liturgy involves repeated actions of remembrance, worship, and resetting our life for the present and the future. Liturgy reaches the parts of us that conscious argument does not reach. Liturgy can touch the subconscious attitudes and outlooks. And we need to recognize the journey is gradual and time consuming.

## The Role of Liturgy

Perhaps the most important contemporary writer on the formation of ethical disposition is Timothy Sedgwick.[5] He credits F. D. Maurice as

5. This section of the essay draws on ideas originally formulated in my essay "The Survival of Conscience."

the one who sees "the task of Christian ethics is to describe life before God."[6] What Sedgwick loves about Maurice is that, for Maurice, one is invited to critique the deepest passions and loves of a life, one is invited to ground those loves in Jesus Christ, which is radiated through the practices and theology of the Church. Sedgwick sees this as "practical piety." He explains:

> Christian faith is a life lived in the presence of God. Christian ethics is a description of that life. As a matter of practical piety, the Christian life is understood as sacramental, incarnate, and corporate. First, this life is revealed and effected by Jesus Christ as known through the church, specifically in scripture, worship, and the life of the Christian community. In this sense, Christ is the sacrament of God. Second, this life is incarnate. The presence of God is experienced in daily life. This presence is experienced as the power in the relationships that gives meaning to life itself. Third, this life is corporate. Life in God connects us beyond ourselves. We transcend our individual, solitary worlds and are brought into a unity or community with all being itself. In this sense we are drawn into a new covenant as we come to participate in the divine life.[7]

One can see the ethical impact on a life is far reaching if one is able to truly exercise "practical piety"—live life in the presence of God. For Sedgwick, this state of closeness to God impacts us deeply. We encourage Christ in the life of the Church (which he terms sacramental); we then encounter a relationship of depth with God (which he calls incarnational); and we make this journey with others—in community (which he calls corporate). This vision of the moral life is wide-ranging. It is an intimate relationship with God that learns from the Church and permeates every single moment of every single day. And to prevent this image of discipleship becoming too individualistic, Sedgwick insists on incorporating the obligation to journey with others—the corporate dimension of living life within the body of Christ. Taken all together, the arena for God's work is both the conscious life of thoughts and decisions and the subconscious life of habits, fears, assumptions, and prejudice. God is everywhere.

It was back in 1987 that Sedgwick grounded his analysis of the ethical in the sacramental. In his classic, *Sacramental Ethics*, he argues for the centrality of the paschal mystery in the formation of the Christian life. In

---

6. Sedgwick, *The Christian Moral Life*, 50.
7. Sedgwick, *The Christian Moral Life*, 51.

the act of participating in the Eucharist, the Christian finds community, with a fresh (and redeemed) self-understanding, and is invited into new life in Christ. Working with an account of worship, Sedgwick explains how it can be transformative:

> Worship is mythic as it mediates between the worshiper and reality; it is also parabolic as it dissolves the taken for granted attitudes and perceptions that distance the self from reality. In other words, worship mediates reality and relates us to God as it expresses and challenges our relation to reality and, in turn, celebrates and effects that relation.[8]

Sedgwick has a vision of a circular motion: worship is an engagement with "reality"—the real that at times we only partially see. As we worship, certain "taken for granted attitudes and perceptions" are challenged because these attitudes and perceptions do not accord with reality. As a result of worship, then we can engage more rightly with "reality"—so we are back at the beginning, where the cycle will begin again, because reality is always complex and our attitudes and perceptions are difficult to adjust.

Sedgwick goes on to stress the fourfold movement of the Eucharist. We hear the Word proclaimed; we respond to the Word by offering our prayers, our gifts, and, in so doing, ourselves; in the Great Thanksgiving, our offering is accepted by God; and then as a redeemed people we are dismissed into the world. In these four movements, there is the cosmic drama of God's engagement with all humanity. In the first movement, we hear of God—the challenge, the truth, the reality—culminating in the preaching of the sermon. In the second movement, we respond in the prayers, especially confession, and offertory, which is an act of giving ourselves to God. We are inviting, in the light of the proclaimed Word, God to work on our lives. In the third movement, we learn of what God has done for us on the cross—the Great Thanksgiving is God's yes to our offering. And then finally, in the fourth movement, we are sent out—redeemed and restored to work for the kingdom in the world.

This beautiful description of the liturgical pattern of the Episcopal Church demonstrates how God can form us—how the potter can work

---

8. Sedgwick, *Sacramental Ethics*, 34–35. Sedgwick acknowledges his debt to John Dominic Crossan for the mythic and parabolic distinction. Perhaps in the notes, I might just express a slight anxiety that Crossan's account of religious language is insufficiently realist. I want to advocate for the idea that the liturgy is also descriptive of a God that has acted in Christ and is acting in the church.

on the clay. We are given a sense of how the liturgy forms us. Our worldview is transformed; our liturgy shapes our self-understanding of our place with each other and with God.

Liturgy works in the non-rational realm. It is not that we are consciously thinking as we participate in the various steps of the liturgy. Instead, the liturgy's very pattern helps us see the world differently. In the Eucharist, the human life is placed in the context of eternity and divine action in creation. Our hopes and concerns are shaped through confession and the hearing of the Word. Values inculcate us without us realizing that they are being inculcated. Even if the service was boring; there was a work that the Potter was doing through the liturgy that made a difference even if we didn't consciously realize that it was the case.

## Who Then Can Lead the Sacraments?

The argument thus far is this: an instrument of grace is the liturgies, of which the sacraments are a key part. This is an instrument that God wants to use on our lives to transform us into vehicles of grace and holiness. However, this clearly raises an important question: can only the virtuous be sacramental leaders?

This question was especially acute in the early church. Perhaps the best illustration was the debate over Donatism. It was in the fourth century, that the Romans, as they persecuted the church, insisted that Christians surrender any copies of the Bible so that the Romans could destroy these texts. In an attempt to save their lives, some Christians, including some priests and Bishops, did indeed hand over copies of the Bible. The question then divided the church: could these priests and Bishops still perform a valid sacrament? Surely, we should expect behavior free from sin from our priests and bishops?

It is important to remember as we consider this controversy that, at this time, there were high expectations for conversion and even higher expectations for those "set apart" for holy orders. In addition, many Christians had refused to hand over their Bibles; and as a result were martyred for their faithful witness. Augustine of Hippo is the bishop responsible for articulating the position that became the Christian orthodoxy. The Donatists were wrong. William Placher explains the practical nature of Augustine's response:

If the Donatists were right, and a priest's sin renders the sacrament he performs invalid, then, if a priest (or the bishop or ordained him, or the bishop who ordained that bishop) was secretly an unrepentant sinner, then those he had ministered to were not really married, did not receive Communion, were not truly baptized, and so on. Most leaders of the church agreed with Augustine that we cannot ask people to have so much depend on the unknowable moral purity of the priesthood. In securing the condemnation of the Donatists, Augustine made it clear that priest's authority rests on his proper ordination, not his personal virtue. That made Christian authority purely hierarchical, dependent only on one's place in an institutional structure, but it gave people priests whose legitimacy they could trust.[9]

Fortunately, for all priests and bishops since, we are not expected to be sinless. The priest is also a piece of clay that God is working on. The priest is also fallen and comes to God seeking repentance and resources for a life that is ever growing closer to the image of Christ. Both lay and ordained are all making the journey together. Both are striving to get nearer to being the person that God intends for us all.

## Conclusion

Becoming a vehicle of love is hard work. Every human being struggles with this work. We all have grudges; we all find it difficult to forgive those who have wronged us; and we all imagine that we really cannot live without this or that additional object (car, clothes, or vacation) in our lives.

The mistake many of us made is to imagine that all we need to do is to simply resolve "to do better." But sin has an addictive quality. Our inner selves surface and displace our rational commitment to the resolution. Overcoming our sinful propensities is not a matter of a rational decision. Instead, we have to go deep. We need a vehicle that works on our assumptions, habits, hopes, fears, and aspiration. We need a vehicle that exposes our vanity and laziness.

Herein is the power of the liturgy. As Sedgwick shows, the very pattern of the service does the hard work of relocation and transformation. We are relocated from the ephemeral and immediate to the world of the enduring and eternal. We are then transformed through the listening to the Word, through the offering of the self, through the acceptance of the

---

9. Placher, *A History of Christian Theology*, 114.

self (in all our weakness and fragility), and then and only then invited to seize the moment and live afresh as an agent of love in the world.

But, even then, (and it is a big and important "but") the Donatist controversy teaches us all that you live at the heart of the liturgy and still be—very much—a work in progress. A priest can still do the work of the liturgy, despite their failings. But even the priest needs the work of the liturgy to be used by God. We all need to fall in love with love. We all need to challenge the worlds of conscious and unconscious sin. It is a project requiring a lifetime. And in truth is never complete until we are made perfect in the presence of Christ.

## Bibliography

Augustine, St. *City of God*. London: Penguin, 1972.
Baard, Rachel Sophia. *Sexism and Sin-Talk: Feminist Conversations on the Human Condition*. Louisville: Westminster John Knox, 2019.
Markham, Ian. "The Survival of Conscience in a Post-Freudian and Post-Nietzsche World." *Sewanee Theological Review* 62 (2020) 573–90.
Placher, William C. *A History of Christian Theology: An Introduction*. Louisville: Westminster John Knox, 1983.
Sedgwick, Timothy F. *The Christian Moral Life: Practices of Piety*. Grand Rapids: Eerdmans, 1999.
———. *Sacramental Ethics: Paschal Identity and the Christian Life*. Philadelphia: Fortress, 1987.

# 10

# Moral Imperatives Brought on by our Sacramental Participation

CAYCE RAMEY

## Introduction

FROM THE ARMENIAN GENOCIDE to the pogroms of Stalinist Russian; from the slaughter of indigenous people across North and South America to the Rwandan genocide; from South African Apartheid to the dehumanization of women throughout the ages, there is no shortage of heart-breaking examples of fratricide within the human family, including what is arguably the most present sin in Western culture today, white supremacy. The church is as mired in these sins as anyone else. From papal bulls to a city on a hill; from Manifest Destiny to sermons of "slaves obey your masters" to owning slaves, to opposing civil rights, to hoarding wealth from stolen land and stolen people, the church continues with the world around it, to live in broken communion. Standing on the battlements of the Cape Coast slave-trading castle on the shores of Ghana in 2017, I could feel the direct, bitter, violent connection between my Christian forebearers who ran that fort and my own life as a priest in the Episcopal Church in Virginia, a diocese and denomination built on our participation in and the wealth of colonization, the betrayal and murder of indigenous people, and the enslavement of millions of African people.

Such violence and brokenness is anathema to the life of Christ witnessed in scripture. Jesus' living, preaching, teaching, and healing testify to his demand for communion among his children as he transgresses law after law that would deny the sanctity of God's created order of human kinship. Healing on the sabbath and teaching people to love their neighbors as much as they love themselves, Jesus even goes so far as to tell the people that reconciliation must precede worship at God's altar.

In a divisive and divided world, such gospel truths challenge our preferred independent existence. It's much easier inside and outside of the church to live as a benevolent benefactor or an ardent anti-establishmentarian, anything to keep a safe distance between ourselves and our neighbors. Relationship in community complicates our practice of faith and with our mental, emotional, physical, and spiritual resources feeling like so much unrenewable energy in this age, Jesus' demand for interdependence that impacts our existence is nearly unbearable. Yet we must bear it. We must be in communion with each other if we ever hope to be in communion with our Lord. Our longing to participate in the life of our savior, particularly through the sacrament of holy Eucharist, challenges us to ask how we should understand our current sacramental life in the midst of brokenness? What can we make of our embodied theology whereby we continue a sacramental practice in discord with Christ's gospel? Particularly in light of the Church's participation in the white supremacy of the transatlantic slave trade and the ongoing effects of the systems of chattel slavery which built the West, Jesus' demand and our desire for communion create a new moral imperative. Jesus requires communion with neighbor to be in communion with him. Yet we are not without hope. Even in the depths of our darkest history and most violent present, Christ's redeeming love assures us we can be saved from our sin. To find communion with Jesus, we must leave our gifts at the altar and first go and be reconciled to our siblings, sisters, and brothers.

## Biblical

Throughout the Gospels, Jesus demonstrates that, "the human being is worth more than any religious rule."[1] While Puerto and Perroni make that claim based on Jesus' interactions with women in the book of Matthew, we can see in all four Gospels Jesus choosing divine restoration

---

1. Navarro Puerto and Perroni, *Gospels*, 284.

over human regulation and prioritizing right relationship over required worship. Jesus heals on the sabbath—a woman with a spirit in Luke 13, a blind man in John 9, and a man with a withered hand in Mark 3 and Matthew 12. Later, in summarizing the Law and declaring what is most necessary to the life of faith, Jesus says plainly in all three Synoptics that people are to love God with all they are and love their neighbors as they love themselves. Holding these two maxims, loving others as ourselves and choosing people before piety, we begin to see that we must be in communion before one can receive communion.

Particularly resonant with our own day and powerful in its portrayal of these principles, the Gospel of Matthew shows Jesus engaging a community where division among the faithful was common, where political and religious leaders had been "coopted," where "the great majority" of people held no formal power, and where inside and outside status was separated by stark delineation.[2] In Matthew, Jesus challenges allegiances and empire,[3] Jewish and Roman kinship understanding, complacent religious leaders, and "well-off" congregants.[4] Jesus (re)defines qualifying membership in community based not on geography or family lineage but on baptism, faith, and obedience, i.e., doing the will of the Father.[5] The Gospel of Matthew warns the believers that "loyalty to Jesus will disrupt households,"[6] and reiterates that "ethical integrity" takes precedence over the "obligations of the cult."[7]

In the Sermon on the Mount of chapter 5, particularly in verses 21–24, Jesus, echoing Moses on Mt. Sinai, engages what it means to be in right relationship with God. Jesus deepens the crowds' understanding of the law as a love-focused life driving for "radical obedience to God's commands" that reaches "not only to the level of action but to the intensions and dispositions that lead to action."[8]

'You have heard that it was said to those of ancient times, "You shall not murder"; and "whoever murders shall be liable to judgement." But I say to you that if you are angry with a brother or sister, you will be liable

---

2. Case-Winters, *Matthew*, 351.
3. Case-Winters, *Matthew*, 1.
4. Levine and Brettler, *Jewish Annotated New Testament*, 466.
5. Levine and Brettler, *Jewish Annotated New Testament*, 465.
6. Levine and Brettler, *Jewish Annotated New Testament*, 465. Cf. Matt 10:34–37.
7. Senior, *Matthew*, 54.
8. Senior, *Matthew*, 53.

to judgement; and if you insult a brother or sister, you will be liable to the council; and if you say, "You fool," you will be liable to the hell of fire. So when you are offering your gift at the altar, if you remember that your brother or sister has something against you, leave your gift there before the altar and go; first be reconciled to your brother or sister, and then come and offer your gift" (Matt 5:21–24)[9]

While Jewish tradition required reconciliation with neighbor before one could be reconciled with God,[10] Jesus expands the understanding of what actions required reconciliation, moving well beyond physical violence to encompass the more prevalent verbal traumas and "microaggressions," the inner anger and outward speech that can lead to violence. Here again, Jesus prioritizes right relationship with brother or sister even over such central acts of Jewish worship as Temple sacrifice.

What's more, Matthew 5 speaks forcefully to the power of the "other" in the life of the faithful. Even if one had travelled miles at great cost and risk to reach the temple, Jesus commands people to think *before* approaching the altar of the Lord, not only about how they understand their relationship to God and neighbor but also to consider how the "other" views that same relationship. In doing so, Jesus locates the power to determine right relationship outside of oneself. Jesus demands believers consider the views, opinions, and understandings of another, and that they *act* on them. We all must leave our gift and "go"—turning, repenting of an unreconciled approach to God's altar, surrendering priority of place in the Temple worshipers, and seeking the one who believes they have been wronged. Truly, one must be in communion before one can partake of communion.

## Sacramental Imperative

Holy Communion has at its core a drive toward unity and identity. Unity with and identity in Jesus. With holy Eucharist particularly, among the Christian sacraments shared across denominations, the intimacy of sharing and receiving the body and blood of Christ is unequaled. Regardless of what one believes about *how* Christ is present, Christians unite themselves with Jesus and seek to "become what [they] receive."[11]

---

9. Unless otherwise noted, all biblical citations in this chapter are from the NRSV.
10. Levine and Brettler, *Jewish Annotated New Testament*, 11.
11. Augustine, "Sermon 272."

Yet from the first human longings for such intimacy, we are drawn into and challenged in our sacramental participation by Jesus' teachings. Not only does Jesus place right relationship before even sacramental piety, but also he goes further, indicating in the parable of the sheep and the goats (Matt 25), that the righteous and the unrighteous will be separated and selected by the way they treat the other. While readings and reflections on this passage usually stop with verse 45, ("Then he will answer them, 'Truly I tell you, just as you did not do it to one of the least of these, you did not do it to me'"), it is verse 46 that shifts our imperative understanding from the need for right action to the realm of our salvation, "And these will go away into eternal punishment, but the righteous into eternal life.'" Our relationship with Jesus, our salvation, is defined by our actions with and toward the other. 1 John puts it another way, "Those who say, 'I love God,' and hate their brothers or sisters, are liars; for those who do not love a brother or sister whom they have seen, cannot love God whom they have not seen. The commandment we have from him is this: those who love God must love their brothers and sisters also" (1 John 4:20–21).

Sacramentally, then, to participate in communion with Christ we must be in communion with our siblings, sisters, and brothers. Yet today, as we face the realities of the global pandemics of racial injustice and COVID-19, we are not, in fact, in communion with our siblings. Nowhere is that clearer than in the ongoing sin of white supremacy; not (just) the white-robed cross-burning instantiations, though certainly those still exists, but the beliefs and systems that enshrine white bodies, white comfort, and white history, knowledge, and values as being of ultimate worth. The church incarnates this through the ongoing effects of our participation in the stolen land and stolen people of the colonial endeavor and chattel slavery.

## Historical Sin

From humanity's first steps out of Eden, God warns the children of Eve and Adam that "sin is lurking at the door" (Gen 4:7) and from the first family of human creation one sibling seeks to deal with his own insecurities by visiting murderous violence upon the other. Humanity then carries this fratricidal inheritance through centuries of atrocities, the colonial genocide of indigenous peoples of the Americas, the Holocaust, the Cambodian genocide, and others.[12] Each of these vile periods requires exploration and reflection in the context of sacramentally driven moral imperatives, yet, it is white supremacy, most evident in the ongoing effects of our systems of chattel slavery in the United States and the colonialism of the church in western Europe, that is currently present and powerful in a unique way in American culture—what one mainline ecclesial body called, "the most salient and pressing issue we face, and a deeply entrenched and pervasive obstacle in our common life."[13] Witnessed through inequalities in healthcare, education, housing, employment, policing, and more, White supremacy is *the* example of broken communion with God and our neighbor, traceable as the defining strand through so much of the violence of our past and the driving force of our present. White supremacy denies the *imago Dei* of all but a small minority of the people of this earth and seeks to supplant the authority of our Savior with the lordship of white men, largely, and white people more generally. Such insidious dehumanization of "other" people based on their race and the idolatress deification of white men denies the very nature of Love incarnate and becomes the root from which we can trace all manner of dis-oriented relationship. White supremacy distorts the order of creation, making white, cis-gendered, straight, men as gods to fashion a world which they declare "good" for the perpetuation of their power.[14] So we need not create a false opposition among the claims of indigenous, LGBTQ+, disabled, Latinx, women or other peoples and groups to focus here on the particular way that our Black sisters, siblings, and brothers have "something against" us in the ongoing effects of the transatlantic slave trade and to claim that the church is compelled by our sacramental participation in the life of Christ to address it.

The white churches of the Global North built significant wealth as well as their social, cultural, and political power on the foundations of the transatlantic slave trade. This deep historical connection with systemic white supremacy is displayed in our church buildings and the myriad images of white Jesus in art, stained glass, bulletin covers and elsewhere;[15]

---

12. It is a particularly twisted perversion of the faith, then, that white people would apply the mark of Cain not to the people doing the killing but to those being killed.

13. House of Bishops Theology Committee, *White Supremacy*, 1.

14. This idea was originally posed to me and should be credited to the Rev. Jabriel Ballentine in a conversation that occurred in 2020.

15. Loth et al., *Windows of Grace*, 16. For just one of a myriad of examples see the "Lee Memorial Window" of St. Paul's Richmond, in which two different depictions of

in the racial makeup of congregations;[16] in our governance structures and documents explicitly defending the institution of chattel slavery;[17] in the church's silence in the era of lynching in America;[18] and the list goes on. Persistent and repeated critiques by Black Liberation Theology, Womanist Theology, Feminist Theology, Postcolonial Theology, and others, go unheeded while white supremacy remains to beloved community. Even the church's most sacred aspect of worship, the sacrament of holy Eucharist, is today built on, influenced by, and subject to the forces of white supremacy and the ongoing effects of chattel slavery. From de jur and de facto segregated congregations, to separate seating during eucharistic services,[19] to attempts to found entirely separate racially segregated dioceses,[20] the current enacted and doctrinal eucharistic theology of the church continues unaffected by the events of the transatlantic slave trade. Yet the impacts of our participation in those events remains.

## Cape Coast

Cape Coast Castle was established as a trading outpost by the Swedish and later captured by the British and built into a castle in the 1600s. At its most profitable, approximately seventy thousand people annually were sold through the castle as slaves.[21] I was visiting the castle as part of a renewed ministry partnership between churches in Ghana, the UK, and the United States. Our tour began in the male slave dungeon and spiraled through the female slave dungeon, the "Door of No Return," and the offices and residences of the castle garrison. The tour ended at the chapel.

---

Moses resemble General Robert E. Lee, commander of the Southern forces during the U.S. Civil War, inverting the Exodus narrative and casting the man who was leading the military fight to keep people enslaved instead in the role of liberator of white life.

16. Lipka, "Racially Diverse U.S. Religious Groups."

17. Shattuck, *Episcopalians and Race*, 9. Particularly, see the creation of the Protestant Episcopal Church in the Confederate States of America

18. Shattuck, *Episcopalians and Race*, 25. The Episcopal Church was silent from revival of the KKK in 1915 until the 1919 General Convention when it passed the first "churchwide" antilynching resolution, born mostly out of racial paternalism rather than justice.

19. Shattuck, *Episcopalians and Race*, 8.

20. Prichard, *Episcopal Church*, 179.

21. Ghana Museums & Monuments Board, "Cape Coast Castle."

The chapel at Cape Coast Castle was the site of the first Anglican celebration of holy Eucharist in Ghana[22] and was built directly above the male slave dungeon. There is even a large shaft outside the door to the chapel so that the guards could attend services while they monitored the captives below. Standing in that chapel, I realized that holy Communion, the very body and blood of Christ, was offered, blessed, broken, and received on top of the bodies and blood of thousands of enslaved Africans being captured, bound, broken, and sold. I had, just minutes before, heard our guide detail the eighteen-inches of compacted detritus, excrement, and human remains excavated from the dungeon below and so I stood in that chapel, my reality forever transformed, and was compelled to ask myself, "where was Jesus in this Eucharistic moment?"

My faith, my heart, and my vocation were broken open in that moment. There before me was the foundation of my church laid bare. There below me was the truth of the poverty of the theology and traditions in which I had been trained. Those things which I had been taught were universal truths were instead exposed as the warped perversion of God's love. Christians were making Eucharist, *thanksgiving*, over the tortured traumatized captive children of God and claiming that Jesus—the great liberator, the good shepherd, and the bringer of justice—was fine with it. I was no longer fine with it, the very sacraments by which I was supposed to know my Lord most intimately were now suspect.

For the remainder of the ten-day trip to Ghana and the throughout the years that followed, I kept asking myself, "Where was Jesus?" I didn't have an answer. The standard answer—that Jesus was present both in the dungeon and in the chapel—was insufficient even to my own experience as a cis-gendered, straight, white American man. Tragically, the answers arising from the experiences of the men and women held at Cape Coast Castle have been lost. However, the chaplain of the fort captured a revealing and convicting reality, none the less, in a report to his superiors in September, 1766. The Rev. Philip Quaque, the second Anglican chaplain of the fort, wrote that though he was performing his duties as chaplain to the best of his abilities, he "still found none, of what sect or Denomination soever that was willing or disposed to commence Communicants, or embrace the Rapture of the Lord's Supper, and the only plea they offer is

---

22. According to the staff of Cape Coast Castle in Cape Coast, Ghana. Additionally, the Castle has a shaft outside of the chapel door that opens to the dungeon below to enable even the guards to attend services while still being able to monitor the men below.

that while they are here acting against Light & Conscience, they dare not come to that holy Table."[23] The men tasked with guarding the enslaved refused to attend services because they knew too well that if they should stand before God and receive holy Communion while participating in the violence and evil of the transatlantic slave trade, they would be condemned. The soldiers understood that the moral imperative of the eucharistic moment required their own voluntary excommunication.

From Ghana to America and from 1766 to the present, then, is a small step. My own Anglican tradition is directly connected to the earliest Jamestown settlements. Alexandria and Richmond, Virginia, the sites of two of the largest slave trading operations in the U.S. for decades, remain parts of the Episcopal Diocese of Virginia. Our wealth, land, power, and prestige are inexorably linked with our national and ecclesial foundations in the economy of stolen land and stolen bodies.[24] A number of our chapels and altars including the altar at which I, as an Episcopal[25] priest, serve, sit atop the body and blood-soaked lands of former plantations.[26] Yet unlike the garrison of Cape Coast Castle, we persist in celebrating and receiving holy Communion.

## Theological

Just as the church's history is enmeshed in its participation with chattel slavery, so too our current eucharistic theology is steeped in white supremacy. Despite white theologians' general lack of engagement with their own whiteness, they have, in fact, been writing and talking about race all along,[27] though few are willing or able to explicitly center "white theology," "white supremacy," or the events of the transatlantic slave trade in their work.

Two important exceptions are James W. Perkinson's seminal work, *White Theology: Outing Supremacy in Modernity*, and Katie Walker

23. Carretta and Reese, *Philip Quaque*, 41.

24. Kendi, *Stamped from the Beginning*, 1–158.

25. The Episcopal Church is the recognized Anglican church of the Worldwide Anglican Communion in the United States.

26. Massey and Massey, *Colonial Churches of Virginia*, as well as an inquiry of diocesan clergy returned at least eight parishes known to have transitioned directly from plantation land to church property. The original boundaries of the Diocese of Virginia included all of the Commonwealth.

27. Perkinson, *White Theology*, 190.

Grimes' powerful eucharistically-centered, *Christ Divided: Antiblackness as Corporate Vice*. Perkinson takes an interdisciplinary approach to examining white culture in the United States and the foundations of white supremacy as an inherently theological framework for living.[28] Grimes focuses tightly on a Catholic Christian Ethics approach to critiquing "white privilege" and "white supremacy" on her way to advocating for the alternative term "antiblackness supremacy" and a recognition that "Catholic theology has yet to recognize chattel slavery's fundamental theological significance"[29] through a shift in eucharistic practice in the Catholic Church.[30] These few white theologians advocate for the centrality of truthful grappling with white supremacy flowing from the events of the transatlantic slave trade in theological work. Citing the deep need for white theologians and theology to face the death, violence, trauma, and suffering caused by white supremacy throughout history and the present, Perkinson, for example, advocates broadly for the end of white supremacy as white culture has constructed it and the radical reorientation of white life overall.[31] By contrast, Grimes narrowly focuses on critiquing holy Eucharist by declaring "antiblackness supremacy" a "vice" and advocating for a "sacramental realism" whereby the church eschews the "cultic eucharist" in favor of a "real meal" as a praxis-grounded antidote for the current state of Catholic eucharistic practice.[32] Perkinson and Grimes call for radical transformation and re-imagination, which requires recognizing and admitting different understandings of history, different understandings of the threats facing the church,[33] and a new understanding of vocation for white Christians.[34] Instead of "consuming" Black life, the white church and its theologians must be formed under Black authority and shaped by Black culture and spirituality through the work of white people themselves,[35] without requiring Black heroes to teach or to save,

---

28. Perkinson, *White Theology*, 2.

29. Grimes, *Christ Divided*, xvii.

30. I will discuss the space Grimes tries to occupy between liturgical praxis and theological foundations later in this work.

31. Perkinson, *White Theology*, 214.

32. Grimes, *Christ Divided*, xvii, 205–6, 221–22, 230.

33. Grimes, *Christ Divided*, 210.

34. Perkinson, *White Theology*, 236–37.

35. Perkinson, *White Theology*, 241–43.

because, as it stands now, the white church is limiting or even preventing the celebration of Eucharist.[36]

Yet overall, white theologians exploring whiteness, white supremacy, or slavery and holy Eucharist are few.[37] When Eucharist is addressed in the context of white supremacy, communion-hoping-to-create-future-unity is usually the primary framework for reflection. Gutierrez' work is often sited and is still both representative of and influential in understanding the liturgical celebration of the Eucharist as a driving force for future unity among people to transform society at some point.[38] Future-unity focused critiques speak of the power of a shared meal and the joining of participants into the body of Christ[39] and argue that the very act of sharing in the liturgical celebration, regardless of the reality or relationships within the community, can transform white-supremacist structures.

Far more than these and other critiques, Postcolonial Theology does address eucharistic praxis and theology.[40] For example, in his 2015 collection, Carvalhaes engages sacramental theology, including the Eucharist, around the world with the pointed echo of Audre Lord's words reverberating throughout, "The master's tools will never dismantle the master's house."[41] Similarly, Suna-Koro argues for the necessary centrality of sacramental theology while advocating for "confronting and working through history to free sacraments." Suna-Koro even challenges the sacramentality of the sacraments when justice is not present.[42]

Ultimately, however, like Suna-Koro and most theologians, white and Black, even Perkinson and Grimes leave the fundamental nature of contemporary eucharistic theology unchanged, and echo the contention that the violent history of Christianity "does not exhaust [the Eucharist's] redemptive thrust and healing potential."[43] These critiques present only a mild rebuke to the congregation at Cape Coast Castle four-hundred years ago and make a similarly mild adjustment to modern churchgoers,

---

36. Grimes, *Christ Divided*, 201, 227.
37. Van Wyngaard, "White Theology in Dialogue," 1.
38. Albertine, "The Eucharist," 356.
39. Albertine, "The Eucharist," 356–57.
40. Though Jagessar and Burns, writing in 2007, do note that Christian worship has not yet been critiqued to the same degree as systematic, biblical, and other theological disciplines. Jagessar and Burns, "Liturgical Studies and Christian Worship," 39.
41. Carvalhaes, *Liturgy in Postcolonial Perspectives*, 1.
42. Suna-Koro, *In Counterpoint*, 187.
43. Suna-Koro, *In Counterpoint*, 173.

claiming we only need to understand better what we've always done. Together, these critiques offer an insufficient answer to those held in the dungeons of Cape Coast and on the plantations of Virginia and throughout the West.

## New Imperative

By approaching the altar of the Lord before we are reconciled with our siblings, we are celebrating the Eucharist "unworthily" (1 Cor 11:27) to our condemnation. Our eucharistic participation in the life of Christ requires a new imperative. Jesus teaches the humility of right relationship before worship, yet the church continues to practice a depraved sacramental theology that affirms, rather than challenges, the status quo of shattered communion among God's children. Instead, we need new eucharistic theology with the humility to: (a) take seriously the experiences of oppressed and marginalized people as necessary sources of eucharistic theology, (b) heal the moral injury of those perpetrating oppression, and (c) enable eucharistic theology to become a driving force for God's love as justice in our world. Yet, humility in Western Christianity—often in the form of a sacrificial or servanthood ethos—has brought violence and oppression to the perceived enemies of straight white cisgender male leadership of the Church for hundreds of years;[44] and in the context of the sin and violence of white supremacy, both inside and outside of the church, our current understanding of humility is insufficient to the task. Required instead, is a theology of eucharistic humility as the practice of acknowledgement, submission, and transformation that enables us to live in right relationship with God and our neighbor. Eucharistic humility applied to the reality of white supremacy demands that the white

---

44. I.e., calls for submission of wives to husbands even unto violence and death, justification of chattel slavery, theologies of sacrifice or servanthood unequally applied, and more.

Black Liberation, Feminist, and Womanist theologians rightly declare that, "servanthood, in this country, in effect, has been servitude." These critiques help to set the limits of any proposed theology of eucharistic humility, particularly one which includes submission, and demand that humility moving forward be (re)defined not as the weapon of violence it has been but as submission of power, privilege, and all of who we are—including submission of our identity within white supremacy culture, even our Christian identity—to God's justice rather than our wills. Further, these critiques highlight the necessity of applying such a theology of eucharistic humility firmly within the bounds of the white church.

church, like the soldiers at Cape Coast Castle, recognize we have and continue to act "against Light & Conscience," living in and perpetuating broken relationship with our siblings, and that we: (a) take seriously the experience of BIPOC, (Black, Indigenous, People of Color) as necessary sources of a new eucharistic theology, (b) heal the moral injury of white people whose own relationship with God has been perverted by the idolatry of whiteness, and (c) enable and allow our new eucharistic theology to drive the white church into the world for love as justice, working to undo white supremacy in the systems we've created and perpetuated all these centuries. This work for unity in right relationship with God and our siblings demands the white church leave our gifts at the altar, voluntarily excommunicating ourselves, and go first to be reconciled through acknowledgement, submission, and transformation.

*Acknowledgement:* Eucharistic humility requires acknowledging three fundamental truths underlying current theology in the church: (a) the interrelatedness of historical, economic, and theological realities with holy Eucharist; (b) our current eucharistic theology perpetuates violence against our siblings; (c) and acknowledging that contemporary eucharistic theology perpetuates moral injury. Specifically, this work in undoing our white supremacy eucharistic theology means acknowledging the inequality of our embodiment.

Throughout the violence and oppression of Western colonial conquest and economic exploitation, we have continued to celebrate holy Eucharist. Yet the inextricable bond of our eucharistic theology with transatlantic slavery and white supremacy remains largely unacknowledged, demonstrating that such realities are inconsequential. We do not require equality to embody our eucharistic theology. Similarly, despite the distorting and damaging nature of white-centered spaces, we claim that (white) Jesus is present in our worship. White supremacist art and images across the church are legion. The stained-glass imagery alone is testimony enough that holy Eucharist can cohabitate with whiteness in spaces which perpetually deny the humanity of Black people.[45] We are serving the eucharistic Feast at the 'whites only' lunch counter.

---

45. Perkinson, *White Theology*, 177, observes: "Space cooperates with whiteness; white people have 'place'"—places built on plantation land, by the labor of people enslaved, or with money from the slave-economy, or filled with looming portraits of old white male clergy enslavers serve as white eucharistic spaces which deny the humanity of African Americans.

Additionally, our eucharistic language is full of white-dominated values.[46] This, in turn, reinforces the value of white modes of speech and associates white linguistic patterns with the divine rites of soteriological grace bound in holy Eucharist, excluding people that deviate. Our silence incarnates "whiteness [as] a conspiracy of silence about history."[47] We neither talk about race nor acknowledge whiteness in our liturgy. We exclude vast swaths of Black experiences and history, damaging Black lives in the process.[48] Such a "silence about history" is antithetical to anamnesis, the foundation of our enacted eucharistic theology.

White speech and silence are not only damaging to Black people but also perpetuate the moral injury of our white parishioners.[49] Moral injury as, "the psychospiritual impact of participating in the subjugation, abuse, and murder of other human beings," recognizes that these acts "violate our core beliefs about what it means to be human, to be moral, and to be Christian."[50] Our current eucharistic theology is locked in a "fiction of independence" that it and we can somehow persist in a state of grace

---

46. "It [white speech] is periodized in well-regulated time and timing, wedded to segregations of meaning, and turn-taking in argument, and clarity of intentionality rooted in a thing called an 'individual.'" Perkinson, *White Theology*, 182.

47. Perkinson, *White Theology*, 182.

48. While much of our eucharistic language in particular and our *Book of Common Prayer* language as a whole is biblically-based, there is still more than sufficient room within our liturgies to incorporate modern concepts. For example, Eucharistic Prayer C (p. 370) reads, in part, "At your command all things came to be: the vast expanse of interstellar space, galaxies, suns, the planets in their courses, and this fragile earth, our island home." Surely if we can find room in our liturgical language for modern concepts like "interstellar space" then there is room enough for the concept of racial justice.

49. The concept of moral injury grew out of work with combat veterans in the 1990s, following the Persian Gulf War when PTSD-like symptoms were reported by soldiers, sailors, airmen, and Marines who did not have an accompanying triggering event that met the formal definition for trauma. Pastoral Theologian Larry Kent Graham defines moral injury as "the burden of harm and the diminishment of vitality that arises in individual and communities when we (or others) violate our moral compasses. . . . Moral injury comes about when our lives and the lives of our social groups diverge from what we believe to be the best in ourselves, or when our moral actions lead to a diminishment of value for self and others." Graham, *Moral Injury*, 13.

50. Walker-Barnes and Harper, *I Bring the Voices of My People*, 72. The white church has practiced a eucharistic theology that allowed communing congregants separately by race, when Black parishioners were admitted to a church at all. We continue to practice a eucharistic theology that countenances inviting the presence of Christ to inhabit elements sitting under the watchful eyes of Confederate "saints" who killed, fought, and died to keep people enslaved. See St. Paul's RVA, "Bending Toward Truth."

entirely separate from both the full humanity of our Black and Brown siblings and our own whiteness.

Acknowledgment in eucharistic humility for the ongoing sins of white supremacy demands we leave our gift at the altar and cease receiving holy Eucharist unworthily. Voluntary excommunication acknowledges publicly, through action not just more empty words, the status of our broken communion and the beginning of our understanding of the depths of our responsibility and the severity of our sin. We cannot repair that which we never admit. Our own excommunication serves not as punishment but as the ultimate and necessary acknowledgement of the broken reality which already exists—our broken relationship with God, (which is our very salvation), and our broken relationship with our siblings, sisters, and brothers (which is one and the same). Then we will be able to begin our repair by submitting to God's justice.

*Submission:* The foundation of eucharistic humility is acknowledgement. The incarnation of eucharistic humility is submission.[51] Not submission as it's been used to subjugate and control but submission which shifts the church from too-quick reconciliation toward the deep repentance required for restoration. Submission to God's justice requires public exposure of the sinful excuses and false identities used to keep supremacist leadership and evil systems in control. Submission to God's justice requires restorative actions, like those of Zacchaeus, paying back fourfold (Luke 19:8), with the wealth, buildings, and altars with which we enact our eucharistic theology. Specifically, this work in undoing our white supremacy eucharistic theology means the white church must submit by accepting the consequences of our actions and beginning to make repair and restitution.

Reconciliation as currently defined and practiced, "does nothing to repair the harm of systemic racism or to dismantle the system of white supremacy. It is a therapeutic approach designed to make white people feel better about the unjust system in which they live and with which they are complicit."[52] The white church must abandon our ego-centric ineffective efforts at reconciliation.

Instead, submission to God's justice in the context of undoing white supremacy eucharistic theology invites the white church to accept our

---

51. Augustine demonstrated that "submission to God is the characteristic expression of humility." Submission of our will to God's justice compels us to act. Dunnington, "Humility," 29.

52. Walker-Barnes and Harper, *I Bring the Voices of My People*, 86.

own excommunication. We have broken communion with God, accepting broken communion with our BIPOC siblings. Exploring eucharistic theology in relationship to the violent regime of Chilean dictator Augusto Pinochet, Cavanaugh concludes that excommunication be reserved for sins "which impugn the identity of the body of Christ"[53] and that excommunication was the proper response to torturers or to those in a position to stop it who fail to do so.[54] The church has been both the torturer and the one failing to act.[55] We must accept the need for our sacramental separation without controlling the outcome. We must go to the land (of justice) that God will show us, surrendering control of the timeline and milestones, accepting that we will not define the terms or conditions of our parole and trusting in God that when we submit and surrender to God, God will be faithful and just.

Voluntary excommunication is a necessary piece of eucharistic humility in submission to God's justice for us, so that our common life may be transformed into right relationship with God and our neighbor.

*Transformation:* Christians believe we have a right to comfort that extends to our eucharistic theology. We believe the sacraments should bring us peace. We believe Jesus is always present, giving grace alone, and act as if Christ loves us without challenge or conviction. We come as consumers and leave when we're satisfied. We seek amazing grace and omit the demands of discipleship, trusting uncritically in a eucharistic theological system built to reinforce the status quo. We must instead empty ourselves of the unequal distribution of power and privilege we have created in the West and offer our selves, our souls and bodies, to be transformed. Specifically, this work in undoing our white supremacy eucharistic theology means we must be transformed by the redirected application and surrender of the unjust power we have amassed and inherited through the ongoing effects of the transatlantic slave trade enshrined in our cultural, governance, and economic structures, and in our theology.

White people have been made gods by white supremacy. We daily exercise the power of life and death over Black bodies in the United

---

53. Cavanaugh, *Torture and Eucharist*, 247.
54. Cavanaugh, *Torture and Eucharist*, 254, 256.
55. Episcopal Church, "Door of Return."

States, with our system of policing,[56] the law of stand-your-ground,[57] or unjust education, healthcare, voting, and housing policies; and when we daily exercise that power, we are, once again, being conformed to the culture white supremacy has made.[58] White people believe we have a right to comfort[59] that extends to our eucharistic theology. We believe white Jesus is always present, giving grace alone to the saints assembled in congregations which through purpose and apathy remain white spaces for white people. We make no repentance for the wealth we've amassed, the privileges we enjoy, or the power we exercise. We claim we are loved without any challenge or conviction that requires us to alter our altars or our traditions. We believe worship should bring white people peace and that holy Eucharist is never about judgement or correction. We believe we can trust the [holy] system, just like we trust all the systems made for our benefit;[60] so we trust uncritically the eucharistic theological system built largely from the experiences of and by white Western European men. We must instead empty ourselves of the power and privilege we have seized through the transatlantic slave trade and white supremacy. We need transformation.

Transformation requires white people to face "the midnight horror of [our] own racialized history."[61] We must immerse ourselves in the historical and ongoing realities of our sin. We cannot be set free by a truth which we deny. Transformation continues through humble submission to God's justice, whereby "oppressors must give up or lose oppressive power, as oppressed people are empowered for discipleship."[62] We must both use and share the power we have to transform the way we do theology, the way we disciple believers, the way we form our clergy, the way we believe, so that the lives and experiences of our BIPOC siblings are not just present but central to how and what we believe. Transformation requires a kenotic self-emptying of our identity in deified whiteness by

---

56. George Floyd, Sandra Bland, Trayvon Martin, Pamela Turner, Breonna Taylor, Tamir Rice, Stephon Clark, Natasha McKenna, Eric Garner, Michelle Shirley, Atatiana Jefferson, and more.

57. These are just a few examples of the way in which white people and structures exercise power over Black and Brown bodies.

58. Walker-Barnes and Harper, *I Bring the Voices of My People*, 78.

59. DiAngelo and Dyson, *White Fragility*, 100.

60. Walker-Barnes and Harper, *I Bring the Voices of My People*, 78.

61. Walker-Barnes and Harper, *I Bring the Voices of My People*, 187.

62. Townes, *Troubling in My Soul*, 216.

adopting a eucharistic humility in a redeveloped eucharistic theology. We must transform our selves and our theology as part of our voluntarily excommunicating so that and until we are able to answer, "Where was Jesus at the Cape Coast Castle celebration of holy Eucharist atop the male slave dungeon?"

Acknowledgement, submission, and transformation must all take place in community, in the church. Through it all, we cannot give up meeting and worshiping together. Just as God does not desire the death of the sinner so too must we not destroy ourselves and our community. Our sin must die. Our sinful systems must die. We must die to our sin and be resurrected. All of which requires us to stay in relationship, broken as it is, with one another and with Jesus. We cannot hope to be transformed without Christ. Our deep longing for the substance of holy bread and wine, for the intimacy of most holy body and blood, can and will continue to keep us returning to Jesus. Like any fast, voluntary excommunication will draw us closer and help us experience the love, justice, and grace we need to make the changes required for right relationship in ourselves, our church, and our world. And like any fast, having pushed us to repentance, voluntary excommunication will end. Exactly what and how an end is not for the white church to decide even though such uncertainty and lack of control is new and frightening to us. We must hold to the promise that God is faithful and just, that having confessed our sin, we can and will be restored. Until then, I do not know exactly what our liturgies might look like or how a rhythm of life for a community could operate, and a full exploration and development of such questions is beyond the scope of this work, I believe that we can and must find a worshipful embodiment of a theology of humility that encourages our eucharistic longing; supports our acknowledgment, submission, and transformation; works to rebuild trust with our BIPOC siblings; and leads us as a church-resurrected back to the altar of God.

## Conclusion

The communion Jesus demands has been and continues to be broken by unimaginable violence and systemic sin, including the most present sin in Western culture today, white supremacy. Genocide, conquest and colonization, the murder and enslavement of millions—the inseparable history of the church and empire has littered our past with the blood of the slaughtered while twisting theology to insulate us from the consequences of our actions. There is a direct, bitter, violent connection in our sacramental worship between the chapel of Cape Coast Castle built atop a slave dungeon and the altars of our Lord sitting atop plantation land, in chapels built by the wealth of chattel slavery.

The gospel both compels us to right relationship with God and our neighbor and shows us the way. Jesus' life on earth shows us radical, challenging, revolutionary love and all the ways that such Love will reorient our lives, topple empire, and defeat death itself so that we might live in communion with Christ and one another. "Do this in remembrance of me." Our desire for sacramental participation in that sacred life of Love demands we submit in humility, repent and be saved. Yet, our current eucharistic theology continues mired in white supremacy. Our efforts toward reconciliation without repentance, toward justice without truth, toward Eucharist without communion are beyond ineffective, they are actively perpetuating the evil and violence they claim to counter.

In order to address the historical violence, theological failings, and the biblical mandate of our participation in the sacrament of holy Eucharist, we must work to undo the white supremacy of our church, our liturgy, and our theology in order to undo the white supremacy of our governments, schools, and societies. We must recognize that we have already affected our own separation, our own exclusion from full communion with Christ through our exclusion from full communion with our BIPOC siblings, sisters, and brothers.

The work begins with voluntary excommunication—the moral imperative of our sacramental participation and the first step toward answering the challenge of white supremacy and our participation in chattel slavery. The work continues as we claim the authority and agency required to live in humility and submission to Jesus, recognizing the experiences of BIPOC as authoritative sources of theology, and recontextualizing sacramental participation outside the boundaries of Sunday morning church walls (physical or electronic) and into the movements around the globe for justice and liberation.

Voluntary excommunication will draw us closer to the source of the love, justice, and grace we need to make the changes required for right relationship in ourselves, our church, and our world and to be restored. This is good news. God has not abandoned us nor barred the way or our return. We can rejoice that there is a path of redemption offered us to redeem even that which feels broken beyond repair between the peoples of the world. We can know the love and peace of restoration and resurrection. We will and must, then, continue being, worshiping, and ministering together while we work out with fear and trembling the path ahead. So that compelled by our desire to participate in the sacramental life of Christ and by Jesus' sacramental participation in our lives, we will be able to transform our theology from an affirmation of our superiority into a ritual of submission and humility that leads us to reconciliation. Then, in remade communion with our neighbors we will find communion with our God.

## Bibliography

Albertine, Richard P. "The Eucharist in a Liberation Context." *AFER* 31 (1989) 352–61.

Augustine of Hippo. "Sermon 272: On the Day of Pentecost to the Infants, On the Sacrament." https://stromata.co/sermon-272-on-the-day-of-pentecost-to-the-infants-on-the-sacrament/.

Carretta, Vincent, and Ty M. Reese, eds. *The Life and Letters of Philip Quaque, the First African Anglican Missionary*. Race in the Atlantic World, 1700–1900. Athens: University of Georgia Press, 2010.

Carvalhaes, Cláudio, ed. *Liturgy in Postcolonial Perspectives: Only One Is Holy*. 1st ed. Postcolonialism and Religions. New York: Palgrave Macmillan, 2015.

Case-Winters, Anna. *Matthew: A Theological Commentary on the Bible*. 1st ed. Belief: A Theological Commentary on the Bible. Louisville: Westminster John Knox, 2015.

Cavanaugh, William T. *Torture and Eucharist: Theology, Politics, and the Body of Christ*. Challenges in Contemporary Theology. Malden, MA: Blackwell, 1998.

DiAngelo, Robin, and Michael Eric Dyson. *White Fragility: Why It's So Hard for White People to Talk about Racism*. repr. ed. Boston: Beacon, 2018.

Dunnington, Kent. "Humility: An Augustinian Perspective." *Pro Ecclesia* 25 (2016) 18–43.

Episcopal Church. "Door of Return: Racial Truth and Reconciliation Pilgrimage to Ghana." https://www.episcopalchurch.org/video/ghana-reconciliation-pilgrimage/?wchannelid=5qemgoevv4&wmediaid=bxpdbfhtt5.

Ghana Museums & Monuments Board. "Cape Coast Castle, Cape Coast (1653)." https://ghanamuseums.org/forts/cape-coast-castle.php.

Graham, Larry Kent. *Moral Injury: Restoring Wounded Souls*. Nashville: Abingdon, 2017.

Grimes, Katie Walker. *Christ Divided: Antiblackness as Corporate Vice*. Minneapolis: Fortress, 2017.

House of Bishops Theology Committee. *Report for the House of Bishops from Its Theology Committee: White Supremacy, the Beloved Community, and Learning to Listen*. https://www.episcopalchurch.org/wp-content/uploads/sites/2/2020/11/bbc_hob_theo_cmte_report_on_white_supremacy.pdf.

Jagessar, Michael, and Stephen Burns. "Liturgical Studies and Christian Worship: The Postcolonial Challenge." *Black Theology* 5 (2007) 39–62. https://doi.org/10.1558/blth.2007.5.1.39.

Kendi, Ibram X. *Stamped from the Beginning: The Definitive History of Racist Ideas in America*. New York: Nation, 2016.

Levine, Amy-Jill, and Marc Zvi Brettler. *The Jewish Annotated New Testament*. New York: Oxford University Press, 2011.

Lipka, Michael. "The Most and Least Racially Diverse U.S. Religious Groups." *Pew Research Center*, July 27, 2015. https://www.pewresearch.org/fact-tank/2015/07/27/the-most-and-least-racially-diverse-u-s-religious-groups/.

Loth, Calder, et al., eds. *Windows of Grace: A Tribute of Love, the Memorial Windows of St. Paul's Episcopal Church, Richmond, Virginia*. Richmond: St. Paul's Episcopal Church, 2004.

Massey, Don W., and Sue Massey. *Colonial Churches of Virginia*. Charlottesville: Howell, 2003.

Navarro Puerto, Mercedes, and Marinella Perroni, eds. *Gospels: Narrative and History*. Society of Biblical Literature. The Bible and Women 2.1. Atlanta: SBL, 2015.

Perkinson, James W. *White Theology: Outing Supremacy in Modernity*. Black Religion, Womanist Thought, Social Justice. New York: Palgrave Macmillan, 2004.

Prichard, Robert W. *A History of the Episcopal Church*. Harrisburg, PA: Morehouse, 1999.

Schjonberg, Mary Frances. "House of Bishops Theology Committee Examining 'Infection' of White Supremacy." *Episcopal News Service*, June 21, 2019. https://www.episcopalnewsservice.org/2019/06/21/house-of-bishops-theology-committee-examining-infection-of-white-supremacy/.

Senior, Donald. *Matthew*. Abingdon New Testament Commentaries. Nashville: Abingdon, 1998.

Shattuck, Gardiner H. *Episcopalians and Race: Civil War to Civil Rights*. Religion in the South. Lexington: University Press of Kentucky, 2000.

St. Paul's RVA. "Bending Toward Truth: History and Reflections." *YouTube*, November 26. 2018. https://www.youtube.com/watch?v=RyQjj9ivtdc.

Suna-Koro, Kristine. *In Counterpoint: Diaspora, Postcoloniality, and Sacramental Theology*. Eugene, OR: Pickwick, 2017.

Townes, Emilie Maureen, ed. *A Troubling in My Soul: Womanist Perspectives on Evil and Suffering*. Bishop Henry McNeal Turner Studies in North American Blackreligion 8. Maryknoll, NY: Orbis, 1993.

Van Wyngaard, G. J. "White Theology in Dialogue with Black Theology: Exploring the Contribution of Klippies Kritzinger." *Hervormde Teologiese Studies* 72 (2016) 1–9. https://doi.org/10.4102/hts.v72i1.3033.

Walker-Barnes, Chanequa, and Lisa Sharon Harper. *I Bring the Voices of My People: A Womanist Vision for Racial Reconciliation*. Prophetic Christianity. Grand Rapids: Eerdmans, 2019.

# 11

# Sacraments and the Transformation of Desire

D*avid* T*remaine*

### A Changing Identity

M*y name has been* Addict *for a long time. Sex Addict, to be exact. It has been my name even before I could say the word out loud, but I can feel that it is time for that name to die. It has come time for that identity to be pruned, not so that it can be cut off and burned in the fire of ill-decision, but so that it might be able to sprout new growth, to create a cut in the bark through which new life might emerge. The name Sex Addict was a blessing and a grace. It helped me to take a breath in the midst of my suffering. It provided a reprieve from the chaos that bubbled up and consumed me, from the endless hours scrolling though pornography, from the lies and deceit and shame.*

*I am grateful for its time in my life, but I see now that calling myself a sex addict was a transition, an invitation, a narrow gate to greater life, to something bigger than a label and a behavior. It was a necessary step in my journey, it allowed me to name my suffering and open up to God in new and unexpected ways, but it was one step, and has pointed beyond itself to a greater, more whole, more uncertain end. I thought that sex was the root of the problem, that pornography was the cause of my suffering, but they were only intermediaries, and themselves were neither good nor bad.*

*I was wrestling with something else completely. Something deeper than pornography, deeper even than sex. It was the very source of life, the depth of God, the depth of myself, the yearning for something transcendent. For something to emerge that had not yet become. For something new.*

## The Development of Practice

In a 2019 article published in *Religious Studies* entitled "Spiritual Desire and Religious Practice," philosopher Clare Carlisle wrote about the distinctions between a practice and a habit. After interviewing religious practitioners from different faith traditions about their spiritual transformation over many years of practice, she wrote that "if practices are habits we deliberately cultivate, rather than fall into accidentally, this difference has effects so significant that practice might be contrasted to habit: in some cases at least, and certainly in the case of addiction, habit is a contraction of a person's sphere of activity and experience, while practice tends towards development and growth."[1] When we enact the behaviors of addiction, or any of the behaviors that cause suffering for ourselves or others, our world contracts, the possibilities become narrow. The purpose of taking on a spiritual practice, either individually or communally, is to transform our behaviors (i.e., our practices) and, rather than narrow our world, open ourselves up to endless possibilities. Through practice, then, the way we express the desires that lead to the behaviors of suffering are transformed, developed, and grown into expressions that make us whole and allow us to reconnect with the depth from which they emerge.

Maybe you identify as an addict, and maybe you do not, but either way we all know what it is to suffer and to cause suffering. Whether that manifests itself in specific addictions or any other painful behavior, it is a universal human experience. As Jesus says in his farewell discourse to his disciples at the end of John's gospel, our sorrow has the potential to turn into joy (John 16:16–24). Our suffering has the potential to be transformed into our greatest strength. The desires that drive our most painful impulses and behaviors have the potential to be realigned with the divine desire from which they emerge. In our lifelong journey of doing this work, how might the sacraments, the communal practices of

---

1. Carlisle, "Spiritual Desire," 431.

transformation, create the container for this work of transformation in and around us? How does engagement with the sacraments transform our desire over the course of our life?

Before we begin this exploration, take a moment to wonder what it is in you that is causing suffering, that is causing tension in your life. Where do you feel most unsure, most ungrounded, most destabilized? Without labelling that thing good or bad, without hating it or attaching to it, hold that place of suffering gently in your heart, and take a deep breath, as if you are giving it vital oxygen for survival, as if you are creating a wind that will sweep over its face. What do you feel in this moment? What does another breath bring you? Can you feel something new emerging where this tension and suffering have been held? Remember this feeling, and for now release this suffering, this tension, this frustration back into your depths, and imagine with me how our journey of transformation might include not just those things we love within us and around us, but those things we wish we would never see again, the places of deepest pain and suffering.

The sacraments can help us cultivate the ability to live with and breathe into our discomfort, our frustration, our anger, our pain, our sadness, and our painful impulses, without the goal of extinguishing that discomfort. The sacraments invite us to bring our painful impulses into daily practice, so that they change and transform slowly, over the entirety of our lives. True recovery from addiction is not abstinence but the transformation of desire, and the recovery of God's desire for us. True recovery means allowing the energy present in our painful desires to be reoriented, engaged, and cultivated into something new. Before we can examine how desire is transformed, we must examine the painful ways we live out desire individually and communally. We must examine suffering.

## Holding Suffering

At its core, Christianity is about suffering, and about creating ways to metabolize experiences of suffering into spiritual fuel for transformation. There are two different kinds of suffering. Most simply, these two sufferings can be defined as *necessary* and *unnecessary*. Necessary suffering is that which is embedded in the very fabric of existence. It is that suffering which is inextricably linked to having a body, being a human in relationship with other humans, and yearning for the divine. These forms of suffering include aging, death, physical illness or injury, love, change, uncertainty, addiction, and longing. Necessary suffering is the raw material of transformation. It is the tool we use to recover our truest identities. It is the path we walk to wholeness. It is our greatest teacher. Jesus' concern with this kind of suffering was not to pretend like it could be ended or avoided, but to teach others how to be with it, how to let it be a catalyst for transformation, and that there was no other way forward. Thus, he said things like "If any want to become my followers, let them deny themselves and take up their cross and follow me" (Matt 16:24 NRSV). Unnecessary suffering, on the other hand, includes all forms of human violence, oppression, disenfranchisement, and all other forms of systemic destruction. This is the kind of suffering that Jesus saw as diametrically opposed to the kingdom of heaven. Necessary suffering is our pathway to the kingdom of heaven, and it equips us to do the work of dismantling the unnecessary forms of suffering in order to bring that kingdom about.

In the face of this individual and communal reality, Christianity would do well to strive for a balance of these two nodes of suffering. Thankfully, there is a well of tradition, practice, and ritual on which we can draw to balance these important realities of our faith journey. Engaging with our individual suffering should lead us to engage with the suffering of the world, and thus to strive for a reduction in those unnecessary causes of suffering (e.g., systemic oppression, racism, violence, etc.) and a transformation of those necessary sufferings (e.g., physical illness, relational pain, anxiety, depression, addiction, etc.) into a deeper sense of self, authenticity, and connection. The goal is for Christianity and its practices to be effective in this transformation, and one part of that effectiveness grows from the communal and individual engagement with the sacraments, specifically in how they transform sources of suffering into sources of healing and salvation.

This is why we see Jesus speak so often about his own suffering as an integral part of his journey. He seeks out and communes with those who suffer the most. He addresses the suffering of the world, not just of individuals, but the suffering caused by systems that oppress, overpower, and disinherit. Of course, Jesus did not stop at simply recognizing or seeking out suffering, instead he taught and then embodied the path of transformation from suffering to joy, from woundedness to wholeness, from death to life. He implored not only his closest friends and disciples, but anyone who would listen, to engage with their own suffering and the suffering around them. Then he lived out that journey in his very body, holding the suffering of the world, receiving the suffering inflicted on him by the systems of oppression, and transforming that suffering into joy, hope, and new life. And yet, Jesus went even further than merely transforming suffering. He showed us that our goal is not to erase suffering and be left with only joy, or erase death and be left with only life, or erase wounds and only be left with wholeness, but to be able to hold it all together, recognize the suffering inherent in joy, the death inherent in life, the woundedness inherent in wholeness. Again, as he showed with his very body, the transformation of wounds does not remove them completely, but makes them sources of life, wholeness, and faith for others.

Even more than that, Jesus' death and resurrection did not end suffering. It did not end the oppressive systems of the world. It did not remove our ability to cause suffering for ourselves and others. If anything, in the almost two thousand years since Jesus' death and resurrection, the myriad ways we cause suffering, both internally and externally, individually and in the systems within which we operate, have grown exponentially. Instead, what Jesus did in his life, death, and resurrection, was give us the road map and the practices necessary to open ourselves up to that same transformation. The salvation he offered, then, was not an evacuation plan to remove us from the suffering of the world, but the way forward and the practices necessary to cultivate the ability to stay in the suffering, and to transform it as we are transformed. Thus, he could say, as he often did, that the kingdom of God was not somewhere over there, and it would not appear then, but was right here and right now. It is ours to cultivate in this life in this place in this time, co-creating with God.

Think of all the ways that you have suffered in your life. What are some ways you are suffering right now? There is no hierarchy of suffering. It can include the extremes of death and destruction, intense physical pain and anguish, as well as the monotonies of daily anxiety, worries, angry outbursts, feelings of inferiority, guilt, shame, and all manner of other experiences. As many ways as there are to suffer, there are that many ways that we cause suffering, both to ourselves and to one another. These could be categorized in several ways, but in the Christian theological tradition we have a helpful word for them all: *sin*.

## Sin and Finitude

Sin is a challenging concept, and for good reason. As helpful as it can be, it has too often been used for destruction, and to exclude and degrade huge swaths of people throughout history. It has been used to marginalized vital spiritual experiences and push important voices outside the bounds of "the church," and even the kingdom of heaven itself. In reclaiming powerful words, like sin, we may be able to rejoin that grand network of prophetic voices ushering in this new kingdom. The queer, feminine, trans, Black, brown, indigenous, and migrant voices that have for too long been excluded will be the very ones that offer the church salvation from itself.

How might we conceive of sin, then, in a way that leads to life rather than death, liberation rather than bondage, inclusion rather than exclusion? The verb "to sin" in the original Greek of the New Testament was ἁμαρτάνω (pronounced *hamartano*). This word does not imply evil action, divine retribution, eternal damnation, shame, or guilt. Instead, the word simply means "to miss the mark." It was originally a term used for archers to denote the action of aiming, shooting, and missing an arrow meant for a target. When we think about it in this way, sin becomes a source of hope, because in order to "miss the mark" we need to be aiming at it. The mark we miss is God's desire for our lives and for the life of the world. It is the divine desire, and we cannot miss it unless we are in some way connected to it. We cannot miss it if it is not our mark in the first place. So sin, rather than being an indication of our separation or estrangement from the divine, is in fact indicative of our inherent connection to the divine. It is the life of God residing in us, the Spirit dwelling in us, the divine desire operating in us that prompts our impulses to act.

When we sin, then, we act out of this desire but in a way that causes suffering rather than healing, alienation rather than love, separation rather than connection. These behaviors can be as simple as an angry outburst or as complicated as substance abuse and addiction. Even in the face of all this suffering, though, we can have hope that every action, even the most destructive and terrible, is a response to the divine desire that resides in us. Returning to Claire Carlisle's research on desire and practice, we see how the ways we respond to the divine desire goes astray:

> Once we understand spiritual desire to be a radically infinite desire for an object (or non-object) that remains at least partially indeterminate and elusive, the function as well as the character

of religious practices becomes clearer. All practices, like habits, give a particular, determinate form to desire: they are ways of channeling our desire, and thereby enacting it concretely. Infinite desires, however, have to be expressed in ways that preserve their infinity or indeterminacy—otherwise they are converted into finite desires, a contraction or displacement that theistic traditions identify as idolatry.[2]

As Carlisle names here, infinite desires, those that emerge from our connection to and yearning for the divine, "have to be expressed in ways that preserve their infinity or indeterminacy." When we cause suffering in the world, either to ourselves or to others, it is because we have made the object of our desire finite, and thus our practice constricts and harms us. As Carlisle says, the name we have for replacing an infinite object (or non-object) of desire (e.g., God, love, wholeness, peace) with a finite object of desire (e.g., pornography, alcohol, drugs, violence) is idolatry. Idolatry is what happens when the object of our desire becomes an end in itself rather than a means to an end. Instead of interacting with graven images as ways of communing with the divine we make them divine in and of themselves. We make money not a means to support one another's thriving, but an end in itself. We make sex about finite pleasure rather than about infinite connection and wholeness.

When we sin, we are missing the mark of the infinite, and responding to a finite object of desire in painful ways: ways that leave us empty, desolate, and suffering. What we require are practices, like the communal practices we know as sacraments, that will help us engage with this suffering and transform the object (or non-object) of our desire over the course of our lives. The sacraments could give us the tools to slowly transform the object of our desire, and help us preserve the indeterminacy, the mystery, of that which we desire.

## Transformation and the Sacraments

The Jesuit priest and mystical theologian Pierre Teilhard de Chardin, in his book *The Divine Milieu*, wrote this reflection about his experience of his own contemplative prayer practice:

> And so, for the first time in my life perhaps (although I am supposed to meditate every day!), I took the lamp and, leaving the

---

2. Carlisle, "Spiritual Desire," 442.

zone of everyday occupations and relationships where everything seems clear, I went down into my inmost self, to the deep abyss whence I feel dimly that my power of action emanates. But as I moved further and further away from the conventional certainties by which social life is superficially illuminated, I became aware that I was losing contact with myself. At each step of the descent a new person was disclosed within me of whose name I was no longer sure, and who no longer obeyed me. And when I had to stop my exploration because the path faded from beneath my steps, I found a bottomless abyss at my feet, and out of it came—arising I know not from where—the current which I dare to call my life.[3]

Our lifelong journey is to reconnect to this bottomless source from which flows our life. In this description, Pierre Teilhard de Chardin shows us what we might find when we intentionally take on practices that lead us to this mysterious abyss. We see, in Chardin's example, the depth of our interior reality, but also the multiplicity of it. He names this bottomless abyss that is, in fact, his source of life, but also how along the way to this depth he recognized the many-faced reality of this depth. At each step of the descent "a new person was disclosed within me of whose name I was no longer sure, and who no longer obeyed me." We all have both this infinite depth of identity and infinite complication to our identity, and an infinite number of parts of ourselves. As Jungian analyst Robert A. Johnsons describes it, we all have a "shadow side" which is "the dumping ground for all those characteristics of our personality that we disown."[4] This is the shadow, this is the Abyss, this is the mystery of our identity.

Beyond that, this depth is not just the place from which our identities flow, or from which emerge the ideas that make up our concept of self. It is the place from which everything within us emerges. It is our connection to God. From this depth is where the desire we have been exploring emerges. It is from this depth that every impulse arises and to which we respond with action. Our journey, then, is to follow the lead of our desires, or our impulses, even when they have hurt us in the past, and in engaging with them let them lead us back to our source—to God. It is spiritual practice that creates the container for this kind of engagement. As Claire Carlisle writes, "All practice is oriented by a desire for an outcome, and uses the repetition of particular processes as a means to

---

3. Teilhard de Chardin, *Divine Milieu*, 76–77.
4. Johnson, *Owning Your Own Shadow*, ix–x.

this end."[5] When we can do this without judgement or closure, the ways we respond to these divine impulses, the desire of God, are transformed from sources of suffering to sources of healing.

At the same time, it is not for us to decide what the outcome of this transformation will be, or if there will be an outcome at all. Instead, it is for us to open up to the journey, to take on the practices that will help us engage with the mystery operating in and around us, with the depths of ourselves, and the multiplicity of that depth. Again, Claire Carlisle describes this reality well:

> Spiritual practice differs from skill practice in being "dialectical" and open-ended, and in being oriented to an indeterminate goal, which is understood more deeply in and through the practice. Spiritual practice shares these features with art practice, but its indeterminacy seems more radical; its goal-directed structure is not entirely undermined, but certainly unsettled and problematized; and its animating desire seems to transcend the practitioner's agency, so that we might describe the practice not simply as desiring, but as being-desired.[6]

In the Christian tradition, the sacraments provide a container to help us facilitate this transformation and hold the mystery. The communal practices of Baptism and Eucharist uniquely address these two characteristics of our interior journey: Baptism probing our depths, and Eucharist engaging our infinite multiplicity.

## Baptism: Plunging into the Abyss

The Episcopal Church's *Book of Common Prayer* defines Baptism as "the sacrament by which God adopts us as [God's] children and makes us members of Christ's Body, the Church, and inheritors of the kingdom of God."[7] We tend to think of this action as a once and for all type of ritual, that when we are baptized is when we become children of God, members of Christ's body, and inheritors of the kingdom of God. The adopting, making, and inheriting, though, are not once and for all actions, but a process of *becoming* that we take part in with God throughout our whole lives. As outlined in the ecumenical statement on baptism in the *Baptism,*

---

5. Carlisle, "Spiritual Desire," 436.
6. Carlisle, "Spiritual Desire," 441.
7. Episcopal Church, *Book of Common Prayer*, 858.

*Eucharist, and Ministry* document created during a 1982 gathering of protestant, Roman Catholic, and Orthodox theologians, "Baptism is related not only to momentary experience, but to life-long growth into Christ. Those baptized are called upon to reflect the glory of the Lord as they are transformed by the power of the Holy Spirit, into his likeness, with ever increasing splendour."[8]

In this way, Baptism is not just a rite that initiates an individual into a static community of believers, but it is the communal recognition of the task ahead, of the journey that is required of every one of us. We plunge people, young and old, into the depths of the water, to remind ourselves that we are all invited to take that plunge every day into the chaotic waters that surge in us, the depth that exists in every one of us. Not only that, but we do this in community to communicate to the baptized, or their sponsors, that they are not alone in this journey. We are all on this path of continuously dying with Christ and rising with him, as Paul says in the letter to the Romans. Baptism is our communal practice of remembering how to dive into the depth of ourselves, to re-engage with the chaos churning in us, from which our greatest energy and potential emerges.

This process, though, is not for the faint of heart. It will be gut wrenching, it will be exhausting, it will be never end. But the more we do it, like any practice, the more capable we are of sitting with the discomfort of it. When we have an interaction that elicits an overly strong response from us, or we behave in a way that leads to feelings of shame and guilt, or we are confronted with our own behavior that has caused suffering, our instinct is often to retreat from those feelings that emerge from our depths, to push them back down, to run away from them, or to manifest that emergence in painful behaviors (e.g., addiction, anger, destruction, etc.). Instead, Baptism calls us to dive in, to let ourselves be submerged, and remember the waters of creation, the Tehom, the deep, from which all forms of new life emerged.

Theologian Catherine Keller, in her book *Face of the Deep*, reframes creation through the lens of the pre-existent, and still existent, depth of creation, arguing for a *"creatio ex profundis,"* a creation from the deep, rather than a *"creatio ex nihilo,"* the orthodox Christian doctrine of creation from nothing.[9] It is from the deep, the Tehom, rather than from absolute nothingness, that God brings forth creation. This deep, then,

---

8. World Council of Churches, *Baptism, Eucharist, and Ministry*, 3.

9. Keller, *Face of the Deep*, 40.

cannot be separated from God, but is "the depth of God."[10] It is at the same time "the heterogenous depth of divinity and of world"[11] as well as "the *goodness* of our depths, our differences, our spirits."[12] As the first creation story says, there was the deep, the murky, formless chaos, and by the breath of God moving over its face, all forms of life emerge. God, then, is not controlling or ordering this chaotic depth, but engaging, breathing, calling forth, and responding to what emerges.

This chaotic depth is present even in the baptismal rite of the Episcopal Church. The prayer over the waters of baptism calls our attention back to this foundational depth of creation:

> We thank you, Almighty God, for the gift of water. Over it the Holy Spirit moved in the beginning of creation. Through it you led the children of Israel out of their bondage in Egypt into the land of promise. In it your Son Jesus received the baptism of John and was anointed by the Holy Spirit as the Messiah, the Christ, to lead us, through his death and resurrection, from the bondage of sin into everlasting life.[13]

Our baptism brings us back to the beginning, but not so we may keep that process of creation there and then. It calls us back so that we can see the beginnings that continue to emerge here and now from our depths, the depth of God, to which we are all connected.

Former Archbishop Rowan Williams, in his book *Being Christian: Baptism, Eucharist, Prayer, Bible*, similarly calls our attention to these depths, writing that "baptism means being with Jesus 'in the depths': the depths of human need, including the depths of our own selves in their need—but also in the depths of God's love; in the depths where the Spirit is re-creating and refreshing human life as God meant it to be."[14] The water of baptism, that "outward and visible sign," represents the waters that are in us, and moving all the time. The depth, the Tehom, the formless void of creation was not ordered and annihilated by God back then, but still moves in us now.

Through the Deep moving in us we are inextricably linked to the primordial deep over which God moved, as Keller says, the "*goodness* of

---

10. Keller, *Face of the Deep*, 231.
11. Keller, *Face of the Deep*, 231.
12. Keller, *Face of the Deep*, 235.
13. Episcopal Church, *Book of Common Prayer*, 306.
14. Williams, *Being Christian*, 5.

our depths," and thus have the opportunity at every moment to breath down into these depths and send the breath of God over the face of the deep again and again and again. After all, what breath do we have but the breath of God? The practice of Baptism is not just the sacramental rite itself, but our daily plunge into the baptismal waters—the deep, swirling in us. It is the catalyst and container for an engagement with depth that we would never be able to do alone, or without the promise that new life awaits on the other side of this death and authenticity awaits on the other side of this discomfort.

When we have a desire to act in a way that we know will cause suffering—for ourselves or others, externally or internally—we have a new opportunity to remember our baptism, to remember creation, and to engage with the Tehom. We can breathe over the face of this deep, sit in the discomfort of new life, and allow something novel to emerge. This, of course, will not be a once and for all task, any more than creation was or Baptism is. It will be the work of a lifetime, of incremental change, of slow but steady unfolding. A new way will emerge, and it will be messy, and it will be painful, but it will also be true, and we will see over the course of our practice that the way we respond to the deep will change. The object of our desire will transform and take on more and more the characteristics of infinity and indeterminacy. The object of our desire will transform into something that opens us up to infinite life, rather than finite suffering.

## Eucharist: Dining with Discomfort

If baptism was about engaging our depths, then Eucharist is an invitation to recognize our multiplicity. In reflecting on the Last Supper—the first Eucharist—we see how Jesus embodied this engagement with discomfort and complication. In the face of his own impending suffering, when Jesus could have run from the discomfort of his own suffering, when he could have withdrawn entirely, when he could have lashed out at his closest friends, what did he do? He sat down, slowed down, and ate a meal with them. But even more importantly, he ate a meal not with twelve perfect followers, not with twelve rock-solid individuals who completely understood what was happening. He ate with people who in a matter of days would let him down completely. Chief among them was his soon to be betrayer, Judas Iscariot.

Theologian Lauren Winner, in her book *The Dangers of Christian Practice: On Wayward Gifts, Characteristic Damage, and Sin*, writes that, while it is not made explicitly clear in all the gospel accounts that Judas was present at the Last Supper, his inclusion in our exegesis of this meal "is crucial for an account of the Eucharist (and of Christian practice more generally)."[15] Why? Because, as she highlights later in the same discussion, the "One who receives immediately betrays the reception (and the Giver), and the betrayer's reception is inseparably the sign of his inability to receive; Judas's reception is about the fact that he will betray the reception."[16]

While Winner sees the betrayal of Judas as indicative of the inherent damage of the Eucharist, we might interpret it instead as a way to recognize the inherent invitation of the Eucharist to engage with suffering and discomfort so that the ways we cause damage in the world might be transformed. What is most important about Judas' presence at the Last Supper is not just that he will ultimately betray Jesus, but that Jesus did not get rid of him in the first place. From the very beginning the gospels make it clear that Jesus knew Judas would betray him, but instead of dismissing his betrayer, what did Jesus do? He kept him around. And not only that, but even at the very end, he knelt down and washed his feet, he loved him in the most intimate and vulnerable of ways. He remained connected to him, he remained in dialogue with him, and finally he dined with him.

This is the invitation we receive every time we take part in the Eucharist. That is what we ingest. The invitation to sit with, as Pierre Teilhard de Chardin named them, each new person that is disclosed within us. Or, as Robert A. Johnson put it, "all those characteristics of our personality that we would rather disown."[17] Jesus certainly had the chance to disown many of the people who were closest to him, chief among them Judas, his betrayer, but also Peter, his constant denier, or Thomas, his doubter. The Eucharist invites us to sit at the table with our betrayer, with our doubter, with our denier, with our fear, and our hate, and our shame, and our guilt, and not coerce them or banish them, but to love them, to wash their feet and know that God is working in them for transformation.

This invitation is twofold, beckoning us to dine both within and without. We never take part in Eucharist by ourselves, so as much as we

---

15. Winner, *Christian Practice*, 20.
16. Winner, *Christian Practice*, 55.
17. Johnson, *Owning Your Own Shadow*, ix–x.

are called to commune with our inner multiplicity, we are also asked to dine with all of the people in our community. The ones we love and the ones that are challenging to love. The ones that bring us peace and the ones that arouse fear, or anger, or anxiety in us. We dine with them, no matter what they elicit from us. And in doing so, in sitting down at this table of discomfort, something new emerges within us. The ways we interact with ourselves and with other people is transformed. What Jesus seemed to desire most was community, but not a homogenous community, made up of people that looked the same, or thought the same, or experienced life in the same way. Instead, Jesus nurtured community that recreated the depth and multiplicity of those creation waters, and when we can stay with those manifold parts, internally and externally, without trying to force an outcome or a resolution, we are transformed, and our community is transformed.

We, like Jesus, can sit with our contradictions and see how their reconciliation emerges. We can create the space for Peter to transform from the denier to the rock of the church, and Thomas from doubter to prober of the wounds. We can, like Jesus, be in relationship with these contradiction without trying to control their fate, letting Peter deny, and Thomas doubt, and Judas betray. Loving and letting go. Engaging and seeing what grows.

And when we accept this invitation, maybe we will be able to imagine what redemption and transformation look like for Judas—for the untouchable, unforgiveable parts of ourselves. Can we bring them all to the table, and see what God does with them when we are able to engage, even when we would rather cast them out to die in a field? Every moment that we can commune with these parts of ourselves, something in us grows, and the object of our desire becomes that of God's.

## Conclusion

What we learn when we engage with our desire and the object of our desire is that it is more than just something to discard or to hate. Individual practices like contemplative prayer, journaling, labyrinth walking, or communal practices like Baptism and Eucharist, create the containers within which we can courageously come face to face with our infinite complexity, with the depth swirling in us, with the guilt, and shame, and fear that arise from those depths. And when we can do this, the object of our desire transforms, and the object starts to look more like the very source of that desire. We will desire the indeterminate, the uncertain mystery, the previously impossible, the murky unfolding of our own creation, and we will become, in the process, people able to heal the world.

## Bibliography

Carlisle, Clare. "Spiritual Desire and Religious Practice." *Religious Studies* 55 (2019) 429–46.

The Episcopal Church. *The Book of Common Prayer and Administration of the Sacraments and Other Rites and Ceremonies of the Church: Together with the Psalter or Psalms of David according to the use of the Episcopal Church*. New York: Seabury, 1979.

Johnson, Robert A. *Owning Your Own Shadow: Understanding the Dark Side of the Psyche*. San Francisco: HarperSanFrancisco, 1991.

Keller, Catherine. *Face of the Deep: A Theology of Becoming*. London: Routledge, 2003.

Teilhard de Chardin, Pierre. *The Divine Milieu: An Essay on the Interior Life*. New York: Harper, 1960.

Williams, Rowan. *Being Christian: Baptism, Bible, Eucharist, Prayer*. Grand Rapids: Eerdmans, 2014.

Winner, Lauren F. *The Dangers of Christian Practice: On Wayward Gifts, Characteristic Damage, and Sin*. New Haven: Yale University Press, 2018.

World Council of Churches. *Baptism, Eucharist, and Ministry*. Geneva: World Council of Churches, 1982.

## 12

# Sacramental Therapy

*Benjamin B. Hawley*

### Introduction and Overview

JESUS THE MESSIAH FULFILLS the promises of God to the Jewish people to set aright the tribulations that Adam and Eve's misjudgment unleashed on all humanity. The Jewish prophets announced these promises and described what the Messiah would do to fulfill them. Read the texts of the prophet Isaiah and recall that Jesus of Nazareth read these same texts as a child and young man. Through the ministrations of his mother, Joseph, and the Holy Spirit, he came to realize that he was the one of whom these texts spoke. His was the task that these texts promised.

> Strengthen the weak hands, and make firm the feeble knees. Say to those who are of a fearful heart, "Be strong, and do not fear! Here is your God. He will come with vengeance, with terrible recompense. He will come and save you. Then the eyes of the blind shall be opened, and the ears of the deaf unstopped; then the lame shall leap like a deer, and the tongue of the speechless sing for joy." (Isa 35:3–6a)[1]

---

[1.] See also Isa 58:6; 62:1–5. Unless otherwise noted, all biblical citations in this chapter are from the NRSV.

> The spirit of the Lord God is upon me, because the Lord has anointed me; he has sent me to bring good news to the oppressed, to bind up the brokenhearted, to proclaim liberty to the captives and release to the prisoners . . . to provide for those who mourn in Zion—to give them a garland instead of ashes, the oil of gladness instead of mourning, the mantel of praise instead of a faint spirit. (Isa 61:1–3)

The gospels show us Jesus performing miracles and signs, often physical healings. But the absence of psychological understandings of the human person limited gospel writers' ability to help their readers see the interior, affective dimension of Jesus' healing acts. Failing to recognize and understand this interior dimension robs readers of the text the hopefulness that these texts offer: the love of the God restoring to renewed life those who suffer the privations Isaiah describes. Emmanuel, God with us, indeed.

This sharing of divine love occurs in concrete moments of human life in a real and direct way, in other words, in a sacramental way, between God and the believer, among believers and among believers and those who do not yet believe. "Sacramental" in this case indicates Jesus' dynamic presence (a faith claim) in the power of the Holy Spirit, revealing the Father as love, as distinct from a symbolic or metaphorical presence.

These moments can occur in highly formalized settings, such as in eucharistic/communion celebrations, as well as in daily events, such as interactions between human beings in social settings or human experiences of Beauty in nature. These moments can also occur when believers join together in faith to invoke God's love on behalf of a person, or people or a situation. In the aftermath the discerning eye can recognize the divinely-inspired effects of this prayer.

This chapter will describe this process of divine love being offered to suffering human beings through human agency, as suggested in scriptural texts and perceived in the modern mind in psychological language. The chapter will also describe how people of faith can engage this process to experience God's restorative love themselves and how they can act on behalf of others who suffer.

In this chapter, I write as a Jesuit Catholic priest, drawing on principles of Roman Catholicism in a way that invites believers of other Christian denominations and perhaps people of faith traditions more broadly into this ministry of healing and the building of God's kingdom of peace on earth.

## Human Suffering and the Hope for New Life

> O my people, what have I done to you? In what have I wearied you? Answer me. For I brought you up from the land of Egypt and redeemed you from the house of slavery. (Mic 6:3–4)

Through myth the story of Adam and Eve shows how the human temptation to autonomy and choice-for-self create human suffering. Adam and Eve shared an idyllic life, yet succumbed; Cain and Abel succumbed as well, the one murdering the other out of jealousy. God's covenant invited human beings back into relationship with God and one another, and the prophets repeated the invitation. And yet, in the mid-first century, the Letter to James describes with penetrating psychological insight the ongoing workings of the Adam-and-Eve temptation:

> Those conflicts and disputes among you, where do they come from? Do they not come from your cravings that are at war within you? You want something and do not have it; so you commit murder. And you covet something and cannot obtain it; so you engage in disputes and conflicts. You do not have, because you do not ask. You ask and do not receive, because you ask wrongly, in order to spend what you get on your pleasures. (Jas 4:1–3)

Judaism and Christianity assert God's desire to assist human beings to find resolution from the effects of this temptation through the promised Messiah, offering God's salvation, freedom from Cain-and-Abel-style dysfunction and freedom for renewed and restored life in renewed and restored relationship within the human community and with God. Freedom from the effects of this dysfunction came through Jesus' miracles that are explicitly physical, e.g., healing from blindness, and implicitly psychological, e.g., physical healing that restores lepers to a sense of belonging to their community. This coming into freedom is what St. Paul calls "healing," as a gift of the Spirit (1 Cor 12:9)[2] through the process described by the author of the Letter of James:

> Is anyone among you sick? Let them call the elders of the church to pray over them and anoint them with oil in the name of the Lord. And the prayer offered in faith will make the sick person

---

2. See the entire chapter for St. Paul's description of the gifts and the working of the Holy Spirit through them.

well; the Lord will raise them up. If they have sinned, they will be forgiven. (Jas 5:14)

Drawing on the Pauline-Jamesian tradition the emerging Catholic hierarchy in the second century established the Anointing of the Sick as a formal sacrament. In succeeding centuries, however, the theology of the sacrament of the anointing of the sick moved away from the sacrament's healing character in favor of an absolving-of-sin character offered near death in preparation for the beatific vision, understood in Catholic tradition as full communion with God in the next life.

Vatican II brought the sacrament of the anointing of the sick more into line with its scriptural origins. If in the future this sacrament could be further reformulated in ways consistent with the presentation below, then "healing" could take on its full potential as freedom from hurt and privation and freedom for new life through God's salvific action. Such reform could also empower the laity to take their full role as bearers of God's healing love in genuine partnership with priests and deacons in the ministry of healing.

## Approaching the Topic of Healing

The term "healing" as it is used here is understood as God's promised resolution to the effects of the Adam-and-Eve temptation, experienced in two ways:

- *The sin I do:*[3] individual thoughts and behaviors (actions, speech) and repeated over time as habitual thoughts and behaviors, arising from past and present day events. This category includes not only sins I do to others and God, but also sins I do to myself, e.g., not forgiving myself or indulging in self-destructive thoughts and behaviors, because of my cravings and conflicts, per the Letter of James; and

- *The sin done to me:* individual acts and behaviors (actions, speech) and repeated over time as habitual thoughts and behaviors, visited upon me by individual people, systems of people (families,

---

3. This phrase is explicit in the invitation at the beginning of the Roman Catholic Eucharist. The complementary phrase "the sin done to me" is intended as a counterpart understanding of hurt visited upon us. This chapter will not undertake a discussion of sin as a Catholic theological category.

workplaces) and institutions in the past and present, because of their own cravings and conflicts, per the Letter of James.

*Corollary*: the sin I do often arises from the sin done to me, where the sin done to me is usually much greater than the sin I do. This corollary, though generally true in many ministerial settings, is subject to significant qualifiers, such sin done by people under the influence of addictive substances, excessive sin done to them (childhood abuse, neglect), or psychological sociopathy or narcissism.

*The divine remedy* comes to us as one dimension of God's salvation, "soza" in Koine Greek, which in its original usage meant deliverance, preservation in a physical sense (as, for example, in a ship wreck), a return home after a journey, or a guarantee of safety and security against danger. Other dimensions, beyond the scope of this article, include guiding us toward life-giving work, family, and friends that would offer us freedom from hurt and freedom for richer life.

The end point of God's salvation, the telos or goal toward which healing is directed is the fullness of life for each human person, described, for example, by St. Ireneus as, "The glory of God is the living man, and the life of man is the vision of God,"[4] more popularly cited as, "The glory of God is a human being fully alive in Christ." Jesus describes this telos in the Gospel of John:" I came that they (you) may have life, and have it abundantly" (John 10:10);" I have said these things to you so that my joy may be in you and that your joy may be complete" (John 15:13).

Making sense of these ideas of healing and telos as integral realities of human life obliges twenty-first century people—believers, wonderers, non-believers—to straddle two thought worlds:

*First, the world of the scripture narrative that records God's remedy and prioritizes God's communal people.* This remedy begins with the covenant with Abraham and includes the giving of the Law and the land, and the promise of the Messiah; then the epic narrative of Jesus of Nazareth the Messiah who is the fulfillment of the Law, the prophets and of Israel, who is the Savior of the world, who brings the good news, whose death and resurrection breaks through sin and death, who gives rise to the church, and who now sits at the right hand of the Father as the risen Christ in glory.

The language of this orientation is mythical, universal, theological, abstract, and ancient. Moral precepts are stated in theological and

---

4. Ireneus, *Against Heresies*, 20.4.7.

abstract terms. In this orientation sacrificial atonement resolves personal and communal sin against moral precepts. Healing responds to physical illness by forgiving personal sin, without specific reference to emotional healing. Anointing for healing offers preparation for death and meeting God in the afterlife.

*Second, the world of the twenty-first century people in the affluent West that prioritizes personal, individual, emotional well-being and self-actualization.* The language of this orientation is intellectual/rational, psychological, and spiritual in a psycho-emotional terms. Healing is understood as resolution of and relief from the harm done to me and preparation for a yet-more fulfilling life in this world.

The distinctively Catholic sacramental imagination bridges these two thought worlds. This sacramental imagination sees God present and active in an epic narrative addressing communal human life in ways perceptible by the individual person in a language addressed to the individual person that also creates a common language describing the spiritual experience of individual persons gathered in community. This common language is established and reinforced by individual and communal reading and interpreting of scripture, in the sacraments and sacramental encounters in the *communio*—the gathered community—of the church.

This Catholic sacramental imagination will also allow us to bridge the lay-clerical gap to be proposed below, thus moving toward the unity of the faithful, per Vatican II.[5]

> Though they differ essentially and not only in degree, the common priesthood of the faithful and the ministerial or hierarchical priesthood are nonetheless ordered one to another; each in its own proper way shares in the one priesthood Christ.[6]

This sacramental vision recognizes the church as the people of God ordered hierarchically, which seeks increasingly to embrace the people of the Abrahamic covenant, thus raising the "church" to being the light of the world (Isa 2:2–4).[7]

---

5. Suenens, *Theological and Pastoral Orientations*, 55–60.

6. *Lumen Gentium*, no. 10, in Flannery, *Vatican Council II*, 361.

7. "The one People of God is accordingly present in all the nations of the earth, since its citizens, who are taken from all nations, are of a kingdom whose nature is not earthly but heavenly." *Lumen Gentium*, no. 13, in Flannery, *Vatican Council II*, 364.

## The Scripture's Understanding of Healing

Jewish and Christian scripture texts cite the need for physical healing from physical limitations (blindness, speech impediments, defective limbs) and generic diseases (leprosy, hemorrhage). Other texts cite the need for relief from injustice (taxation, merchants, temple elite); indifference (widows, orphans, immigrants); social prejudice (women, foreigners); or moral disapproval (women adulterers, lazy, dishonest household workers).

Since scripture writers lacked psychological insights, we of the twenty-first century must bring these insights to our interpretation of scripture. This article focuses on the psychological need for healing that arises from the above modes of privation and identifies God's love as the remedy. A few examples will suffice:

A. The Psalms:

- He heals the brokenhearted, and binds up all their wounds (Ps 147:3).
- Have mercy on me, Lord, For I am faint; heal me, Lord, for my bones are in agony. My soul is in deep anguish.... Turn, Lord, and deliver me; save me because of your unfailing love (Ps 6:2–4).

B. The Beatitudes recognize human distress (the poor, those who mourn, those who thirst for righteousness) and suggest divine care (theirs is the kingdom of heaven, they shall be comforted, they shall be filled), without explaining how this divine care is to be received.

C. The prophecies of Isaiah cited above.

D. Jesus' commission

- Jesus went through Galilee, teaching in their synagogues and proclaiming the good news of the kingdom and curing every disease and every sickness among the people, ... those afflicted with various diseases and pains, demoniacs, epileptics, and paralytics, and he cured them (Matt 4:23–24).

## How Did Jesus Heal in a Way That Also Forgave?

Recognizing that scripture records God's efforts to healing human beings, we now need to examine what Jesus actually did to offer this healing:

³⁶ One of the Pharisees asked Jesus to eat with him, and he went into the Pharisee's house and took his place at the table. ³⁷ And a woman in the city, who was a sinner, having learned that he was eating in the Pharisee's house, brought an alabaster jar of ointment. ³⁸ She stood behind him at his feet, weeping, and began to bathe his feet with her tears and to dry them with her hair. Then she continued kissing his feet and anointing them with the ointment. ³⁹ Now when the Pharisee who had invited him saw it, he said to himself, "If this man were a prophet, he would have known who and what kind of woman this is who is touching him—that she is a sinner." ⁴⁰ Jesus spoke up and said to him, "Simon, I have something to say to you." "Teacher," he replied, "speak." ⁴¹ "A certain creditor had two debtors; one owed five hundred denarii, and the other fifty. ⁴² When they could not pay, he cancelled the debts for both of them. Now which of them will love him more?" ⁴³ Simon answered, "I suppose the one for whom he cancelled the greater debt." And Jesus said to him, "You have judged rightly." ⁴⁴ Then turning towards the woman, he said to Simon, "Do you see this woman? I entered your house; you gave me no water for my feet, but she has bathed my feet with her tears and dried them with her hair. ⁴⁵ You gave me no kiss, but from the time I came in she has not stopped kissing my feet. ⁴⁶ You did not anoint my head with oil, but she has anointed my feet with ointment. ⁴⁷ Therefore, I tell you, her sins, which were many, have been forgiven; hence she has shown great love. But the one to whom little is forgiven, loves little." ⁴⁸ Then he said to her, "Your sins are forgiven." ⁴⁹ But those who were at the table with him began to say among themselves, "Who is this who even forgives sins?" ⁵⁰ And he said to the woman, "Your faith has saved you; go in peace." (Luke 7:36–50)

For Jesus, love is the engine of simultaneous forgiveness and healing: her choosing to love in the midst of her suffering and his loving her in that place release her from the sin she has done and from the sin done to her, thereby giving her freedom for hope for a better life. The narrator does not describe her renewed interior state that opens us this freedom for hope. But we can reasonably believe that she is beginning to feel a share in Jesus' offer of his complete joy and the hope for more abundant life (John 10:10; 15:11).

The narrator does not tell us what her many sins were nor what may have led her to sin, though tradition claims that she was a prostitute. We thereby risk seeing her, as tradition has, as a cardboard character of little interest beyond showing off Jesus as savior and miracle worker.[8] This unreflective, demeaning valuation of her obscures the story's insight into what Jesus means by healing and why his healing offers us real hope. So we must take her seriously and try to understand her as she is in this story.

Feminist social science research asserts that childhood abuse, family dysfunction, poverty, drug addictions and unemployment contribute to women (and men) entering or being forced into prostitution.[9] The woman in the Lukan story may well have been forced into prostitution by any of these factors and then shunned by her culture as "sinful," a clear case of her culture's double standard and of the sin done to her leading her to her own sin and then leading her to yet more sin done to her.

Whatever the reasons for her becoming a "sinner," those reasons must have severed whatever family ties she may have had and intensified her feeling of being outcast and abandoned, a sense of being unloved and unworthy of love, of hopelessness in the present about her future life. Newly broadened applications of the concept of PTSD and moral injury would describe her emotional state and its implications in similar terms.[10]

And yet, remarkably, she continued to love and to display an amazing courage, generosity and faith. This continuing to love is the linchpin of the story. At some point before the story opens, she must have heard about Jesus or heard him speak. On this basis she must have intuited that this Jesus might hold the key to relief from her suffering. In other words, her coming to Jesus was already a faith claim about him, though we cannot tell what this "faith" might have been: in him as a person, a rabbi, as a miracle-worker? Whatever the intuition, whether with words or without words, it was an intuition of sufficient strength to motivate her dramatic appearance at the dinner.

Her tears and kissing his feet suggest the dispirited humiliation of one who is lost, what the first Beatitude calls poverty of spirit (Matt 5:3). And yet her walking uninvited into a Pharisee's all-male dinner party suggests an extraordinary courage and hopefulness against the odds. Her coming with the jar of oil for anointing suggests a generosity of spirit in the midst of her poverty: what must have such a jar of anointment cost, given her income?

---

8. Schneiders, *The Revelatory Text*, 188.

9. See the research conducted by Catherine MacKinnon, Andrea Dworkin, Melissa Farley, and Julie Bindei.

10. Sherman, *Afterwar*.

What Jesus sees—and names with his usual penetrating wisdom—is not simply her faith, but also her willingness to continue to love, which Jesus names as her central characteristic. Her decision to continue to love nourishes her faith, and this faith, which must have been in some way be connected with something beyond herself, what today we might call a "higher power," gave her the ability to continue to love. And not just to continue to love but also to be courageous and generous at quite extraordinary levels, given her low social status and financial poverty.

As she encountered Jesus, she experienced the kingdom of heaven: being noticed, appreciated, respected, and loved, despite whatever she has done or become, just what the first Beatitude promises: "Blessed/fortunate/well-situated are the poor in spirit for theirs will be and is the kingdom of heaven" (Matt 5:3). "The kingdom of heaven is in you/in your midst" (Luke 17:21), and she experiences the kingdom of heaven present to her as she encounters Jesus through her own initiative as a matter of her faith.

The encounter with Jesus' love heals the sin done to her and forgives the sin she had done in a single dynamic action, leaving her free to experience yet more of the love, courage, generosity and faith she has already demonstrated and at some point to offer it to others. Jesus tells her to go in peace, and we can assume that she does.

Since her active expression of love, courage, generosity and faith drives the narrative, an analysis of the story adequate to the present-day reader must come to understand the reality and interaction of these qualities, not just as abstract virtues, which they are, but also dynamic realities requiring psychological, affective language to provide an adequate explanation. An abstract version of the story, one that sees her as no more than a prostitute, as the tradition has, might say that she left in peace, a "bad" person having become a "good" one. But this "becoming good" remains an abstraction, in the sense of "becoming morally good," with no explanation about the interior dynamics at work in her, nor about how "being morally good" opens for her the hope for freedom for new life and hope. This abstract account offers neither a response nor even an acknowledgement of the sin done to her. Such a failure leaves the account quite insufficient, even unjust. The morally abstract expectation that she must simply forgive those who have hurt her seems compounds the injustice. It seems quite clear that the abstract moral statement lacks explanatory power.

We encounter here a concrete instance of present-day people of faith needing to bridge the gap between the ancient thought world of the text (and its continued presence in Catholic theology) and the modern thought world.

Where abstract moral language has limited explanatory power, our present-day use of affective language broadens our ability to analyze this encounter: she leaves in peace, an actual human emotion, because in the encounter Jesus honored what was true about her in its fullest sense in a manner that was loving, compassionate and affirming without being in any way condemning. Jesus offers her freedom from her sin combined with freedom from the sin done to her and freedom for a new, deeper peace as the foundation to a new version of herself and perhaps a new way of living. His love released the emotional, psychological burden of responsibility for past behaviors and became the indwelling matrix of her personality.

By contrast, Jesus heals where the Pharisee cannot, because the Pharisee thinks of her "a sinner," an ontological and therefore permanent category, as opposed to a descriptive assertion, like "she has sinned." This happens in our own time when people are imprisoned in such ontological categories as "He is a criminal" or "They are addicts." This categorization asserts an unchangeable, morally unworthy condition and thereby a death sentence to any hope for life in wider society.

When Jesus asks him, "Simon, do you see this woman?" Jesus already knows the real answer: No, he does not see this woman. He does not see any woman, least of all a sinful woman. Simon, living in the ontological category of "the upholder of the Law," has lost the opportunity to offer compassion and forgiveness before the story even starts. This, of course, is Jesus' primary criticism of the Pharisees and the rest of the religious elite: they know the Law but do not understand its deeper meaning nor can they connect the abstract Law to the concrete reality of human life. They have the keys to heaven but won't enter themselves nor will be allow (much less facilitate) other people's going there,[11] and they do not recognize their own blindness.[12]

---

11. "But woe to you, scribes and Pharisees, hypocrites! For you lock people out of the kingdom of heaven. For you do not go in yourselves, and when others are going in, you stop them" (Matt 23:13–14).

12. "Some of the Pharisees near him heard this and said to him, 'Surely we are not blind, are we?' Jesus said to them, 'If you were blind, you would not have sin. But now that you say, "We see," your sin remains'" (John 9:40–41).

This story and the above analysis show us the working out and fulfillment of the promises the Messiah will offer. God's covenant with the Jewish people and the renewed covenant with the Christian people embody mutual, loving relationship of which obeying the commandments are expressions with fuller and more abundant life and sharing Jesus' joy as their telos.

How then might that love be made concrete by believers? That is the question to which we now turn.

## Sacramental Ministry: The Priesthood of All Believers in Sacramental Community

> But you are a chosen race, a royal priesthood, a holy nation, God's own people, in order that you may proclaim the mighty acts of him who called you out of darkness into his marvelous light. (1 Pet 2:9)

A priest is a baptized believer to whom God has granted authority to invoke God's presence on behalf of another person or other people for ministerial purposes. A clerical (ministerial) priest does so in the formal sacraments with the authority of the ministerial priesthood. A lay person does so in sacramental actions, such as prayer for healing, with the authority of the royal priesthood of Christ.

In addition to bestowing these fundamental modes of authority, God gives each person—both clerical and lay—particular gifts of the Spirit that guide their apostolic work, e.g., preaching, teaching, healing, service, wisdom, administration, faith, among others (1 Cor 12).[13]

> Allotting his (the Spirit's) gifts according as he wills (cf. First Corinthians 12:11), he also distributes special graces among the faithful of every rank. By these gifts he makes them fit and ready to undertake various tasks and offices for the renewal and building up of the church, as it is written, "the manifestation of the Spirit is given to everyone for profit" (I Corinthians 12:7).[14]

Drawing on the authority of the royal priesthood of Christ and making use of the spiritual gifts empower the laity to take on priestly ministry. Though ministerial priesthood differs "essentially and not only

---

13. Waddell, *Catholic Spiritual Gifts Inventory*.
14. *Lumen Gentium*, no. 12, in Flannery, *Vatican Council II*, 363.

in degree"[15] from that of the royal priesthood of Christ, the latter complements ministerial priesthood, offering the people of God the fullest expression of God's love through the ministry of both ministerial and lay priests. A child or adult with a serious illness, for example, profits both from the sacrament of the anointing of the sick as well as from the prayers of family and friends. The healing of a person's emotional hurts from the past may well be better addressed through ongoing prayer by friends, family and prayer partners for their specific needs than by the formal sacrament. Because of its sacramental nature, the latter would be offered with far less frequency and less specificity than the ongoing prayer necessary for emotional healing.

Lay people offering this mode of prayer represents a concrete expression of their participation in the royal priesthood of Christ. If this expression of priesthood is unwelcomed in its fullness by anyone, whether in positions of authority or not, then the idea of "the royal priesthood of Christ" is robbed of any concrete reality. By contrast by drawing on both sacramental rites, sacramental prayers, and the spiritual gifts granted to those offering the rites and prayers, ministerial priests and lay priests are united in ministry. All then become full participants in the priestly, sacramental life of the church. This united ministry is constitutive of the church as the people of God.

> One of the most important developments in the (Charismatic) Renewal is the move towards community. This emphasis upon Christian community, where clergy and laity alike share their lives, stands in contrast to the individualism of today. Such community life is marked by various ministries based on charism where there is a mutuality of service. The large participatory character of community life and worship is a reflection of the nature of the church where the charisms are the principle of order and structure. The Renewal asks whether the revitalization of the structures of the Church is not to be found in this shared ministry.[16]

---

15. *Lumen Gentium*, no. 10, in Flannery, *Vatican Council II*, 361.
16. Suenens, *Theological and Pastoral Orientations*, 59.

## Forming the People of God for Sacramental Ministry

Bringing into concrete reality this collaboration between ministerial priests and lay priests necessitates deeper formation for all believers.

1. The foundation of such formation is growing in faith-filled, personal relationship with Jesus through participation in the sacraments, daily personal prayer, scripture reading, and conversation with a small prayer group and spiritual companion, and—quite possibly—a therapist. The therapist's contribution is to help the believer disentangle the realities of their past lives and to name precisely how to pray for their own healing. This is an exercise in "Physician, heal thyself."

    This call to relationship with Jesus requires a recentering and reordering of the believer's life such that discernment of spirits and reflection on experience are the guides to the believer's forward movement in their lives of which the search for inner healing is a part. This deeper relationship is essential to discerning giftedness, dismissing forces of evil that distract from prayer, and ensuring the deeper humility and generosity essential to the healing ministry.

    Jesus' desire to heal us arise from his experience among us:

    > For we do not have a high priest who is unable to sympathize with our weaknesses, but we have one who in every respect has been tested as we are, yet without sin. Let us therefore approach the throne of grace with boldness, so that we may receive mercy and find grace to help in time of need. (Heb 4:15)

    Jesus' being dismissed, abandoned and ridiculed in his public ministry and his passion help him sympathize with our own comparable experience and offer us freedom from the sin we do and the sin done to us and the freedom for new life.

2. Discerning of individual gifts and growing in the use of these gifts. Gifts must discovered, nurtured and guided in their use through personal prayer with a personal companion/spiritual director and ongoing affirmation by the praying community. To be resisted are temptations of spiritual pride and envy of other people's gifts. The fundamental virtues for this growth are humility, generosity of spirit, and indifference.

3. Learning to listen as a sacramental act. Listening deeply to another's story with compassion and empathy creates the interior space in

which God's love can pour into the encounter, offering relief to the one suffering. Such listening, contrasted to simply hearing, embraces the person as he/she is. The listener's learning to ask questions that evoke without prying nor judging nor advising can help the sufferer understand their own story. Questions can become an invitation to reflection, provided that the listener remains always within the limits of sacramental listening and avoids crossing the line into clinical therapy.

When the one seeking healing experiences being listened to and being heard, their first reaction can be relief. Then they may experience the opening of a greater interior space in which to discover their "voice," their story as they themselves tell it in their own words. They can discover their authentic selves speaking what has hitherto been unspoken out of fear or unheard though spoken and so come to realize their fundamental goodness in God's eyes. In other words, "the eyes of the blind shall be opened, . . . and the tongue of the speechless sing for joy" (Isa 35:4–5).

4. Growing in community and into community. A grouping of believers becomes a healing community when clerics and laypeople gather to use their gifts in complementary prayer for a particular person or perhaps a group.

## Finding Freedom from Hurt

The Lukan story of Jesus healing of the woman cited above demonstrates that prayer for healing offers resolution of emotional pain that may give rise to dysfunctional ways of thinking and acting. Those seeking such healing and those praying for them need to be attentive to the following needs:

1. Discover the root cause of the hurt. Jesus asks us to take responsibility for our own healing through faith in him and the hard work of psychological exploration. He asks of the blind man seeking healing, "What do you want me to do for you?" (Mark 10:51), and he asks the same of us. To be uncovered is the root cause of the sin done to me and of the sin I do or have done and the relationship between the two. Root causes often lie in one's family of origin or schooling and may be the result of personal trauma, e.g., PTSD

or moral injury, or generational trauma, e.g., alcoholism, physical dislocations, emotional abandonment, or abuse. The point is not to blame earlier generations, but rather to understand the causes of one's present-day suffering.

Of special note in cases of using pornography and other modes of acting out is the possibility that the pornography being watched or the modes of acting out are re-enacting one's own historical trauma, e.g., rape pornography as an act of violence against the mother. Resolving the distress creates the possibility of reducing or eliminating the use of pornography or acting out.

2. Reframing repeated individual acts that create ongoing guilt (sin I do) as ongoing hurt needing God's ongoing love and healing. Routine temptations to sexual acts, including pornography, become focused on the cross one bears that lead to prayers for strengthening, patience and perseverance, rather than perpetuating feelings of guilt. This reframing is grounded in a faithful trust in Jesus that

> "My grace is sufficient for you, for power is made perfect in weakness." So I will boast all the more gladly of my weaknesses, so that the power of Christ may dwell in me. (2 Cor 12:10)

3. Identifying where healing is impeded by the actions or inaction, conscious or unconscious of the one seeking healing, e.g., lack of desire to be healed, lack of prayer.[17]

4. Praying for knowledge of one's hurts arising from family of origin and multiple generations. As healing comes to one family member, some resolution may extend to other family members, a process known as healing the family tree.[18]

## Conclusions and New Opportunities

Sacramentality, the experience of Jesus present in the power of the Holy Spirit revealing the Father as love, constitutes the inner dynamic reality of what can properly be called sacramental actions and as such represents a sure sign of hope for suffering humanity. The sacramental imagination sees this divine presence in the beautiful efflorescence and mathematical

---

17. MacNutt, *Healing*, 193–204.
18. Sears, *Healing the Family Tree*; Hampsch, *Healing Your Family Tree*.

precision of Creation and in the beautiful if infuriating human people that can be either—and sometimes both—the glory of God and the horror of Satan in the figurative and even literal senses of those designations.

This presence is mysterious. It is mystery—*mysterion*—in that it is real, present, discernible to the practiced eye and efficacious in the believer, and yet of divine origin and therefore ultimately unknowable. This presence, offering love-in-relationship, gives rise to hope for the resolution of the damage caused by that which tempted Adam and Eve through the workings of sacramental healing. This coming of the Spirit of love-in-relationship into individual human lives and into human communities dissolves the hurt in human hearts and creates the freedom for fuller and more abundant life.

Sacramental healing, which offers renewal, wholeness, and empowerment, carries with it the hope for a renewed ministerial priesthood, where priestly service is increasingly based on a discernment of spiritual gifts in a mature spiritual community, and the hope for a renewed mutuality between ordained clergy and lay people through the priesthood of all believers.

This sacramental renewal also offers a channel by which to heal the divisions between Western Catholicism and Protestantism, Western and Eastern Catholicism, and between Christianity and Judaism, the Jews being the people of the original olive tree onto which Christianity was grafted by God (Rom 11).

This renewal also poses new opportunities for Catholics for a richer embrace of their Catholic faith. Might Jesus' washing his disciples' feet at the Last Supper (John 13) be raised to the level of a formal sacrament? Might such a sacrament be confected by lay people without clerical presence? One could easily imagine it as such a sacrament for lay chaplains or family members in a nursing home, hospice, or hospital, in a prison, with immigrants, with those contemplating divorce, and with those rejected by the hierarchical church, like the divorced and remarried, LBBTQUIA+, et al. Similarly, this renewal might lead to Christian believers discovering ways of sharing a sacramental meal in the manner of a Jewish seder as a family/home-based eucharistic-like celebration.

The final word is also the first word: God has been faithful and has always offered to all human beings God's own self for renewal and restoration through the manifold healing of our human hurts and privations so that believers can come to experience fuller and more abundant life and complete joy and contribute to the building of the kingdom.

## Bibliography

Flannery, Austin, ed. *Vatican Council II: Conciliar and Post-Conciliar Documents.* Collegeville, *MN*: Liturgical, 2014.

Hampsch, John. *Healing Your Family Tree.* Huntington, IN: Our Sunday Visitor, 1989.

Irenaeus. *Against Heresies.* Translated by Alexander Roberts and James Donaldson. Edinburgh: Ex Fontibus, 2017.

MacNutt, Francis. *Healing.* Notre Dame: Ave Maria Press, 1999.

Schneiders, Sandra. *The Revelatory Text: Interpreting the New Testament as Sacred Scripture.* Collegeville, MN: Liturgical, 1999.

Sears, Robert. *Healing the Family Tree.* http://www.familytreehealing.com/.

Sherman, Nancy. *Afterwar: Healing the Moral Wounds of Our Soldiers.* Oxford: Oxford University press, 2015.

Suenens, Leo Joseph. *Theological and Pastoral Orientation on the Catholic Charismatic Renewal.* Notre Dame: Word of Life, 1974.

Waddell, Sherry. *The Catholic Spiritual Gifts Inventory.* 3rd ed. Seattle: Siena Institute, 1998.

# Postscript on Pastoral Liturgy

*Barney Hawkins*

As I CONTEMPLATE THE struggle with pastoral liturgy over the last fifty years, I cannot help but reflect on my journey and formation as a priest in the Episcopal Church. Connecting pastoral ministry to liturgy has often been undermined by "all that's going on." Church changes, church governance, and church management can often divert the priest from being pastor, presider, preacher, teacher and visitor. The priest can become a corporate officer without even knowing it. The priest can do so much away from the parish that the parish suffers. Can the priest function in a parish without being fully present most of the time? The priest can attend to so many meetings and be about managing endless details that there is no time left for ministry to the flock and, thereby, God's mission in the world. The priest can be about doing, rather than about being.

In 1970, in the dark ages, when I entered Duke Divinity School, I was set on a course to get an MDiv and then a PhD with the hope that I would reach religion in a small liberal arts college. My courses in the Divinity School were largely flavored "academic." I thrived on courses in Old Testament (with Roland Murphy); New Testament (Hugh Anderson); Church History (Stuart Henry); Ethics (Waldo Beach and Harmon Smith); and Theology (Cushman). Because I had little interest in parish ministry and was an Episcopalian in a United Methodist seminary, I took no courses in homiletics, liturgy or pastoral theology (as the discipline was then called).

I found my first year at Duke Divinity School very hard. The Vietnam War dominated our lives. Dean Cushman called me into his office to confront me about my obvious unhappiness. The Dean suggested that I study my second year at New College at the University of Edinburgh. I took him up on the full scholarship with money for living and travel. It was a great offer! Little did I know that the year in Scotland would change my life.

Going to New College meant that I would sit at the feet of the Torrance brothers—Thomas, James and David—who for more than six decades had a tremendous influence on the theological world. By the time I arrived in Edinburgh, Hugh Anderson who had been a visiting professor at Duke had returned to his position at New College. I will never forget Professor Anderson's grace and hospitality in Durham, North Carolina and in Edinburgh.

What I did not know was that a decision to volunteer at St. Giles Cathedral in Edinburgh would quite literally turn my life upside down. Initially, I was drawn to St. Giles on the High Street because of its architecture, its beauty, and its location near the Palace of Holyroodhouse which is the Queen's official residence when in Scotland. On my first Sunday, I heard about a program to visit the poor, old and sick. It was a bleak, very cold winter in Edinburgh in 1971–72. Many were suffering from isolation and lack of adequate food. I wanted to help. So, I offered to receive the training for home visits.

I began serving one afternoon a week and soon three afternoons a week. I was visiting the poor, the old, and the sick. I found myself or was found, as I entered apartments and homes, offering prayers and the plans the Cathedral had in place for food delivery, medical visits and pastoral care. I had no formal preparation for such a ministry, save for the four training sessions offered by the clergy of St. Giles. I became a believer in visiting.

For a long winter I looked forward to my visitation ministry in neighborhoods a long way from the Cathedral and the Palace of Holyroodhouse. I discovered that practicing ministry changed the way I came to the liturgy and sermons on Sunday. When I would sit in the grandeur of St. Giles, I would have with me the faces and stories of those I would visit. I connected what I was doing with what I was a hearing and sensing in the services of worship.

## Postscript on Pastoral Liturgy

I sent a letter after a few months to Dean Cushman. First, I expressed my gratitude for the amazing opportunity of a year at New College. I then told him that I loved my lay ministry at St. Giles. I told him I wanted to return to Duke but that my focus would be parish ministry not graduate school. I shared with the Dean that I wanted to seek ordination which was something about which I had been hesitant. Almost immediately it seemed, Dean Cushman sent a reply. The letter was rather short. He said my vocation need not be either/or. "You should do the PhD to prepare you for preaching and teaching in the parish and university."

I returned to Duke. I finished Divinity School. I entered the arduous ordination process. I entered the Graduate School of Duke University. Because of my experience of St. Giles, I knew that always liturgy would be connected to pastoral care. In Duke's Graduate School, I focused only on the "life of the mind." I took courses in Philosophical Theology, Church History, and French Symbolism (with Wallace Fowlie). There was also growing in me "the life of faith."

While a graduate student, I worked part-time as the Lay Pastoral Assistant at St. Philip's Church in Durham. My first rector was The Rev. Eugene Bollinger who began his priesthood as a Lutheran. I loved my ministry at St. Philip's. Preaching in a true "town and gown" parish was a wonderful challenge. It was in the pulpit at St. Philip's that I learned that preaching was always drawn from the scripture for the day, the life of the parish (pastoral issues), local politics and national/international news. My preaching also drew texture and truth from literary sources, film and art. St. Philip's was my first and best laboratory for preaching.

Because I was the Lay Pastoral Associate, my involvement in liturgy was insignificant. When Fr. Bollinger suddenly resigned from "battle fatigue," I was thrust into a leadership role. The Vestry decided not to have an ordained interim. I was placed in charge, asked to preach more often, and given the responsibility of recruiting guest priests to preside. I fell in love with parish ministry. I loved planning liturgy with the organist, Kent Otto, and others.

So, if it were at St. Giles that I "found" myself (or was found) and the importance of pastoral ministry, it was at St. Philip's that I connected the "life of faith" with the "life of the mind;" where I connected preaching and presiding at the liturgy with pastoral care and caring.

I was ordained a priest in 1980. In 1981 I completed my graduate work at Duke. My first position as an ordained person was at Trinity Church in Asheville, North Carolina. I was called the Curate. That appellation and that assignment brought it all together for me. My first rector as a deacon and then priest, the Rev. Graham Butler-Nixon, told me when I asked for my "job description:" "No job description. It will be hard work. You are here to be a cure of souls." So it was. That was a revelatory moment.

Let me now turn from my story to our story as the gathered in Christ in the Episcopal Church. I will focus on the "habit of priesthood" (with a nod to George Herbert) and liturgy. I will then suggest a way forward as we practice Pastoral Liturgy.

When I was ordained in 1979, the "Habit of Priesthood" was largely about parish ministry. The emphasis was not on "the life of the mind." In fact, it was difficult to be ordained in many dioceses if you wanted an academic ministry. The Priest's Study, however, was slowly being replaced with the Priest's Office. Job descriptions became more prevalent and complicated, and the emphasis was on doing not being. Growing the Church in the early 1980s became a concern. Stewardship was a focus. Meeting the annual budget became a chore. Goals and outcomes often became more important than the "cure of souls." The parish church became increasingly a business. The rector or priest was called upon to be the CEO and/or the CFO. That was true of pastoral size congregations, as well as large, resource congregations. Priests were called from being presider, preacher and teacher to being managers and fixers. The priesthood became all about multi-tasking in a changing church and a complex world.

A major challenge to what was happening to the priesthood was the irregular ordination of women in Philadelphia in 1974. At the LXV General Convention of the Episcopal Church in 1976 in Minneapolis-St. Paul, Minnesota, our church recognized—at last—that women were rightly part of the ordained in Holy Orders. This "new development" for the priesthood was met by other changes in the Episcopal Church

In 1979, after several tumultuous years of trial liturgies, the Episcopal Church adopted a new Book of Common Prayer to replace the 1928 Book of Common Prayer. The 1979 Book of Common Prayer was not welcomed by all. A distinctive feature of the 1979 Book of Common Prayer was the centrality of the holy Eucharist for our common life. No longer was Daily Morning Prayer assumed to be the Sunday morning service. A celebration of the holy Eucharist was becoming normative for gathered worship. The liturgy looked different, and the roles of priests—men and women—were shifting.

In the early 1980s and increasingly so, being a priest was about being a manager, and liturgy was being transformed by a new Book of Common Prayer. The liturgy continued being refitted as the 1940 Hymnal was replaced by the 1982 Hymnal. The priesthood was certainly impacted by the national church changes in 1976, 1979 and 1982. As many were longing for nothing to change, in 1989 the Rt. Rev. John S. Spong, Diocesan Bishop of the Episcopal Diocese of Newark, ordained an openly gay man as a priest. Traditionalists argued that Bishop Spong was disregarding Christian moral standards. The Rev. J. Robert Williams, ordained at All Saints Parish in Hoboken, New Jersey, was followed by the first openly gay bishop in 2003 when The Rt. Rev. V. Gene Robinson was consecrated as a bishop in the Diocese of New Hampshire.

The consecration of Bishop Robinson divided the church. Some left. Others stayed but all Episcopalians were different. Priests were under pressure to be agents for social change, as they "learned" new liturgies which took time and energy. More and more, serious issues ruled clergy lives, whether women in the ordained ministry or LBGTQI ordinations—not to mention the need to confront injustices and racism on American soil while there was a succession of constant wars on foreign soil.

With all the changes in the 1970s and 1980s, clergy were forced to attend more meetings. Dioceses and governance got more complicated. Church Polity became the fifth Gospel as clergy navigated new and treacherous waters and tried to anticipate the impact of so many earth-shaking changes—which were long overdue. The priest became a conflict manager, a social activist and necessarily a student of new liturgies. Priest as pastor was put on the back burner. Priests had no time for home visits. Getting to the hospital to visit the sick was often an effort.

The 1990s and the first two decades of the twentieth-first century have only brought more changes, more issues, more pressure with which clergy must deal. Thankfully, the scourge of sexual misconduct has required changes in clergy life, church buildings and church governance. The deep political division in the United States has put clergy leadership in a critical place. Many clergy are dealing more with the socio-economic reality of the rich getting richer and the poor getting poorer. The death of George Floyd, the beginnings of the Black Lives Matter Movement and our increased awareness of systemic racism in American society are demanding informed and knowledgeable clergy attention.

In the last 50 years, many years were spent by the Episcopal Church on internal matters—women's ordination, prayer book and hymnal revisions and LBGTQI rights, to name just a few. In the last twenty or so years, there seems to be a slow turning outward by the Episcopal Church, even as we have fewer members. This is good. With cultural and social demands, internal and external, clergy have focused more and more on life in the office. Or, have clergy sought refuge in the office? There is not enough time in the day. This means that priestly counseling and parish visits are often assigned to others or left undone. Too much clergy time may go into helping the parish survive, rather than helping the parish to be whole and healthy.

Church changes with the accompanying pressures means that clergy are under more stress than ever—or at least so it seems. It is no wonder that clergy wellness became a "cottage industry." It is true that a priest's work is a complex relationship network. Without a doubt, efforts to improve clergy health must go beyond eating well and getting exercise. Clergy wellness or self-care mean much more. While we may not have always kept this in mind, clergy wellness is grounded in 3 John 2: "Beloved, I pray that all may go well with you and that you may be in good health, just as it is well with your soul" (NRSV). Clergy wholeness or "good health" seem more appropriate than clergy wellness or self-care. Yes, we need a theology of clergy wholeness, a theology of "it is well with your soul." To many clergy, out of necessity, clergy wellness has become a vocation. The day-off has become sacrosanct for the priest who can often seem entitled. Clergy wellness has become a clergy mantra, and self-care a way of life. Now, this is not surprising because ministry in Christ's Church brings joy and pain, true delights and deep worries.

The "Habit of Priesthood" includes wounds and wholeness. In an article in *The Christian Century* in July of 2021, two academics reminded us: "Woundedness is the predictable price we pay for being sent on outrageous assignments by Jesus." Bishop William Willimon and Professor Stanley Hauerwas go on to say that telling the truth brings pain and "meeting people's needs" is dangerous work in a society where "the more affluent and privileged among us have solved with a credit card most of our biblical needs like food, housing, and clothing." Bishop Willimon noted in their provocative conversation that "to be a pastor today is to risk being nibbled to death by ducks."[1]

There is possibly a way forward. A focus on Pastoral Liturgy could help us find our way. Pastoral Liturgy would celebrate the intrinsic

---

1. Willimon and Hauerwas, "Dangers of Providing Pastoral Care."

connection between priest as pastor and priest as presider. The priest is interested in self-care for her own well-being, but also because she has the care of Christ at the heart of her ministry. For the liturgy to be pastoral, the priest must know well his flock. He cannot be a professional who sits in his office in front of his computer screen. The pastoral priest and liturgist will recover the significance of priestly counseling, hospital communions and home visits.

Denise Levertov, who was born Jewish but became an Episcopalian, offers an image of the priest as pastor, as "A Cure of Souls," the title of her poem. Levertov's poem reflects the best of Anglicanism: generous, open, thoughtful and tolerant. The priest guides "with all his care" for he has "heard." The physically present priest comes to the altar and brings with him his flock. The priest knows that his flock will be bringing their wounds. They are "hungry and need the grass." Pastoral Liturgy is about the healing rituals which are at the heart of Jesus' very ministry. Pastoral Liturgy is prophetic, for priest and liturgy challenge the flock to be whole and well for the sake of God's mission in this world.

Pastoral Liturgy is like the truth of the novel, *The Welcome Table*, by Alice Walker wherein we find numerous invitations to follow Jesus Christ. Indeed, each time the bread is broken in the Holy Eucharist the priest invites the congregation to follow the living Christ of our faith. The pastoral priest is a sacramental person who is also a symbol. The liturgy is pastoral because the faithful gather to be cared for, to be fed, to be sent out, to be the "new creation." Liturgy is about pastoring the flock. Liturgy is the work of the people because it is the care of the people. Pastoral Liturgy may be the priest's most important work. Pastoral Liturgy is not self-centered, parish-centered or priest-centered; rather, pastoral liturgy is Christ-centered for God's mission in God's world.

Pastoral Liturgy is keeping the feast and serving the feast. Pastoral Liturgy is holding up in silence at the fraction the body of Christ for the body of Christ. The broken bread is made one by God's grace. The pastoral priest and the pastoral liturgist is presider, vicar and visitor. Pastoral Liturgy promises wholeness for the faithful in a fractured, suffering world—a world hungry to be fed by priest and people.

## Bibliography

Willimon, William H., and Stanley Hauerwas. "The Dangers of Providing Pastoral Care." *The Christian Century*, July 27, 2021. https://www.christiancentury.org/article/interview/dangers-providing-pastoral-care.

# Conclusion

## Jeremy Means-Koss and Ian S. Markham

*Now when Jesus came into the district of Caesarea Philippi, he asked his disciples, "Who do people say that the Son of Man is?" And they said, "Some say John the Baptist, but others Elijah, and still others Jeremiah or one of the prophets." He said to them, "But who do you say that I am?" Simon Peter answered, "You are the Messiah, the Son of the living God." And Jesus answered him, "Blessed are you, Simon son of Jonah! For flesh and blood has not revealed this to you, but my Father in heaven. And I tell you, you are Peter, and on this rock I will build my church, and the gates of Hades will not prevail against it. I will give you the keys of the kingdom of heaven, and whatever you bind on earth will be bound in heaven, and whatever you loose on earth will be loosed in heaven." (Matt 16:13–19)*[1]

THE FULL BEAUTY OF this text is never fully realized because we do not read it in its original. In the translated English of Matt 16:18, we read Jesus giving Simon his new name, Peter. And we further read that he calls Peter his rock that he shall build his church. But in the Greek we read that Jesus gives Simon the new name *Petros*, which literally means

---

1. Unless otherwise noted, all biblical citations in this chapter are from the NRSV.

a stone. And then says that this small stone will be his *petra*, his massive boulder or cliff. The beauty we miss in the English is see that one person, a person who believes—not with their eyes and hands but instead with their heart—can carry the strength for an entire cliffside.

The title of this book is *Mysterion Seeking Understanding: How Sacramentality Can Save the Body of Christ*. To be very clear, the church is in no danger of dying. It cannot die, irrespective of the fate of any building or ecclesiastical body. But over the course of this collection of essays, the authors have identified fracturing points; points where the church might find miracles for its rehabilitation.

A key theme is that a resource for the church is our sacramental and liturgical life. Instead of seeing sacraments and liturgy as problems that create barriers for the seeker, we share a conviction that these things are a resource. Each contributor has stressed how a sacramental and liturgical sensitivity can be a gateway to engaging with the complexity of living and life.

This book has no denominational affiliation, though each author has a background that they bring which holds a unique beauty Christ has offered to the world. Salient in all their texts however is the primacy of Scripture. Each author has not only brought a different perspective to bear on sacramentality, but they have also brought a scripture as the anchor for their texts. Condensed here are those scriptures for you to consider side-by-side.

- From *Word and Flesh*: "Jesus said to her, 'Mary!' She turned and said to him in Hebrew, 'Rabbouni!' (which means Teacher)" (John 20:16).

- From *The Religiously Unaffiliated*: "He said, 'The one who showed him mercy.' Jesus said to him, 'Go and do likewise'" (Luke 10:37).

- From *The Mysterion of God's Devotedness*: "Then he said to them, 'Oh, how foolish you are, and how slow of heart to believe all that the prophets have declared! Was it not necessary that the Messiah should suffer these things and then enter into his glory?' Then beginning with Moses and all the prophets, he interpreted to them the things about himself in all the scriptures. As they came near the village to which they were going, he walked ahead as if he were going on. But they urged him strongly, saying, 'Stay with us, because it is almost evening and the day is now nearly over.' So he went in to stay with them. When he was at the table with them, he took bread, blessed and broke it, and gave it to them. Then their eyes were opened, and they recognized him; and he vanished from their sight. They said to each other, 'Were not our hearts burning within us while he was talking to us on the road, while he was opening the scriptures to us?'" (Luke 24:25–32 RSV).

- From *What Perfect Love Can Be*: "I do not pray for these only, but also for those who believe in me through their word, that they may all be one. . . . The glory which thou hast given me I have given to them, that they may be one even as we are one, I in them and thou in me, that they may become perfectly one, so that the world may know that thou hast sent me and hast loved them even as thou hast loved me" (John 17:20–23 RSV).

- From *Sacramental and Liturgical Inclusivity*: "Now there were devout Jews from every nation under heaven living in Jerusalem. And at this sound the crowd gathered and was bewildered, because each one heard them speaking in the native language of each. Amazed and astonished, they asked, 'Are not all these who are speaking Galileans? And how is it that we hear, each of us, in our own native language? Parthians, Medes, Elamites, and residents of Mesopotamia, Judea and Cappadocia, Pontus and Asia, Phrygia and Pamphylia, Egypt and the parts of Libya belonging to Cyrene, and visitors from Rome, both Jews and proselytes, Cretans and Arabs—in our own languages we hear them speaking about God's deeds of power'" (Acts 2:5–11).

- From *Wrapped in Paradox*: "Who, being in very nature God, did not consider equality with God something to be grasped, but made himself nothing, taking the very nature of a servant being made in human likeness. And being found in appearance as a man, he humbled himself and became obedient to death, even death on a cross" (Phil 2:6–8 NIV).

- From *Addressing Polarization*: "And God said, 'Let there be light,' and there was light" (Gen 1:3 NIV).

- From *Intergenerational Worship*: "And the king will answer them, 'Truly I tell you, just as you did it to one of the least of these who are members of my family, you did it to me'" (Matt 25:40).

- From *Ethical Formation*: "Put away from you all bitterness and wrath and anger and wrangling and slander, together with all malice, and be kind to one another, tenderhearted, forgiving one another, as God in Christ has forgiven you." (Eph 4:31–32).

- From *Moral Imperatives*: "You have heard that it was said to those of ancient times, 'You shall not murder'; and 'whoever murders shall be liable to judgment.' But I say to you that if you are angry with a brother or sister, you will be liable to judgment; and if you insult a brother or sister, you will be liable to the council; and if you say, 'You fool,' you will be liable to the hell of fire. So when you are offering your gift at the altar, if you remember that your brother or sister has something against you, leave your gift there before the altar and go; first be reconciled to your brother or sister, and then come and offer your gift" (Matt 5:21–24).

- From *Transformation of Desire*: "Then Jesus told his disciples, 'If any want to become my followers, let them deny themselves and take up their cross and follow me'" (Matt 16:24).

- From *Sacramental Therapy*: "One of the Pharisees asked Jesus to eat with him, and he went into the Pharisee's house and took his place at the table. And a woman in the city, who was a sinner, having learned that he was eating in the Pharisee's house, brought an alabaster jar of ointment. She stood behind him at his feet, weeping, and began to bathe his feet with her tears and to dry them with her hair. Then she continued kissing his feet and anointing them with the ointment. Now when the Pharisee who had invited him saw it, he said to himself, 'If this man were a prophet, he would have known who and what kind of woman this is who is touching him—that she is a sinner.' Jesus spoke up and said to him, 'Simon, I have something to say to you.' 'Teacher,' he replied, 'speak.' 'A certain creditor had two debtors; one owed five hundred denarii, and the other fifty. When they could not pay, he cancelled the debts for both of them. Now which of them will love him more?' Simon answered, 'I suppose the one for whom he cancelled the greater debt.' And Jesus said to him, 'You have judged rightly.' Then turning towards the woman, he said to Simon, 'Do you see this woman? I entered your house; you gave me no water for my feet, but she has bathed my feet with her tears and dried them with her hair. You gave me no kiss, but from the time I came in she has not stopped kissing my feet. You did not anoint my head with oil, but she has anointed my feet with ointment. Therefore, I tell you, her sins, which were many, have been forgiven; hence she has shown great love. But the one to whom little is forgiven, loves little.' Then he said to her, 'Your sins are forgiven.' But those who were at the table with him began to say among themselves, 'Who is this who even forgives sins?' And he said to the woman, 'Your faith has saved you; go in peace'" (Luke 7:36–50).

The biblical framing is important. We are locating ourselves within the realm of Scripture. Instead of seeing the Bible as problematic for engagement with the world, our authors have used Scripture as a resource. But seeing these texts side-by-side also gives us a way of trying to find a commonality, a thread and theme that permeate this literature that has been missing from the larger conversation on the wellness of the church.

A logical pragmatist might say, with all the arguments and explorations of sacramentality presented in this text, that dedication to the sacraments—to the visible ways that we encounter God's grace and make sense of it—that after two thousand years why is a church that has been celebrating the sacraments for two millennia, in such decline? And what does this literature bring to bear that has been absent from the conversation so far?

It would be of no surprise to the readers of this text that we would say "empire" was and is the largest weight that brings down the church. But what might surprise you is of which empire we are speaking. In ancient Rome, emperors Theodosius (in the west) and Gratian (in the east) made several shifts that forced the entire population to become Christian. Faith was no longer based on belief. It was based on adherence to the state. Peter's claim to Jesus in the above text was not because someone told him. Peter professed that Jesus was the Messiah because that was what was revealed to his heart by God.

The moment we take revelation away from God and put it into our own hands, we pollute Christ's own praise and reject the Evangelist's word's from his own Gospel that "No one has ever seen God. It is God the only Son, who is close to the Father's heart, who has made him known" (John 1:18). We can never truly *know* God. Only God knows God and can reveal himself to us. Revelation and belief live squarely and only there. And any earthly state that attempts to dictate such forgets this important and powerful point. Though God can create beauty and meaningfulness in any situation, we must also attempt to get out of our own ways and stop making it harder for ourselves to share in the wonder of God.

*What has thus been offered by the authors are ways to pivot, way to help us get out of our own ways and out of the ways we have inherited.*

## So Where Do We Go from Here?

What the authors of this text have shown is that the sacraments are not solely what Augustine described them to be, as visible signs of the invisible grace, but are also embodied graces that can confer revelations and deepen a relationship with the divine.

*Lex Orandi, Lex Credendi* is a common phrase in intellectual liturgical circles because of what it validates. The phrase literally means "the law of prayer, [is] the law of belief" and has come to be the backbone argument for not only sacramental dedication but for liturgical continuity itself.

Authored by fifth-century Christian writer and a disciple of St. Augustine, Prosper of Aquitaine, the full phrase *ut legem credenda lex statuat supplicandi*, "that the law of praying establishes the law of believing," explains for all that by enacting—performing as Judith Butler might put it—the liturgical realities of Christian faith, we are learning from them. Perhaps one of the most iconic phrases to embody this teaching is from the hymn "We Are One in the Spirit" with the line, "and they will know we are Christians by our love"—a line directly inspired from John's Gospel.[2] The authors throughout this book have explained in their myriad of ways, *mysterion* at its most core is grace embodied.

To focus on a more precise example, the question of an "open table" or "closed table" is anathema the sacramental work of the church. *Should* someone who knows nothing of the sacrament of the Lord's Supper come up and ingest it? No. But should the conversation be about who is and is not able to approach the altar and thus by extension approach Christ? Never.

The opportunity yet unrealized by churches around the world is that every *mysterion* is in itself an "altar call"—a time during a church service when a person may come forward and newly declare, in front of their community, their faith in Jesus.

How we attune our churches to align in that way is up to us.

---

2. By this everyone will know that you are my disciples, if you have love for one another (John 13:35).

www.ingramcontent.com/pod-product-compliance
Lightning Source LLC
Chambersburg PA
CBHW050851230426
43667CB00012B/2244